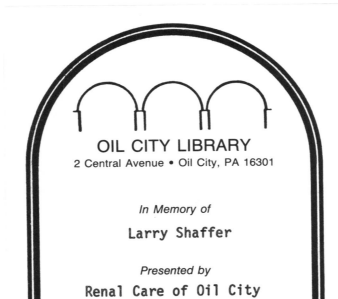

GMC

The First 100 Years

John Gunnell

Published by

krause publications

700 East State Street, Iola, WI 54990-0001
Telephone (715) 445-2214
www.krause.com

Please call or write for our free catalog of publications.
Our toll-free number to place an order or obtain a free catalog is (800) 258-0929.

Library of Congress Catalog Card Number: 2001091081
ISBN: 0-87349-326-5
Printed in the United States of America

Front cover:
2002 GMC Envoy XL (GMC)
1958 GMC 350 platform truck with stake rack body (JMSC)
1955 GMC "Cameo" pickup (Bud Juneau)
1919 GMC Model 16 1-ton truck with express body (FREC)
1948 GMC 1/2-ton pickup (Barry Ferguson)

Back cover:
"Parade of Progress" buses in the 1950s.

Title page:
1919 GMC Model 16 (FREC)
1937 GMC platform stake (KTA)
2001 GMC Sonoma Crew Cab (© General Motors Corp.)

Page 192
1956 GMC pickup (Jess and Rita Ruffalo)

CONTENTS

DEDICATION

To Jesse

You can be like GMC
Look good, work hard
And you'll find success

Dad

ACKNOWLEDGMENTS

When it comes to publishing any book on vintage cars or trucks, one of the hardest jobs is acknowledging all of the people who helped. The following persons made contributions to researching, illustrating or producing this work, but I would also like to thank all automotive enthusiasts, GMC aficionados, *Old Cars Weekly* subscribers and General Motors or Pontiac-GMC employees who have made contributions.

First and foremost, there would have been no 100-year history of GMC without the massive support of Lynn Myers, general manager of Pontiac-GMC Division, who also wrote the introduction to the book. Mark Hitchins also deserves a big thank you for getting the project rolling while he was at Pontiac-GMC Division. A massive dose of credit for general direction, detailed fact checking, photo identifications and several personal photographs go to Donald E. Meyer, Official GMC Truck Historian, who added a wealth of knowledge to this work. Dayna Hart, manager of Media Relations for Pontiac-GMC, was an invaluable link to divisional and corporate research sources. Mary Henige, Director of Communications, did a fantastic job of proofreading the manuscript. Jim Mattison, of Pontiac Historic services, contributed his facility in Sterling Heights, Mich., for research efforts and an important meeting. Very special thanks go to Mike Brazeau, Julie Fiegel, Clyde Hensley, Larry Kinsel and Ken Luttermoser of GM Media Archives, in Detroit, who helped gather over 500 images of GMC-related vehicles.

As for published sources, *GMC Trucks The First 80 Years: A History of GMC Trucks From 1900-1980* compiled by Donald E. Meyer in 1995 was a valuable research tool. Huge credit should also be given to author Gini Rice, who wrote the pioneering book *Relics of the Road #1: GMC Gems 1900-1950* published by Hastings House Publishers, of New York, in 1971 and 1973, and to Ken Goudy, Jr., who illustrated sections of the book. Another fabulous source of information was R.A. Crist's *GMC Truck History: Chronology of Significant Dates and Events*, a corporate history that was updated several times and which Robert J. Stevens later used as the basis for an informative series of articles in *Cars & Parts* magazine during the mid-1980s. *The GMC 6 x 6 and DUKW: A Universal Truck* by Jean-Michel Boniface and Jean-Gabriel Jeudy, published by EPA in 1978 and republished by Haynes Publishing Group in 1990, was helpful in researching GMC's World War II experience. Also informative about GMC military vehicles was *The Standard Catalog of U.S. Military Vehicles 1940-1965*, which Thomas Berndt compiled for Krause Publications. Portions of the 1997 book *Modern Intercity Coaches* published by bus historian Larry Plachno — editor and publisher of *National Bus Trader* magazine — largely guided our research on GMC transit coaches.

The following individuals were also involved in the research and photo gathering phases of compiling this book: Bob Adler (Adler's Antique Autos); American Truck Historical Society; The Antique Automobile Club of America; the Auto Collection at the Imperial Palace, Las Vegas, Nev.; Michael Ball (Futurliner Restoration Project); Bill Baron; Jim Benjaminson; Paul Bergstrom; George Bossie III, Fire Chief, Dunbar Fire Dept., Dunbar, W.V.; Bill Bryant; Ken Buttolph; Dave Carlson; Chapdelaine Truck Center, Lunenburg, Mass.; Bob and Kathy Christiansen; Gene Clarey; the late Henry Austin Clark, Jr., Long Island Automotive Museum, Glen Cove, N.Y.; Richie Clyne (director, Imperial Palace Auto Collection), Las Vegas, Nev.; Albert C. Cochrane, advertising director DAC News, (the Detroit Athletic Club), Detroit, Mich.; Ken Corl (Valley GMC), Centre Fall, Pa.; Jim Crame;

DailyRadar.com; Heather DeBaille (Cat Scale Co.), Iowa 80 Truck Stop, Davenport, Iowa; Frank DiPaola; Bill Dorney; Ralph Dunwoodie; Roy J. Eaton, City Manager, Decatur, Texas; Joe Egle; Ralph Ehrhardt; Ron English; John Ernst; Francis R. Everett; Barry Ferguson; George B. Field; Russ Fisher (FATSCO Transmission), Fairfield, N.J.; *The Flint Journal*, Flint, Mich.; Earnest C. Fordor; Bill Forner; Scott Fraser; Fullington Auto Bus Co., Clearfield, Pa.; John P. Garrett; General Electric Co.; GM Furturliner Restoration Project /National Automobile and Truck Museum of the United Stated (NATMUS), Auburn, Ind.; Mark D. Goldfeder; Michael Goodfellow; Ren Gorette (Futurliner Restoration Project); John A. Gunnell Collection; William Gwodz; Clinton H. Hardenbrook; Cecil C. Harris; Brad Hartley; the Hays Antique Truck Museum, Woodland, Calif.; David Heise; Greg Holmes; Frank Holzem; Lee W. Hoovler; Clyde Horst; Ross Hubbard (Krause Publications Photographer); Indianapolis Motor Speedway Corp., Indianapolis, Ind.; Randy and Donna M. Ingelse (Lanser Garage & Towing, Inc.), Belgium, Wis.; David N. Jacobsen (Jacobsen's Services), Inc., Argyle, Wis.; Richard and Peg Jansen (Mostly Toys), Denmark, Wis.; Thomas M. Jevcak (Classic Images Photography), Tampa, Fla.; Bud Juneau; Howard Keith, Jr.; Bruce D. Keivit; David H. Kenny; Kenworthy Truck & Auto; Ron Kowalke; Jay and Trici Knowles; Chester L. Krause; Roy Krueger; Alan Lapides; Mike Larsen; Russell Lewis; Robert B. Loudon; Allen J. Martin, Jr.; Jack Martin; Don Mayton, Director of Futurliner Restoration, Zeeland, Mich.; Martha Addington-McCormick; Marty McGuire; John Merchant; Gregg D. Merksamer; *Military Vehicles* magazine, Iola, Wis.; Carolyn Moon (Iowa 80 Truck Stop), Davenport, Iowa; Motor Vehicle Manufacturer's Assoc.; LeRoy D. Mudge; Roy Nagel; National Steel Products Co.; Larry Nicklin; Harold F. Overton; *Old Cars Weekly* collection, Iola, Wis.; Al Phillips; David Reed; Glenn L. Reimel; James Renn (Madison Fire Dept.), Madison, N.C.; Jack R. Robinson; Michael Rose (Michael Rose Productions, Inc.), Santa Monica, Calif.; Robert K. Rostecki; John Sawruk; Robert Scoon; Steve Schultz; James M. Semon (Trains-Trucks-Trolleys), Westlake, Ohio; Carl Sheffer (SEMA), Diamond Bar, Calif.; Clifford P. Shuping; Daryl and Nancy Skaar; Ed Snyder; Robert and Norma Sperling; Jerry Steinhelper; Robert J. Stevens (*Cars & Parts*), Sidney, Ohio; Arthur D. Strain; T.L. Tallentine; Telephone Pioneers of America, Manitoba, Canada; Coy Thomas; Simon Thompson; Leon Trice Photography, New Orleans, La.; Valley GMC Sales & Service, State College, Pa.; Lloyd Van Horn; Conrad Vogel; Gene and Tina Von Gunten; John Wangelin; Ralph M. Wescott; Bob Wessman (Images & Design); Kenneth and Fern Whitcher; John W. Whitehead; Wisconsin Power & Light/Alliant Energy, Madison, Wis.; Jim Wrosch; and Bret Zieman.

Finally, I would like to thank Karen O'Brien for a wonderful job of editing my immensely lengthy, contrived and unrefined manuscript and artist Clay Miller for his masterpiece of layout design. Thanks also go to all members of the Krause Publications book division, proofreading and production departments who contributed, in significant ways, to the creation of this book.

John Gunnell

John A. Gunnell
Dec. 3, 2001

INTRODUCTION

GMC marks its centennial anniversary in 2002 with the strongest line-up of trucks in the history of the brand. Since its early days, GMC has focused on trucks and only trucks—longer than any other manufacturer. We believe this expertise uniquely qualifies us to offer products with capabilities that exceed our customers' expectations.

Each decade of our proud history is marked by our industry firsts and achievements. In 1914, we introduced the first light truck with a bevel gear drive rear axle, which made it vastly more efficient, quieter, smoother riding, and required much less maintenance. Soon after, the U.S. military proved its confidence in our trucks' quality and endurance by enlisting them for combat in World War I. In 1925, GMC debuted four wheel brakes to help our trucks stop more quickly and easily. During the 1930s, we again set the standard by introducing the two-speed rear axle and putting more effective hydraulic brakes on light duty trucks.

During the early 1940s GMC concentrated its resources on producing military vehicles for our troops in World War II. During the next decade our innovations came in the form of power steering, strong V-6 gas engines, and we were the first to pioneer air suspension for some heavy-duty models.

Our momentum continued into the second half of the century, beginning with safety enhancements like energy-absorbing steering columns and instrument panel pads, and dual brake systems long before they were mandated. In 1956 GMC offered factory-installed 4-wheel-drive for better off-road performance.

GMC was one of the first to offer a sport utility vehicle, with the birth of the Jimmy 4-wheel drive SUV in 1970. Front disk brakes were another safety advance we made standard on most GMCs during the era.

Four new family members joined the GMC family in the 1980s: the S-15 compact pickup; the S-15 Jimmy compact SUV; the Safari van and the Sierra full-size pickup. Each of these new products reinforced GMCs heritage as an authentic truck company. During the 1990s GMC flew high on the soaring popularity of trucks and SUVs, and had seven consecutive years of record-setting sales to prove it.

By the year 2000, 125 different trucks were available to consumers, many targeted at Baby Boomers in their peak earning years. Our mission today is to satisfy the high standards of these customers, who demand "professional grade" capabilities in many of the products they buy. Drawing on our solid truck heritage, GMC is positioned as the only truck producer offering "Professional Grade" products—products with outstanding capabilities, unique GMC design elements, and giving customers a feeling of confidence when they get in their GMC truck.

Our GMC products continue to pay off our Professional Grade promise, including the introduction of the all-new GMC Sierra in 1999, followed by GMC Yukon and Yukon XL with more sophisticated suspensions, more potent powertrains and unexpected agility in a full-size SUV.

In 2001, Yukon Denali, Yukon XL Denali and the Sierra C3 joined our impressive lineup, all with features unique to GMC. The Yukon Denali and Yukon XL Denali boasted full-time All-Wheel Drive and a 6-liter Vortec V-8 engine with the most horsepower and torque in any full-size 1/2-ton SUV. The Sierra C3 touted the industry's first all-wheel drive system in a full-size pickup. We made it even better by being the first in the industry to introduce 4-wheel steering (Quadrasteer) for unprecedented maneuverability and control in a full-size truck. When we added Quadrasteer we renamed it Sierra Denali.

The all-new 2002 Envoy, introduced in 2001 became the first GMC with a unique exterior and interior plus the best-in-class Vortec inline 6 engine, and superior comfort and roominess. And in 2002, Envoy XL came along with best-in-class, seven-passenger roominess with the addition of a third row seat.

Thanks to these product advances, today we have the strongest, most capable stable of professional grade trucks in our history—and our portfolio is growing. That's good news in a market where trucks are half of all vehicles sold and growing

Looking to the future, our momentum will continue to build. Soon, GMC will introduce an environmentally friendly Parallel Hybrid truck, with dramatically better fuel economy. Mid-decade, we'll offer another engine that will boost fuel efficiency by automatically shifting between 4 to 8 cylinders, depending on the vehicle's need.

Our future looks bright, with all the essential elements needed for continued success. Our rich heritage gives us an unshakable foundation from which to grow. We have a strong lineup of Professional Grade products, with more on the way. And we have extraordinary people in every segment of the organization laying the groundwork for the next 100 years.

Happy 100th Anniversary, GMC! We're proud to be part of you.

Lynn C. Myers
General Manager
Pontiac-GMC Division
Detroit, Michigan

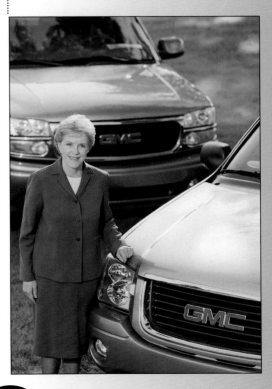

C h a p t e r   1

Laying the Foundation of GMC

1902-1925

Page 6 and 7: The GMC 1-ton Model 16 was also used in civilian applications such as this 1919 express-bodied truck. (FREC)

This model is probably of a 1904 Rapid 1-ton Model D-21. (© General Motors Corp.)

The first truck built by the Grabowsky brothers. Max Grabowsky started experimenting with his Rapid Motor truck in 1900 and sold his first unit in 1902. (© General Motors Corp.)

Rapid Motor Vehicle Co.

It has been 100 years since the keystone was laid in the foundation of one of America's great truck makers—GMC. That took place in 1902 when Max Grabowsky of Detroit, Michigan, sold his first truck to a dry-cleaning company.

Brothers Max and Morris Grabowsky started designing motor vehicles in their mechanical repair and workshop in 1900. They formed the Grabowsky Motor Vehicle Co. to assemble, distribute, and sell commercial vehicles. Their first experimental truck—a small, chain-driven machine with a one-cylinder gasoline engine—was built the following year and test driven on Woodward Avenue, among horse-drawn traffic.

In 1902, executives of the American Garment Cleaning Co. of Detroit, Michigan, ordered one of the Grabowsky brothers' trucks. This company was the first commercial operator of a truck in the "Motor City," and that 1902 model was among America's earliest motor trucks. Like the prototype of 1900, it had a one-cylinder horizontal engine, double-chain drive, right-hand steering, and wood spoke wheels. Later in 1902, the Grabowsky Motor Vehicle Co. was reorganized in Detroit as the Rapid Motor Vehicle Co. and the company sold 75 trucks between 1902 and 1904.

The Grabowsky brothers formally organized and incorporated the Rapid Motor Vehicle Co. in Detroit in March 1904, with financial backing from Barney Finn and Albert Marx of the American Garment Cleaning Company, purchasers of Grabowsky's first truck in 1902. All four were listed as the incorporators. The firm was started with an initial capitalization of $13,000.

During 1904, Albert G. North began building Rapid trucks in his Pontiac Spring & Wagon Works in Pontiac, Michigan. North and his partner, Harry G. Hamilton, started their buggy-building firm on July 13, 1899. North

This photo of Max Grabowsky (left) was taken during the years 1945-1953, when Morgan Douglas (right) was general manager of General Motors Truck & Coach Division. (© General Motors Corp.)

was president and Hamilton was secretary and treasurer. By 1904, carriages were starting to give way to motor vehicles and North and Hamilton saw some wisdom in giving financial support to the Rapid Motor Vehicle Co. By 1905, they gained control of the truck maker and broke ground for a plant on a site on Rapid Street in the city of Pontiac, not far from where GMC Truck & Coach operations were carried on in later years. The company's first sales catalog was also issued in 1905.

North was president of Rapid Motor Vehicle Co. and Hamilton became treasurer of the company. The Grabowsky brothers remained on for a while, with Max serving as vice president and Morris serving as secretary.

Rapid's 1905 line included about 20 one-cylinder models, as well as a new 15-hp two-cylinder Model B "Power Wagon" that was featured in the company's new sales brochure. The 1-ton Model B had a two-cylinder engine rated at 15 hp mounted under the driver's seat. The 1,900-lb. truck rode on an 80-in. wheelbase and had $1,250 price tag. A planetary gearbox transmitted power to a single-chain drive system that turned the rear wheels. A 1 1/2-ton version with a slightly larger engine was also offered.

Rapid moved into a new plant at 107 Rapid Street in 1905. The new facilities enabled Rapid to turn out an incredible 200 trucks and buses during the company's first year in Pontiac. In the same year, a new Model C delivery wagon was offered in 1-ton and 1 1/2-ton models.

For 1907, Rapid introduced the Model D-21, which could be ordered with a buggy top (at extra cost) to protect the driver from bad weather. The D-21 was a 1-ton delivery van.

During 1907, Max Grabowsky became disgruntled with his associates because they were trying to force him out of the Rapid Motor Vehicle Co. In March, he left the company to start the Grabowsky Power Wagon Co., which set up shop at 110 Champlain St. in Detroit. Grabowsky

continued in business until 1913, advertising that, "The power wagon will do the work of three or four horse drawn wagons and do it better and cheaper!" In October 1907, Harry Hamilton became general manager of Rapid, succeeding Max Grabowsky who had held the titles of vice president and general manager.

Rapid Motor Vehicle Co. displayed eight 1908 models at the Grand Central Palace Automobile Show in New York City from October 24-31, 1907. They were basically the 1902 chassis models carried over with a variety of new body styles. The Model E-62 was a 1-ton truck with a two-cylinder horizontal engine that sold for $1,600. The E-21 was a 1-ton truck with the same 5 x 5-in. bore and stroke 24-hp engine and $1,600 price. The Model E-11 teamed the same power train with a full-paneled body and cost $1,650. The E-132 was a 12-passenger bus, again with the same engine, priced at $1,800. The E-152 was a 16-passenger wagonette with the same engine and a $2,000 price tag. The E-222 had the same motor and a $2,400 price. The most expensive vehicle was the Model 2-182, a 12-passenger bus with the same motor. It sold for $4,000. The E-44 was a 1 1/2-ton truck with a different two-cylinder horizontal engine that had a 5 1/4-in. bore. It also carried a 24-hp rating, however, and it sold for $2,000.

An advertisement in the November 1, 1907, edition of *Cycle and Automobile Trade Journal* promoted a line of 12- to 25-passenger sightseeing cars, any style delivery car, several models of trucks, and what Rapid called, "anything desired for special service." Pictured was the E-11 panel delivery truck, plus an E-72 freight wagon that was not displayed at the New York Show (but may have been seen in the Chicago show). In the announcement, Rapid Motor Vehicle Co. sales manager B.M. Henry invited sales agents to write him for information about selling "the best commercial cars in the world."

During 1908, William C. Durant started buying up the stock of the Rapid Motor Vehicle Co. Although it remained an independent firm, Rapid came to be represented by the sales force of Durant's General Motors in 1909. Durant had organized GM as an "umbrella" company that bought up many firms and brought them into one corporation. GM was experiencing strong growth and brought Rapid into the GM family as a division in 1909. However, the GMC logo would not be on trucks seen by the public until the New York Auto Show in January 1912.

During 1909, Rapid published its first fully illustrated, full-line sales catalog. It showed 28 "F" models, including an ambulance, a patrol wagon, a fire engine, and 9- to 22-passenger buses, as well as 1-ton and 1 1/2-ton trucks. Both 24- and 36-hp two-cylinder double-opposed engines were available. Rapid advertised that its commercial cars "Pay for themselves in one season." Six trucks, an ambulance, and two buses were exhibited at the New York Auto Show in January.

In addition to Rapid's new sales catalog, other types of product promotions were arranged to help B.M. Henry sell his line of Rapid trucks. Pikes Peak Mountain, near Manitou Springs, Colorado, had impressed Americans since 1806, when Lt. Zebulon Pike (who was never able to reach the top of the mountain that came to bear his name) viewed it from over 100 miles away. In 1901, a Locomobile Steamer became the first automobile to reach the summit of Pikes Peak at 14,110 feet above sea level. On August 1, 1909, a Rapid truck left Colorado Springs at 6:15 a.m. and began a journey to the summit, which it reached the following morning, making it the first truck to ever complete the climb.

Rapid offered a line of 1-, 2- and 3-ton trucks during 1910 and the two larger sizes were all-new models. The 2-ton sold for $2,750 and was a conventional truck with its engine under a hood in front of the driver. The 3-ton model, which was priced at $3,500, was of driver-over-engine design. (You can't say cab-over-engine design because a cab was not standard equipment.) A new four-cylinder engine powered both trucks, while the 1-ton model, priced at $2,300, retained the previous two-cylinder engine. The larger trucks were manufactured with GMC logos in late 1911 and the 1-ton evolved into a 1 1/4-ton GMC model.

This 1905 Rapid 6-9-passenger sightseeing bus was part of the Imperial Palace Auto Collection of Las Vegas, Nevada. (IP)

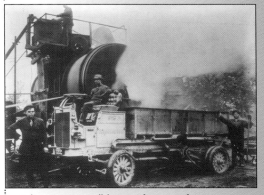

Reliance was well known for manufacturing large trucks. This 1908 Model G4 was rated at three tons capacity. (© General Motors Corp.)

Left: When photographed by prominent automotive historian Henry Austin Clark, Jr., this 1907 Rapid Model E 12-passenger sightseeing bus was in the collection of Mr. Harold F. Overton. (HACJ)

An early milestone in GMC history was this 1909 Rapid, which served as a service truck for the Glidden Tour and became the first truck to climb Pikes Peak. (© General Motors Corp.)

Reliance Motor Truck Co.

The Reliance Motor Truck Co. was another building block in the makeup of GMC. This firm started in business at 61-89 Fort Street in East Detroit in 1902 as the Reliance Automobile Manufacturing Co. E.O. Abbott and W.K. Ackerman, formerly of Cadillac, were the designers of the company's first two-cylinder car. In 1904, the firm reorganized as Reliance Motor Co., putting J.M. Mulky in charge, but Fred O. Paige soon replaced Mulky. The Reliance was advertised as a "Car too Good for the Price" (which was $1,250) and as the "Light-Heavyweight Touring Car." Advertisements also emphasized that the Reliance was "All Made Under One Roof."

The under-one-roof reference probably reflected Reliance Motor Car Co.'s 1906 move to Owosso, Michigan, where a commercial vehicle was added to the line. By February 1907, trucks became the company's primary product and rights to the Reliance passenger car were sold in March to a Philadelphia group that continued to produce it as the Crescent automobile. During the winter of 1907, a two-cylinder 3-ton Reliance truck with a special "gearless" friction transmission completed a 304-mile promotional run from Detroit to Chicago in less than four days! At the time, that was considered impressive cold-weather performance for a commercial truck.

Reliance Motor Car Co. displayed three of its new 1908 models at the Grand Central Palace Automobile Show at

The GMC logo first appeared on vehicles in 1911, when the Reliance-built Model KL: 5-ton was manufactured. GMC stands for General Motors Truck Company. (© General Motors Corp.)

the end of October 1907. The Model K used a four-cylinder 60-hp two-cycle engine with a 5 1/8 x 5-in. bore and stroke. It was a 4-ton model and priced at $4,400. The 1- to 3- ton Model H had a two-cycle, two-cylinder vertical engine with a 5 1/8 x 5-in. bore and stroke that gave it 30 hp and a $2,750 price. There was also a 3- to 4-ton Model H with a three-cylinder two-cycle engine that produced 45 hp and sold for $3,500.

An advertisement in *Cycle and Automobile Trade Journal* for November 1, 1907, promoted the use of 1908 Reliance Motor Trucks for freight and passenger service. It pointed out that Reliance models did not evolve from pleasure vehicles and said that they were "designed strictly along truck lines with a surplus of strength in all parts." In a claim that sounded much like those made by Max Grabowsky, the ad read, "A Reliance Truck will do the work of three men and three horse-drawn trucks, with an operating cost about equal to one horse-drawn truck" and offered data and the names of owners who could "prove" this. The ad gave the company's address as 87 Fort Street, E., Detroit, Michigan.

General Motors acquired Reliance late in 1908. In *My Years With General Motors*, Alfred P. Sloan, Jr., classified Reliance as one of the "random gambles" that "Billy" Durant took while building his umbrella company. He said that the Rapid Motor Vehicle Co. and Reliance Motor Truck Co. "were combined and named Rapid Truck."

The last full year that Reliance operated independently was 1910, when it offered the 2 1/2-ton Model G for $2,750, the 2 1/2-ton Model G3 for $3,150, the 3 1/2-ton Model H4 for $3,750, and the 5-ton Model K for $4,400. *The Manual of Automobile Liability Insurance* of January 1, 1916, lists no Reliance models for 1911 and the 1912 listing says "See GNC," which is a typographical error.

Rapid Truck Co. was absorbed by General Motors Truck Co., of 88 Congress Street, Detroit, Michigan, on July 22, 1911. General Motors Truck Co. was formed expressly to handle sales of Rapid and Reliance trucks. A few weeks later, on August 1, 1911, a new GMC trademark was first used in the business of the General Motors Truck Co. At that point, GMC nameplates first started appearing

Sturdy enough to last 94 years, although not in like-new condition, this 1910 Reliance truck belonged to the Van Horn truck Museum of Mason City, Iowa. (LVH)

The pride of the Ipswich, Massachusetts Fire Company in 1912 was this GMC 1 1/4-ton Model V fire truck. It had a four-cylinder engine and a 148-inch wheelbase. This painting was done especially for GM by well-known artist Melbourne Brindle. (BDKC)

Sulzberger's Majestic Hams owned this 1914 GMC Model VC 1 1/4-ton canopy delivery truck. It was designed by Rapid Motor Truck Co. (© General Motors Corp.)

on some—but not all—of the company's trucks. The letters "GMC" were curlier and more ornate than the logo we know today, with the legs of the large "M" in the middle flowing under the other letters. Although some people mistakenly believe the letters first stood for "Grabowsky Motor Co.," GMC was actually an acronym for "General Motors Co."

An engine-under-seat truck was the first model to bear a GMC nameplate. Some sources describe it as a cab-over-engine (or COE) model, but it did not really come from the factory with a cab. A simple wooden cab for trucks had been developed by outside suppliers by 1908 and could be added to the GMC as an extra. However, cabs did not become standard equipment until 1916, when windshields were also added.

With GMC logos, the former Reliance trucks were offered as the 2 1/2-ton Model G for $3,000, the 3 1/2-ton Model H for $3,500, the 3 1/2-ton Model HL for $3,800, the 3 1/2-ton Model HM for $3,700, the 5-ton Model K for $4,400 and the 5-ton Model KL for $4,800.

After GM took over, Detroit became the truck company's headquarters city, although the Reliance factory remained in operation in Owosso until 1913. State historical records tell us that the Estey Manufacturing Co. of Owosso lost a furniture factory to a tornado on November 11, 1911. Following this disaster, A.M. Bentley, the manager of Reliance Motor Truck Co., offered to return $12,000 to the city to help the furniture maker, since it had no insurance against tornadoes. That money had originally been appropriated to help Reliance with an addition to its operations. A.M. Bentley eventually became a director at General Motors, while Fred Paige left Reliance and went on to build the Paige-Detroit automobile.

In January 1912, the new GMC trademark appeared on both Rapid and Reliance trucks displayed at the New York Automobile Show in the city's famous Madison Square Garden. A patent application for the GMC logo (copyright number 88270) was finally filed on August 11, 1912 and was registered on September 10, 1912. Some earlier company histories have these dates slightly wrong, but GMC's official historian Donald E. Meyer, who helped with research on this book, has a copy of this patent in his possession. Nine days before the logo was registered by the U.S. Patent Office, William L. Day became the first

general manager of GMC. He continued serving the "Truck and Coach Division" in that capacity until 1925.

For 1913, GMC listed 10 new gasoline models with 1 1/4- to 5-ton payloads and eight electrics with 1/2- to 6-ton capacities. In the gasoline range, the former Reliance models were the H and K and their variants. The S, V, and W models were those previously marketed as Rapids, with the V being the 1 1/4-ton version of the previous 1-ton, the S being the 2-ton model, and the W being the 3-ton truck. The GMC electric trucks came in 1/2-, 1-, 1 1/2-, 2-, 3-, 4-, 5- and 6-ton models, with prices from $1,200 to $2,500.

During 1913, all of GM's commercial-vehicle manufacturing operations, including Reliance, were consolidated at the former Rapid Motor Vehicle plant in Pontiac, Michigan. After that, the GMC nameplate appeared on all trucks made by General Motors Truck Co.

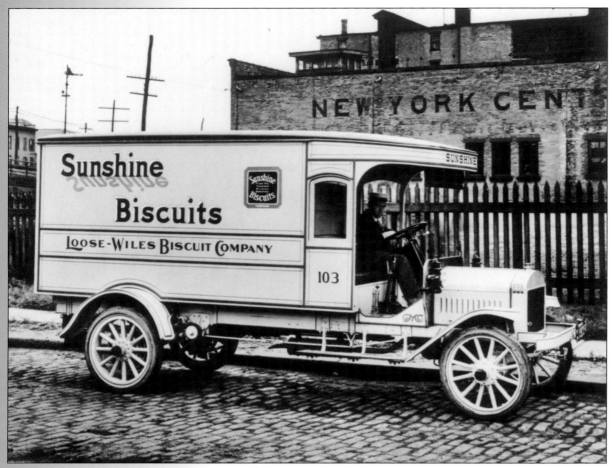

A driver wearing a stylish straw hat makes deliveries for Loose-Wiles Biscuit Co., of New York City, in a 1914 GMC Model VC 1 1/4-ton truck. Wiles was part of the Sunshine Biscuit Co. (© General Motors Corp.)

The Third 'R' — Randolph

A third company absorbed into the GMC family was Randolph, which was originally organized late in 1908, as the Randolph Motor Car Co. According to Shirley Sponholtz, the editor of *Wheels of Time* magazine, the company started in Flint, Michigan, and operated a manufacturing plant at 3900-4000 Union Avenue, in Chicago, Illinois.

E.C. Gage, N.W. Burgstresser, and S. Hyrowitz issued $300,000 in stock to raise money to start a firm to manufacture automobiles and accessories. The company advertised a truck called the Strenuous Randolph. This model came in five capacities, ranging from a light delivery van to a 4-ton flatbed. The smaller models used a two-cylinder engine and all had three-speed gearboxes, solid tires, and double-chain drive. Randolph also planned to manufacture an automobile, but there is no evidence that this machine was ever produced.

W.C. Durant acquired Randolph late in 1908. He then terminated its corporate existence by 1910. The last Randolph trucks were probably produced in 1910, Model 14 as 1911 models. The Hays Antique Truck Museum of Woodland, California, owns a 1911 Randolph 1-ton Model-14 truck. Elements of the company were woven into the combination of Rapid and Reliance trucks. Some sources show Randolph in operation, in Chicago, as late as 1912 or 1913.

1912-1925: General Motors Truck Co.

To briefly sum up the situation that existed in 1911, the General Motors Truck Co.—created specifically to build trucks and buses—came into being through the absorption of Rapid, Reliance, and Randolph, which were already under the control of W.C. Durant's General Motors. Some of the individual brand names were retained until 1911, when production of the first GMC trucks started in the former Rapid factory.

W.C. Durant lost control of GM in 1910 when Buick sales—which had largely financed the corporation's expansion—suddenly dropped. The company literally ran out of money and stockbroker John McClement stepped in to arrange a $15 million bailout loan from Eastern bankers, who then called for the resignations of Durant and other GM directors. By the end of 1912, GM's new president, James J. Storrow, reorganized the firm and had it running smoothly.

By that time, General Motors Truck Co. was able to—as it does today—offer a full range of products to consumers. This was due to the different types of trucks identified with each of the firms it had absorbed. Randolph won recognition for its hardworking 3/4- to 4-ton trucks with two- or four-cylinder engines. Rapid became best known for its medium-sized 1- and 2-ton trucks with four-cylinder engines, four-speed gearboxes, single-chain drive, solid tires, and left-hand steering. The Reliance name was associated with bigger 3 1/2- to 5-ton forward-control trucks with large 6.4-liter engines, three-speed transmissions, and double-chain drive.

The early GMC gasoline models started at 1 1/4-ton capacity and included one 2-ton truck, four 3 1/2-ton versions, and five 5-ton behemoths. In addition, electric-powered trucks were marketed under the GMC trademark from 1911-1915. The smallest electric had a Renault-style "shovel-nose" hood and chain drive. In 1913, 1914, and 1915, the electrics carried model names such as 1, 2, 3…up to 12, in which the numerals indicated the load capacity in pounds. For example, the Model 1 had a load capacity of 1,000 lbs. or 1/2 ton. The gasoline trucks were the same, but some models added a "C" or a "U" in their designations to indicate a different production series or feature.

Note the French front on this 1913 GMC electric truck that the Churchill Drug Co. used to haul paints, oil, and glass. It is a 1-ton Model Z. (© General Motors Corp.)

Left: This 1915 GMC Model SC platform truck with stake sides was painted for *Cars That GM Built*, an album of historic motor vehicles printed in 1956. The truck still belongs to GMC. (BDKC)

Dating from 1916, this is either a GMC Model 70 3 1/2-ton truck or a Model HU. It is fitted with a "C" cab and a dump body. (© General Motors Corp.)

The base prices of electric trucks were lowered in 1913, because batteries were made an extra-cost option. A new 1 1/2-ton electric called the Model 3 was also added that year. In 1914, there were few product changes, but several important historical milestones took place. On January 2, GMC announced a plan to sell trucks only for cash and changed the manner in which it handled service and trade-ins. Prices on gasoline-powered trucks were lowered to stimulate sales.

The first issue of a factory magazine or "house organ" named *GMC Truck Talk* was published with a May 27, 1914 cover date. Later in 1914, GMC put out a special issue of *GMC Truck Talk* to promote the sale of electric trucks. This was followed by cutting prices on the electric-powered models, ranging from $200 to $600. By 1915, the electric-powered Models 6 and 8 were no longer being offered. All other electrics except the Model 12 (which lasted until 1917) were dropped in 1916.

The 3/4-ton Model 15 was introduced in October 1914 as a new 1915 model. It was the first gasoline-fueled GMC light-duty truck. Handsome express bodies were available to fit its 1,500-lb. capacity chassis, which listed for $1,090. Serial numbers for the Model 15s ran from 15851 to 152650. The Model 15 used a Continental Model N four-cylinder 19.6-hp mono-bloc engine with a 3 1/2 x 5-in. bore and stroke. It was the first truck to feature a bevel-gear-driven rear axle instead of chain-and-sprocket drive and the first truck to use standard pneumatic tires. In April 1915, a Jitney Bus version of the Model 15 was introduced. For a short time, it opened up a new line of business.

In 1915 and 1916, the British Army used a number of 3/4-ton Model 15 trucks for war service. An entirely new range of GMC gas-fueled trucks was introduced in 1915 to join the Model 15. The Models 25 and 26 were both 1 1/4-ton trucks priced at $1,800, the main difference being the

use of chain drive on the Model 25 and worm drive on the Model 26. The Model 31 was a 1 1/2-ton truck chassis with worm drive for $1,900. The Models 40 and 41, both priced at $2,375, were GMC's chain-drive and worm-drive 2-ton trucks, respectively. These 2-ton models were powered by a larger Continental Model C2 engine with a 4 1/8 x 5 1/2-inch bore and stroke that was rated at 40 hp.

In 1916, the Model 70 and 71 trucks were added. These were 3 1/2-ton counterparts to the 25 and 26. Both were priced at $3,300. The Models 100 and 101 were 5-ton trucks costing $3,850, with chain drive and worm drive, respectively. They both used large Continental engines with a 4 1/2 x 5 1/2-inch bore and stroke.

After the Samson Sieve-Grip Tractor Co. of Stockton, California, was purchased by William C. Durant, only two of these 1917 Model 10-29 tractors were built under General Motors Truck Co. ownership. (© General Motors Corp.)

This scale model of a 1918 GMC Model 16AA U.S. Army ambulance was made by a prisoner in New York's Attica State Correctional Institution. (© General Motors Corp.)

This restored 1918 GMC Model 16 tanker has been decorated like a Phillips 66 gasoline delivery truck. (LVH)

GMC's first 1-ton gasoline-powered truck, the Model 21, was introduced in 1916, but probably very late in the year. Some sources list it as a 1917 model, although 1916 serial numbers indicate production of a handful of Model 21s in 1916. Serial numbers for 1916 Model 21s were 21101 to 21119, indicating that only 19 were made. Like other GMC trucks, the Model 21 employed a Continental four-cylinder mono-bloc engine. It had a 3 3/4 x 5-in. bore and stroke and produced 33 hp. All GMC trucks of this era featured shaft drive, a three- or four-speed transmission, a straight-bevel axle or worm drive, and a magneto ignition. The Model 31 and 41 GMC trucks used Continental engines until 1922.

W.C. Durant came back to General Motors in 1916. After being ousted from the company in 1910, Durant became involved with Chevrolet. He then used that firm as a springboard to regain absolute control of GM. Charles

Nash resigned as president of GM on April 18 and the board of directors formally accepted his resignation on June 1. Durant then took over as president. On October 13, 1916, Durant incorporated GM, changing its name from the General Motors Co.—a New Jersey corporation— to the General Motors Corp.—a Delaware corporation. At that point, General Motors Truck Co.—along with the company's automobile making and parts manufacturing branches—all became part of General Motors Corp.

In addition to these corporate-level management changes, 1916 was a historical year for the General Motors Truck Co. because of a headline-making "demonstration trip" in which William Warwick and his family drove a 1 1/2-ton Model 31 GMC truck from Washington State to New York and back. The journey to the East, which began in Seattle, Washington, took one day less than two months, but the return leg took much longer.

The Seattle Chamber of Commerce sponsored the trip. Northwest Buick Co., a local distributor of GMC trucks, donated the GMC that Warwick drove, accompanied by his wife and their four-year-old daughter, Daisy. It was loaded with a ton of Carnation canned milk to carry to New York. The truck's large cargo van body also incorporated room inside for the family to camp out along the road. As things turned out, Daisy became sick and was dropped off with relatives who lived in Idaho on the East-bound leg of the journey.

William Warwick had never operated a truck and a woman had never crossed the country by truck before. In spite of these obstacles, no one was allowed to help the Warwicks take care of problems, because the goal was to prove that the GMC truck was able to withstand the hardships of cross-country travel. The couple encountered plenty of bad weather and incredibly bad roads. In one instance, a flood washed the truck down the side of a canyon. Still, the couple continued on and reached New York on September 9. The Warwicks' records showed a total running time of 31 days on the trip to the East.

In New York, the truck was serviced and repainted. This gave Warwick and his wife some time to rest. The couple started their return trip at midnight on October 9, traveling west on the Lincoln Highway. The more southerly route was longer.

When the Warwicks reached 14,000-foot Pikes Peak, near Colorado Springs, Mrs. Warwick challenged William to "Put the GMC over the top or stop right here." So, starting at 1:45 p.m., he drove the GMC truck up to 11,000 feet in second gear. At that level, he started getting "a little pain in the heart." They reached the top after dark and had to tie the truck down with a rope because the wind was so strong. Warwick tried unsuccessfully to light their stove to get warm, but the matches would not burn at that altitude. At about 2 a.m., he drove down to 12,000 feet, where the wind wasn't as strong, but he still could not light the stove. After a cold, sleepless night, he took a photo and descended the mountain.

The Warwicks arrived in Los Angeles and set out for Oregon, but did not reach Portland until January 17,

A 1921 GMC truck with a dump body. (RPJC)

1917, because of treacherous winter weather. When they got to the snowy Siskiyou Mountains, on the border between Oregon and California, their rate of travel slowed to a mile a day. Crossing Oregon's Douglas County took as much time as the entire trip from New York to Los Angeles. However, they refused to give up and reached Portland on January 25, 1917. Five days later, they pulled into Seattle where they were greeted by officials and led by a musical band to the chamber of commerce office.

The Warwicks had traveled a total of 9,513 miles without any major mechanical repairs. Even more important was the fact that William Warwick kept detailed records of the family's trip. The records provided the United States government with information about the condition of the nation's highways. This became very important to the military when the U.S. entered World War I about a month later.

A new 1 1/2-ton Model 30 GMC truck was marketed in 1917 only. This chain-drive model sold for $1,900 and weighed about 5,600 pounds. Like other chain-drive models, it disappeared before the war began. At Durant's urging, GMC also purchased the Samson Sieve Grip Tractor Co. of Stockton, California, in February 1917, to acquire its "Iron Horse" tractor. A Samson farm vehicle that converted from a car into a truck was also devised.

Durant combined Samson with two other firms he controlled, the Janesville Machine Co., of Janesville, Wisconsin, and the Doylestown Agricultural Co., of Doylestown, Pennsylvania. Samson wound up in Janesville, but turned out to be a real money-losing proposition and only two Samson tractors were ever made in Pontiac.

The U.S. declared war on Germany on February 28, 1917. The following June 26, American troops arrived in France, bringing thousands of trucks with them. By the

end of 1917, nearly 90 percent of GMC's truck production was for the war effort. A grand total of 8,512 GMC military vehicles were provided to the United States Army. Civilian production also continued, as evidenced by the fact that GMC built an additional 16,000 Model K-101 five-ton GMC trucks during 1918-1920.

The new Model 16 showed up in the 1918 GMC line and was carried over in 1919 and 1920. Like the Model 15, it was rated for 3/4-ton payloads. It had the same 33-hp four-cylinder engine used in the Model 21 1-ton truck, which was also continued until 1919. With 2,055 assemblies, the Model 16 was a steady seller. In fact, the Model 16 was chosen by the U.S. Army as the Class AA Standard Truck

Fourteenth Aveune Carting Co. put this 10-ton GMC Model 101 highway transportation truck to work back in 1922. (RPJC)

A prisoner in New York's Attica State Correctional Institution made this detailed model of the 1922 GMC K-41 tractor trailer.
(© General Motors Corp.)

Carrying a heavy load of beverage cases is a 1923 GMC K-41 2 1/2-ton bottler's truck.
(© General Motors Corp.)

for the duration of World War I. GMC supplied many ambulances based on the Model 16AA to the Allied forces in Europe. The Model 21 did not sell as well and only 474 were made.

A new 1-ton Model 23 truck with a Continental Model N four-cylinder engine (3 3/4 x 5-in. bore and stroke and 33 hp) was brought out in mid-1918. It was a massive vehicle. A total of 2,401 Model 23 trucks were built in 1917-1918 for the war effort. Most of these trucks were used by the U.S. Army Signal Corps as light aviation-service vehicles. Others were used as artillery-support vehicles.

Due to wartime and postwar demand, Model 16 production was scheduled in four factories in 1919, with a distinct range of serial numbers for each one. Total production was 3,772 units. After World War I ended, the Model 16 became the basis of the classic GMC K-Series truck. Model 21s were made in just one factory in 1919 and production dropped to 335 units, due mainly to declining military demand.

Many trucks ordered by the government were still uncompleted when World War I came to an end. A large number of these were diverted to use by government agencies or sold to private companies. The surplus of trucks existing after the war brought many trucks on the market at low prices and increased the general use of motor trucks in many businesses. It also inspired the government to undertake public-works projects in which these commercial vehicles could be put to good use.

To compete in the over-saturated postwar truck market, GMC announced a $280 price reduction for the Model 16 in the fall of 1918. In early 1919, general sales manager Vance H. Day launched the company's first sales program aimed at the public. The "Consumer Campaign," as

it was called, promoted the Model 16's wartime contributions, as well as its successful use in a variety of different businesses. Dealers were mentioned in factory literature for the first time. Prior to this, those who sold GMC trucks were called distributors or agents.

Starting in the latter part of 1919, new machinery was purchased and new facilities were provided at GMC's Plant One, on Rapid Street, in Pontiac, Michigan, for an anticipated postwar expansion of truck manufacturing. The biggest improvement was the installation of a floor conveyor used in truck-assembly work.

For 1920, the Model 16 was updated to a "3/4-ton to 1-ton model" to cover a wider market niche. This may have been part of an effort to cut back production based on a slackening of late postwar demand due to heavy inventories in the military-surplus market. Production was limited to two factories and fell to 2,623 units.

The Boedeker Ice Cream company operated this 2-ton Model K-41 GMC truck in 1922. (RPJC)

A fabulous scale model of the 1923 GMC Model 23 1-ton GMC panel delivery truck made by a prisoner at Attica Prison in New York State. (© General Motors Corp.)

General Motors Truck Co. also constructed a new storage warehouse at its home plant in Pontiac during 1920. Due to a shortage of railroad cars caused by World War I, the company had to improvise upon its normal ways of doing business. Instead of driving the vehicles onto flatbed freight cars, a system was devised to lift finished trucks into coal tenders and gondolas with a large crane.

In 1921, General Motor Truck Co. switched from Continental engines to engines built by Northway Motor Division of GM, which was based in Detroit. Northway was first incorporated in 1908 and was subsequently acquired by General Motors Co. in 1909. It became a GM subsidiary. The Northway engines used in the trucks were referred to as "GMC" engines and featured removable cylinder sleeves.

Introduced late in 1920 as a 1921 truck was the K-16, a 1-ton postwar model. Other Ks came in capacities up to 5 tons. They had lighter shipping weights than earlier GMCs of the same capacity and the new 33-hp four-cylinder GMC Model-80 engine. The K-15 was a 1/2-ton entry in the new series. GMC built about 276 K-15s in 1921 and K-16 production was higher at 2,026 units, due to its early arrival. A selling point of the K series was that these trucks were specifically engineered to accept a variety of special equipment options from PTOs to tire pumps. Electric lights were standard on all models except the K-15.

Production of both the K-15 (325 units) and K-16 (3,250 units) rose modestly in 1922 and a tractor-truck version was added to the line that December. The K-15 was dropped in 1923, while the 1-ton K-16 was carried over as GMC's smallest truck. There were no changes from 1922 specifications. The GMC four-cylinder Northway engine, used in the Models K-15 and K-16, had a 3 1/2 x 5 1/2-in. bore and stroke and developed 19.6 NACC hp or 33 bhp at 1,810 rpm. The Model K-16X was added in 1923. The X indicated that it had a factory-installed 1-ton express body.

There were virtually no changes in the GMC truck product line for 1924. In April, it was announced that the truck-sales organization of the General Motors Truck Co. had expanded to 10 district sales managers, 25 distributors, 15 branches, and 10 sub-branches.

In early 1925, the 1-ton K-16 and K-16X express were carried over, along with several other models offered the previous year. These were the K-41 models in the 2-ton class, the 3 1/2-ton K-71, and the 5-ton K-101. The K-41 model used a larger GMC Model 84 four-cylinder engine with a 4 x 5 1/2-inch bore and stroke and 37 bhp, while the K-71s and K-101s both employed a 51-bhp four with 4 1/2 x 6-inch cylinder dimensions. These engines were the same as before, but some engineering changes did take place.

GMC added tractor-truck versions of the K-41, K-71, and K-101. These were identified by a "T" suffix. The K-41T was a 5-ton tractor, the K-71T carried a 10-ton rating, and the K-101T was listed as a 15-ton tractor.

While some important keystones in the foundation of today's GMC were laid in the quarter century since Max Grabowsky designed his first truck, the enterprise that existed in 1925 still had many building blocks to set in place. About halfway through that year, a major corporate change took place when the General Motors Truck Co. merged with a Chicago firm to create the Yellow Truck & Coach Manufacturing Co. How this evolved into GMC Truck & Coach will unfold as our history continues.

A well-dressed truck driver of 1924 with his GMC K-41 2-ton truck. (© General Motors Corp.)

This 1925 GMC Model KT1 3 1/2-ton dump-body truck has a new Fisher all-steel cab. (© General Motors Corp.)

Every GMC Mile Pays a Dividend

Whether the work is usual or unusual, hard or very hard, GMC trucks are paying substantial dividends to the GMC users of America.

Dividends in miles, in longer life, in freedom from the need for attention and repair.

Dividends in more miles per dollar of investment because of the many GMC features that increase durability; among others, these: over-strength design of parts, full pressure lubrication of the GMC engine, GMC Two-Range Transmission and GMC renewability of cylinder walls.

Every GMC mile is like every other GMC mile—*it pays a dividend.*

GENERAL MOTORS TRUCK COMPANY
Division of General Motors Corporation
PONTIAC, MICHIGAN

In the Dominion of Canada
General Motors Truck Company of Canada, Limited, Oshawa, Ontario

General Motors Trucks
GMC

Left: An advertisement from the November 1924 *Literary Digest* promoted sales of GMC trucks. (JMSC)

Cabs, Coaches, and 'Cannon-balls'

1926-1939

One of GMC's popular models was the "Big Brute" like this 1927 K102 HD ice truck. The 160-inch-wheelbase truck has a four-cylinder engine with 4 1/2 x 6 1/2-inch bore and stroke. (NSPC/JE)

James Joseph Tunney was known as "The Fighting Marine" because he won the light-heavyweight championship of the American Expediciary Forces in France in April 1919. Tunney was the Heavyweight champion of the world in 1926. (AACA)

1925-1927: Cabs to 'Cannon-balls'

In 1925, General Motors top management decided that the corporation's commercial line should include taxicabs and buses. Bus manufacturing was, at the time, a fast-growing business where automobile makers such as Studebaker and Pierce-Arrow had done quite well. After a series of market surveys, General Motors Truck Co. engineered a merger with Yellow Cab Mfg. Co. of Chicago, Illinois, which included the Yellow Coach Mfg. Co. as a subsidiary.

John D. Hertz—famous for Hertz rental cars—was president of Yellow Cab Mfg. Co. Hertz began his career as a car salesman in Chicago, where he crafted a niche selling taxicabs and advice on how to run taxi companies. Between 1915 and 1922, he sold thousands of Yellow Cabs. His deals were often made on credit or in exchange for shares of taxi companies. Hertz became interested in buses. He obtained the Chicago Motor Bus Co. and its manufacturing arm, the American Motor Bus Co., as well as New York City's Fifth Avenue Coach Co. He joined these together in a holding company called The Omnibus Corp. and built the first Yellow Coach Type Z in 1923. Two years later, GM bought control of Yellow Cab Mfg. Co. from Hertz and his associates for $16 million.

Yellow acquired all the stock of General Motors Truck Co. and General Motors Truck Corp. in exchange for giving General Motors controlling interest in Yellow Truck & Coach Mfg. Co. From 1926 until 1936, General Motors Truck Co. became the sales subsidiary of this new truck-and-bus company, while General Motors Truck Corp. was used as the name of the manufacturing subsidiary. News of the proposed merger made the newspapers on June 27, 1925, with the names of Alfred P. Sloan, Jr. and John D. Hertz appearing in the headlines.

On August 12, 1925, the General Motors Truck Corp. was incorporated under the laws of Delaware by the General Motors Corp. to hold title to the property of the truck plant in Pontiac, Michigan, and to serve as the manufacturing subsidiary of the Yellow Truck & Coach Mfg. Co. The Yellow Truck & Coach Mfg. Co. acquired all the capital stock of the General Motors Truck Corp. from General Motors under the merger terms. The old General Motors Truck Co. continued as a subsidiary of the General Motors Truck Corp. for sales purposes and as the sales and service outlet for the products made by the General Motors Truck Corp.

Yellow Cab Mfg. Co. stockholders ratified the merger on August 17. A new holding company known as Yellow Truck & Coach Mfg. Co. replaced the Yellow Cab Mfg. Co. on August 26. John D. Hertz was named chairman and John A. Ritchie assumed the presidency. The merger of General Motors and Yellow was completed in September. Yellow Truck & Coach also acquired the assets of Northway Motor and Mfg. Co. Yellow Truck & Coach Mfg. Co. then became a manufacturer of trucks, buses, and trailers.

Trucks are the focus of this chapter. Yellow built seven types of coaches, two types of taxicabs, two types of "Drivurself" cars, and several types of 1-ton trucks in its plant in Chicago. GMC did not produce any light-duty trucks in 1925 or 1926. Instead, the Yellow Cab "T" series of light-duty trucks was made available through GMC dealers and distributors. The most popular model was the T-2, a 1-ton truck called the "Yellow Knight." It had a 41-bhp engine built by Yellow Sleeve Valve Engine Works, another Yellow Cab Mfg. Co. subsidiary. A wide range of factory-installed vocational bodies was available. Since the Yellow trucks were priced too high to compete against Chevrolet, Ford, and Dodge trucks, GMC resumed production of light-duty trucks in 1927, with Models T-10 and T-20.

In June 1926, the company consolidated its sales staff at the Yellow Cab plant on Dickens Avenue in Chicago. In July, all engineering personnel from Chicago and East Moline, Illinois, were consolidated into one engineering division at the plant on Rapid Street in Pontiac. General Motors merged its own GMC truck manufacturing operation into Yellow. Truck manufacturing was carried out by the General Motors Truck Corp. in a 500,000 sq.-ft. section of the Rapid Street factory in Pontiac, Michigan.

On February 10, 1926, GM's board of directors approved the purchase of land for a new Yellow Truck & Coach assembly plant. A 160-acre farm south of Pontiac, owned by Alfred Howland, was acquired in March 1927 but the purchase and the company's intent to build a new plant were not publicized until June 13, 1927.

The Northway Motor Division of General Motors Truck Corp., which was now a subsidiary of Yellow Truck & Coach Mfg. Co., was liquidated, with part of its machinery being transferred to the Yellow Sleeve-Valve Engine Works in East Moline. The Northway plant in Detroit was then sold to Chevrolet Gear and Axle Division of Chevrolet

Motor Co. and became known as the Holbrook Avenue Plant.

During the late 1920s, GMC turned to several GM divisions for its truck engines. In 1927, some GMC models switched to a six-cylinder Buick-built motor. A year later, in 1928, the T-11 Deluxe Delivery evolved from a Pontiac truck that had been offered just one year with a Pontiac six engine. Some Yellow Coach buses used Cadillac engines, while other GMC trucks used Oldsmobile engines.

The operations of the holding company—Yellow Truck & Coach Mfg.—were not consolidated into the accounts of General Motors Corp. until the early 1940s, so there are no corporate records of GMC truck production for 1926-1939. However, GMC new-truck registration figures compiled by R.L. Polk & Co. from 1928-1939 reflect an overall growth trend, with some dips that were most likely caused by the Depression. The registration figures looked like this:

1928	14,300	1934	10,449
1929	17,568	1935	11,442
1930	9,004	1936	26,980
1931	6,919	1937	43,522
1932	6,359	1938	20,152
1933	6,602	1939	34,908

The 1926 GMC lineup—announced in 1925—had many changes in model numbers, engines, and capacities, so it was obviously a year of transition. There was no standardized look to a 1926 GMC truck. Some had painted radiator grilles, logos with "GMC" as freestanding letters, and thin, tightly spaced hood louvers like the 1925 models, while others had bright radiator grilles, logos with the letters "GMC" inside an oval badge and fewer, wider-spaced hood louvers like 1927 models.

GMC K-16 1-ton trucks became K-17s and had a larger, more powerful four-cylinder engine. A new K-32 1 1/2-ton truck shared that motor. The K-41 2-ton truck became the K-52 2 1/2-ton truck, but retained the same 4 x 5 1/2-in. bore-and-stroke engine. A new K-54 3 1/4-ton model was added. The K-54 featured the larger 4 1/2 x 6 1/2-inch bore-and-stroke GMC four-cylinder engine that produced 53 hp. Models K-52 and up included a Fisher all-steel closed cab as standard equipment.

The GMC K-71 became the K-72 and kept the same 3 1/2-ton rating and four-cylinder engine. In fact, this larger engine was used in all large GMC trucks. The 70-series 10-ton tractor was dropped. The 5-ton K-101 became the K-102 and used the 53-bhp engine, but the 15-ton K-101T tractor was also discontinued.

Two other 1926 additions were the "Big Brute" K-10T, a 10-ton tractor-truck, and the K-15T, which was a 15-ton tractor-truck. Both of these shared use of the 53-bhp "big four." The K-15T was the first GMC truck to crack the $6,000 price barrier. These were the final examples of GMC's classic K series and reflected a move toward

manufacturing large, heavy-duty trucks. They had the words "Big Brute" on a bar in front of the radiator and were among America's biggest trucks of the 1925-1929 era. They were commonly seen around the docks of seafront cities working as drayage rigs.

In January 1927, John A. Ritchie was elevated to the position of vice chairman of the board of Yellow Truck & Coach Mfg. Co. and GM installed Paul W. Seiler as president and general manager. The general offices of Yellow Truck & Coach Mfg. Co., General Motors Truck Corp., and General Motors Truck Co. were all moved to 11-253-257 General Motors Building on West Grand Boulevard in Detroit. P.W. Seiler and his staff were located there until completion of a new factory administration building in early 1928.

The purchase of the Howland farm was finally announced on June 13, 1927, when Michigan newspapers reported plans to build a modern truck and coach plant, costing $8,000,000, at the site in Pontiac. On July 5, 1927, ground was broken for construction of the new factory and administration building on South Boulevard. The contractors worked on this project 24 hours a day for the rest of the year.

The introduction of the first of the new "T" series, in 1927, marked a major advance in GMC truck styling. Its headlamps were relocated next to the radiator. The fenders were more deeply crowned and the radiator was chrome plated. It was a handsome commercial vehicle and combined sales for 1927-1928 raced to 20,000 units. With the "T" models, GMC introduced a new 221-cid six-cylinder valve-in-head engine built by Buick, a three-speed manual transmission, and a new clutch.

In 1928, Reo Motor Car Co. of Lansing, Michigan, took the six-cylinder engine from its 1927 Speedwagon Six 12-passenger bus and put it in a 1/2-ton truck that it named the Junior Speed Wagon. However, despite its catchy

Sam Dill's Circus made use of several GMCs, including this 1927 Model T20 1-ton truck. (© General Motors Corp.)

This Buick-powered 1927 GMC T50 2-ton truck was used by a glazier to carry window glass. (© General Motors Corp.)

"Cannon-ball" Baker

Top Left: The 1927 GMC 3-compartment tanker went from New York to San Francisco with a capacity load. (© General Motors Corp.)

Top Right: A scale model of the famous "Cannon-ball" Baker truck of 1927 made by a prisoner at Attica Prison in New York State. Lettering like that used on the real truck was added to this model later. (© General Motors Corp.)

Middle Left: Though the trip was done in record time, "Cannon-ball" Baker stopped his 1927 GMC T40 long enough to snap a photo of the truck next to Charles Lindberg's "Spirit of St. Louis" airplane. (© General Motors Corp.)

Middle Right: Stunt driver "Cannon-ball" Baker drove this 1927 GMC T40 2-ton truck 2,493 miles cross country in 5 days, 17 hours and 16 minutes. (© General Motors Corp.)

Bottom: This photo shows "Cannon-ball" Baker, at the end of his 1927 trip, putting water that he carried from the Atlantic Ocean into the Pacific Ocean near San Francisco. (© General Motors Corp.)

name, the famous Reo Speed Wagon was not really the first truck of its kind. GMC offered "speed trucks" with Buick engines even earlier than Reo. The six-cylinder-powered GMC T-20 1-ton truck, T-40 bevel-drive truck, and T-50 2-ton worm-drive truck made big news in 1927. "It had to come," read a sign on the first of three GMCs driven through the streets of Chicago to advertise the new models that year. "The modern six-cylinder speed truck with Buick engine," said the second truck's sign. "As only General Motors would produce it," the sign on truck number three announced.

To promote the new motor, "Cannon-ball" Baker—a well-known racing, endurance, and stunt driver—made a record-breaking run from New York to San Francisco driving a 1927 GMC 2-ton truck. Bold lettering on the bed of the truck's three-compartment tanker body read, "GENERAL MOTORS 2 TON TRUCK POWERED WITH BUICK 6 CYLINDER ENGINE." The tank was filled with a "capacity load" (550 gallons) of Atlantic Ocean water to pour into the Pacific Ocean. Baker left New York at 8:48 p.m. on September 6, 1927, and made the 3,693-mile trip in five days, 17 hours, and 36 minutes. His average speed was 35.5 mph. GMC poured some heavy promotional backing into publicizing the truck's power, driver comfort, and closed-cab construction. The journey was heralded as "the ultimate test of man and machine."

The 1/2-ton T-10 model was introduced soon after the larger "T" models appeared. It was powered by a Pontiac flathead six-cylinder engine and sold for $585 f.o.b. (freight on board) from Pontiac, Michigan.

Toward the end of the year, John D. Hertz stepped down from active involvement in the Yellow Truck & Coach Mfg. Co. and J.A. Ritchie became chairman of the board, a position he held until 1931. On October 27, 1927, O.L. Arnold left Ford Motor Co. to become GMC's vice president and director of truck sales.

1928: Deluxe Delivery

On January 5, 1928, the first truck rolled out of the

new South Boulevard Factory (Plant 2), which had been built in only six months. By March, it was cranking out 150 trucks per day. Also completed that month, adjacent to the factory, was the new administration building. It was quickly filled by members of the sales staff, who relocated from Chicago, and executives who previously worked in the GM Building in Detroit.

A new 1928 model was a fancy panel that started as a Pontiac. The 1/2-ton Pontiac Deluxe Delivery truck had been introduced (as a 1927 model) in October 1926. In late 1927, some details of the radiator design were changed and this truck became the GMC T-11. *Branham's 1930 Automobile Reference Book* lists Deluxe Delivery and T-11 versions as 1928 GMC models. This source suggests that units with serial numbers 145000 through 197183 were built as Pontiac Deluxe Deliveries, units with numbers 197184 through 227163 were built as GMC Deluxe Deliveries, and units with serial numbers 227164 and up were built as GMC T-11 panels. All of these were identical,

This 1928 GMC 2-ton stake bed truck with a Pontiac engine is one of 100 made. It was restored by the Telephone Pioneers of America of the Manitoba (Canada) Telephone System. (RR)

T. Eaton Co.'s "Santa Claus Toyland" express was a 1928 GMC screenside delivery. (OCWC)

Yellow Truck & Coach Mfg., Co. Subsidiaries—1928

The annual report for 1928 showed the following subsidiaries of the Yellow Truck & Coach Manufacturing Company:

Finance
  Yellow Manufacturing Acceptance Corp. –GM Building, Detroit, Michigan
Manufacturing
  General Motors Truck Corp. –Pontiac, Michigan
  Yellow Sleeve Valve Engine Works, Inc. –East Moline, Illinois
Sales
  General Motors Truck Co. –Pontiac, Michigan
  Canadian Yellow Cab Manufacturing Co., Ltd. –Montreal, Quebec, Canada
  General Motors Truck Co. of Canada –Oshawa, Ontario, Canada
Drivurself
  Hertz Drivurself Corp. –Wilmington, Delaware
Foreign
  Yellow Cab Manufacturing Co. –(England) Ltd. London, England

Note: Information compiled from R.A. Christ's *GMC Truck History: 1900-1950*, courtesy D.E. Meyer.

Right: A 1930 GMC truck with a cement mixer body. (RPJC)

A 1929 GMC T-19 1-ton truck used by the Socony Vacuum Oil Co. as a mobile repair shop throughout Egypt. This 1978 photo was taken in the Sudan, North Africa, when the truck was being used as a display unit. (© General Motors Corp.)

In the shop for service are a 1929 GMC T11 panel and a T30 1 1/2-ton dump truck. (© General Motors Corp.)

except for their radiator badges and fuel-gauge locations. Pontiacs had the gauge on the gas tank and GMCs had it on the instrument panel.

Both the Pontiac and GMC version of the Deluxe Delivery sold for $585 and weighed 1,820 lbs. The engine was the Pontiac L-head six, with a 3 1/4 x 3 3/4-in. bore and stroke and 186.5 cid. The engine used convex (rather than concave) interior cylinder walls and was the first to have a fuel pump, rather than a vacuum-feed fuel system. It developed 36 hp at 2400 rpm. The engine had mechanical-valve lifters and a one-barrel Carter carburetor. The trucks both had a 110-in. wheelbase and 4.75 x 20 tires.

Other than the T-11, the 1928 GMC line was much like 1927's. According to the *1930 Branham Automobile Reference Book*, even the prices and weights remained the same. There were 19 lines of trucks in eight weight classes. In addition to the T-11, there was the 1-ton T-19 and four models identified as the T-30, T-42, T-60, and T-80 that had capacities ranging from 1 1/2 to 4 tons. Five different engines were used with NACC horsepower ratings of 16.90, 20.30, 25.60, 29.40, and 32.40. On September 1, 1928, a personnel department was established and William A. Raache became GMC's first personnel director.

1929: Last Big Year

For 1929, GMC decided to emphasize six-cylinder models and only the three "Big Brute" 5-ton tractors, which were making their last appearance, continued using the big 4 1/2 x 6 1/2-in. bore-and-stroke, 32.40-hp four. The T-11 1/2-ton panel and T-19 1-ton panel stayed with the flathead Pontiac six and all other trucks (there were 24 other models of 1 1/2-ton, 2-ton, 3-ton and 4-ton capacities) shared the use of two other sixes, both of which were sourced from General Motors' Buick Division. One with 3 5/16 x 4 5/8-in. bore-and-stroke measurements and 26.30 hp was used in models up to 2 tons and the other with a 3 5/8 x 5-in. bore and stroke and 31.50 hp was used in all 3- and 4-ton trucks. This would be GMC's last big sales year before the Depression.

On October 27, newspapers in Pontiac, Michigan, announced that the Yellow Sleeve-Valve Engine Works was transferring all of its employees and equipment from East Moline, Illinois, to Pontiac. Then, the Yellow Truck & Coach plant in Chicago was sold and manufacturing and production work was centralized in two plants in Pontiac. Finally, in early 1930, all engine production for GMC trucks was housed in Plant One at Pontiac.

1930: The Depression Hits

The 1930s brought many product improvements, but GMC and other truck manufacturers wound up struggling to find buyers in a nation brought to its knees by the Great Depression. Wall Street crashed in on itself on "Black Monday" in October 1929 and the following year saw truck business in the United States and Canada combined drop by some 26 percent. Over the 10-year period 1929 to 1939, the production totals for all truckmakers looked like this:

Year	U.S. Truck Production
1929	.771,020
1930	.571,241
1931	.416,648
1932	.235,187
1933	.346,545
1934	.575,192
1935	.694,690
1936	.784,587
1937	.893,085
1938	.488,100
1939	.710,026

Judging by the new-truck registration figures shown earlier, GMC sold 49 percent fewer trucks in 1930 than in 1929, but this had nothing to do with the product itself, which had many appearance and engineering advances. Four models using a larger Pontiac six were available: the T-11 (3,800-lb. gross vehicle weight rating); the T-15 (5,400-lb. GVWR); the T-17 (6,500-lb. GVWR); and the T-19 (8,500-lb. GVWR). These models were actually 1/2-ton, 1-ton, and two 1 1/2-ton trucks in respective order, but the industry went to straight ratings and recommended GVWRs this year, with load weights given in pounds.

The larger 200 4-cid Pontiac six-cylinder engine had 3 5/16 x 3 7/8-in. bore-and-stroke measurements and produced 26.33 hp (60 hp at 3000 rpm in brake horsepower terms). Three wheelbases of 110-, 130- and 141-in. were offered. The torque-tube drive used previously in the Pontiac drive train was replaced by a Hotchkiss system.

Standard features of these trucks included a three-speed manual transmission, single dry-plate clutch, hypoid, semi-floating rear axle, mechanical four-wheel brakes, and pressed-steel wheels. Bumpers were optional.

The 257.5-cid Buick Standard Six engine was used in the 1 1/2-ton GMC T-25 (8,500-lb. GVWR) and all six 2-, 2 1/2 and 3-ton trucks. It had a 3 7/16 x 4 5/8-in. bore-and-stroke and 80.5 gross horsepower at 2800 rpm. Three models of 3 1/2-ton GMC trucks utilized the 331.3-cid Buick MasterSix motor, with a 3 3/4 x 5-in. bore-and-stroke and generated 99 bhp at 2800 rpm.

In all, there were two each of 2-, 2 1/2-and 3-ton models, plus three 3 1/2-ton models and a wide variety of bigger 4- and 5-ton models. Prices started at about $770 for a 1/2-ton T-11 chassis that weighed 1,980 lbs., and ran up to $2,685 for a 3 1/2-ton T-60-A that had a weight of 6,375 lbs. The larger trucks were even pricier and heavier.

By July 1930, a new General Motors Truck Co. engineering building was completed at Plant 2 in Pontiac. After that, all engineering activities were carried out in

A 1931 GMC T15 1,500-lb. panel used to deliver Klee's Trule fruit flavored beverages. (© General Motors Corp.)

F.M. Kirkpatrick, the official photographer for Indianapolis Motor Speedway, used this T15 GMC 1,500-lb. platform stake truck at the 1931 Indy 500. (IMSC)

Left: This July 11, 1931, photo shows a pair of GMC T15 panels being hauled by a T31. The rear truck was bound for a customer in Milwaukee, Wisconsin. The other trucks were going to Omaha, Nebraska. (BDKC)

A 1931 GMC T11 panel was carried on a 1931 GMC F19C Chassis & Cab as part of a study of vehicle shipping methods conducted by a railroad for General Motors Truck Co. The smaller truck was destined for a buyer in Murfreesboro, Tennessee. (BDKC)

Gerber Products Co. of Fremont, Michigan, started producing baby food in 1928 and used this GMC T95 truck and tandem trailer to deliver its baby foods in 1931. (© General Motors Corp.)

This February 12, 1931, photo shows three GMC T19 trucks on their way to a rail line for shipment to Omaha, Nebraska. (BDKC)

the west wing that adjoined the main factory on South Boulevard. The company began conducting customer surveys to create a profile of its buyers and determine the best vocational markets for its trucks. Some corporate shuffling also took place in GMC's Canadian operations in 1930.

1931: Transcontinental Test Run

The GMC truck line was expanded again in 1931 with 16 models and 56 chassis in the T Series. Due to the effects of the Depression, prices were reduced $50 to $600 per model. There were hundreds of tire-and-wheel combinations. Nine factory bodies were offered and tandem rear-axle units were among the 16 new models.

On September 8, 1931, a GMC T-95-C double unit 6-x-4 truck and full trailer owned by Southern California Freight Lines Ltd. set out from Los Angeles on an eight-day run to New York City. The GMC truck was fitted with a refrigeration unit so it could carry a test load of perishable fruits, vegetables, and eggs from coast-to-coast. This promotion was considered a "scientific experiment" in the long-distance transportation of perishable goods. Close records of every aspect of the trip were kept. When the truck and trailer, which averaged 27.3 mph, arrived on the East Coast 117 hours later, the produce inside was in good condition at 35 degrees.

GMC's Pontiac-powered lineup was carried over in 1931. The 1/2-ton T-11 had an approximate payload capacity of 1,100 lbs., making it a heavy 1/2-tonner. Prices started at $625 for the chassis and cowl. Pickup, canopy,

screen-side, panel, and sedan delivery bodies were available at extra cost. The 1-ton T-15 was carried over in the same models for about $20 more. It was certified for 1,675-to 2,875-lb. payloads. F.M. Kirkpatrick, the official photographer for the Indianapolis Motor Speedway, used a T-15 1-ton range GMC stake body truck that was lettered up for race-day promotions. The 1 1/2-ton Model T-19 was also carried over in 1931. It had a GVWR of 8,500 lbs. and sold for $745.

Also using the Pontiac engine were the 1-ton T-15 and T-17 and a new T-18 model that was developed as a reaction to the country's economic downturn. It was a 1 1/2-ton truck with a 141-in. wheelbase and a 1,645-lbs. to 3,050-lbs. payload rating. It sold for only $595 in chassis-and-cab form. The cab came from Chevrolet, which had purchased the Martin Parry Body Co. in November 1930. After renaming the firm the Chevrolet Commercial Body Co., Chevrolet started making "factory" truck bodies. In the beginning, only the Chevrolet cab was mounted at the GMC factory, while other bodies were available through GMC factory branches.

In 1931, Buick dropped six-cylinder engines and offered only inline eights. GMC developed its own version of the 257.5-cid Buick Standard Six with its 3 7/16 x 4 5/8-in. bore and stroke. GMC fitted this engine with hydraulic valve lifters and a seven main-bearing crankshaft. Repair manuals of the era called it the "Buick eng. 257." Trucks more than 3 1/2-ton used a GMC-modified version of the larger Buick Master Six. Buick-based engines were used in some GMC trucks until 1960 and grew as large as 707 cu. in.

Around this time, General Motors management decided that the Chevrolet Division should specialize in smaller trucks. GMC, it felt, should focus on larger models in capacities up to 15 tons, as well as on advanced technical development work. The 10-ton T-95 and bigger models had tandem-rear axles.

Two of the largest truck models offered by GMC up to this time were released late in 1931. Models T-110 (38,000 lb. GVWR) and T-130 (50,000 lb. GVWR) were designed for off-road construction service. Some T-130s were sold to the Tennessee Valley Authority for dam building. Also, GMC started building trailer chassis in 1931. Initially, 21 models were offered, including semi and full trailers ranging from 4 tons to 22 1/2 tons gross trailer weight. Later, fifth-wheel units (semi-trailer lower couplers) were produced.

Late in 1931, John A. Ritchie resigned as chairman of the board at Yellow Truck & Coach Mfg. Co. He explained that he wanted to devote more of his time to the Omnibus Corp., a holding company associated with John D. Hertz.

1932: Honest-to-Goodness

For 1932, "Pontiac 200"-powered models were cut back to the T-11, T-15, T-18, and T-19. Models were also pared from the larger series, probably due to declining sales impacted by a worsening Depression. GMC was a honest-to-goodness truck company, rather than a car company that made trucks. This allowed it to produce models in small runs or as semi-customized trucks designed for a specific buyer. In many cases, the history of an individual truck can be determined.

> ### Yellow Truck & Coach Mfg., Co.
> ### Subsidiaries—1932
> **Finance** Yellow Manufacturing Acceptance Corp.
> **Manufacturing** General Motors Truck Corp.
> **Sales** General Motors Truck Co.
> **Transport** Hertz Drivurself Corp.
> Terminal Cab Corp.
>
> **Notes:** Information compiled from R.A. Christ's *GMC Truck History: 1900-1950*, courtesy D.E. Meyer.

For example, a 10-ton Model T-95-C straight-bodied delivery truck was held in inventory at the Seattle GMC branch until June of 1932, when it was sold to Sunset Motor Freight. At that time, another of the company's trucks was stranded on Old Highway 99 between Seattle and Tacoma. Driver Gordon Eaton took the big-engined GMC out to pull in the stranded truck. In the process, the big "tow truck" slid on a flooded highway and ran off the side of the road where it sank in the floodwaters. Eaton and the truck both escaped without major problems and Sunset's No. 6 truck, with its handsome louver-door hood treatment, survived to make many trouble-free runs through Snoqualamie Pass.

In 1932, a number of heavy-duty engines were available in GMC's heaviest trucks. GMC Historian Donald E. Meyer has compiled a chart of these from GMC sales specifications. All of these heavy-duty engines were valve-in-head inline six cylinders designed and built by GMC:

A 1932 GMC T85 truck with a dump body made by National steel Products Company. (NSPC/JE)

1933: Slip-in Bearings and Sleepers

Five all-new GMC trucks appeared in 1933 and 10 were carried over. The T-15 continued to be the smallest model, but it was offered only in the early part of the year. GMC light-duty truck production was then suspended until 1935. Also available only in the first 1933 series was the 1 1/2-ton Model T-19. The 1 1/2-ton T-18 and T-23, were also included in the first series with "Pontiac 200"-powered models. When the second series arrived, only the T-18 and T-23 remained and both used a new six-cylinder engine with a 3 3/16 x 4 5/8-in. bore and stroke. This was listed in *Chilton Flat-Rate Manuals* as a "Buick type eng. 221" engine. These smaller trucks also had slip-in main and rod bearings, four-speed transmissions, and Huck brakes.

In 1933, a GMC Model O-10 panel delivery truck had a starring role as a "publicity car" in a contest used to promote a motion picture about tugboats that was shot in Seattle, Washington. "Skipper" Don Mills, dressed in a snappy sea captain's uniform, appeared with the truck at film premieres, such as when the film opened at the Ideal Theatre in Stanwood on June 24. The manager of GMC's Seattle branch, Mr. Sweet, posed with the captain and his "luxury liner" in a publicity photo. The truck was a handsome rig with deluxe trim, a sidemounted spare tire, and chrome-plated full-wheel discs bearing the GMC logo.

Truck Models	Displ. (Cu. In.)	Bore (In.)	Stroke (In.)	Max. HP @ rpm	Max. TQ @ rpm
T-90	400	4.13	5.00	110 @ 2300	296 @ 800-1600
T-95	468	4.25	5.50	115 @ 2200	340 @ 800-1600
T-95	525	4.50	5.50	130 @ 2200	380 @ 800-1600
T-95, T-130	616	4.88	5.50	149 @ 2100	450 @ 1000
T-95	707	5.00	6.00	173 @ 2100	550 @ 1000

Used with permission of D.E. Meyer.

Truck driver J.R. Caldwell used a big 1932 GMC T85 tractor with a 24,000-lb. GVWR to haul tires from Akron, Ohio to the GMC factory in Pontiac, Michigan. (© General Motors Corp.)

This 13,000-lb. GVWR 1933 GMC T33D cowl and chassis was fitted with a very large van-type body. (© General Motors Corp.)

This 1934 GMC T23B tractor trailer belongs to Carolyn Moon, whose family owns the Iowa 80 truck stop in Davenport, Iowa. It was purchased new and picked up at the GMC factory by Jake Iles of Mt. Pleasant, Iowa. Lee Snyder of Minburn restored the truck. (CM)

A sleeper cab was introduced for 1933 GMC heavy-duty models and downdraft carburetors were adopted. The overhead-valve six was used in 2-ton trucks, while the 707-cid 173-hp six was specifically designed for the heaviest trucks. These engines used twin-plate clutches and five-speed main transmissions with three- or four-speed auxiliary transmissions available from the factory. Worm-drive axles were used on models with tandem axles and the largest trucks got Bendix-Westinghouse air brakes.

J.P. Little, who formerly worked for Chevrolet, replaced O.L. Arnold as general sales manager at GMC late in 1933. Little totally reorganized the department, setting up three divisions, 34 zones of operation, six factory retail stores, 21 distributors, 1,769 dealers coast to coast, and 101 other sales outlets by July 1. This basic structure lasted for years at what GM called its "Truck & Coach Division."

1934: Bigger is Better

In 1934, the T-15 was replaced by the T-16. This truck had a 1 1/2-ton payload rating and was the smallest GMC product available. It sold for $570 and weighed 3,140 pounds. The T-16 used a 213.3-cid "Olds-type" L-head six with a 3 5/16 x 4 1/8-in. bore and stroke. The motor was good for 90 hp at 3400 rpm in Oldsmobiles. In GMC trucks, brake horsepower was 84 at 3500 rpm. It developed 152 lbs.-ft. of torque at 1200 rpm. The T-18 and T-23 stuck with the Buick-type 221-cid motor. Their prices climbed to $645 and $795, which represented an increase of $80 and $40 respectively.

Trucks larger than 1 1/2 tons offered either a 70-hp side-valve six or 120-hp overhead valve six. Vacuum-servo brakes were introduced for medium-size trucks and five-speed transmissions became standard for heavy-duty models. Sharing a restyling with some Chevrolet trucks, the appearance of larger GMC cabs became more streamlined in late 1934 with the introduction of a line of cab-over-engine (COE) models for the 1935 selling season. The initial offerings in this style included the T-73, T-75, and T-78 models. These cab-over-engine (COE) models had their engines mounted on sub frames that rolled out from the front to make repairs easy. Later, a T-74 model was added.

The Milwaukee Wisconsin Police Department took its 1935 GMC Police Patrol Van to the annual Wally Rank Car Show operated by the Rank & Son Buick-GMC dealership. (OCWC)

Building large trucks to order was common in the truck manufacturing industry and in late 1934, GMC put together a custom job for Victor Salvino's North American Motor Express Co. in Seattle. It was a T-74-H-C cab-over-engine tractor with a built-in sleeper compartment.

1935: Streamlined

In 1935, GMC returned to light-duty truck manufacturing. No new models were released in 1935, but there were important changes and improvements over the 1934 models. According to the January 26, 1935 issue of *Automotive News*, the redesigned light- and medium-duty trucks included seven models. The T-16 (10,000-lb. GVWR) was a 3/4-ton model. It sold for $620 and had 213.3-cid Olds six. New styling features included a sloping grille and fender-mounted headlamps. The T-18, T-23, and T-33 were continued. They had GVWRs of 11,500, 13,000, and 15,000 lbs. respectively, and were priced between $777 and $1,655. Larger GMC models included the T-43 (17,000 lb. GVWR and $1,795), the T-46 (19,000 lb. GVWR and $2,285), and the T-46H (22,000 lb. GVWR and $2,625).

Hydraulic brakes were a new feature for GMC trucks in 1935. A Hydro-Vac system was used on medium-duty models and a full air-actuation system was designed for larger trucks. Another new feature for larger rigs was a two-speed rear axle sourced from Eaton.

On September 1, 1935, Irving B. Babcock replaced P.W. Seiler as president of Yellow Truck & Coach Mfg. Co. This change reflected a shuffling of the company's board of directors, which gave General Motors more representation. Mr. Babcock's first directive was an order to revise the 1936 program to make the trucks look as up-to-date as

A prototype cab-over-engine tractor created by GMC in 1936. (© General Motors Corp.)

passenger cars. More importantly, he decided to re-enter the competitive 1/2-ton light-truck market to compete against Chevrolet, Ford, and Dodge.

1936: New Suburban, New Name

The 1936 GMC truck lineup included 12 conventional cab and 11 COE models. The smaller GMCs adopted more streamlined cabs shared with Chevrolet trucks and featured skirted front and rear fenders and a rounder grille with prominent vertical bars. There was also a larger, fin-like hood ornament. The use of a "blister" type sun visor over the windshield was discontinued. Directly below the "General Motors Truck" nameplate on the hood sides were five bright horizontal moldings. A handsome "veed" bumper was seen up front.

Styling advances such as these helped to boost 1936 GMC truck production an amazing 300 percent over 1935. Of course, another factor was the improvement in economic conditions as the nation emerged from the Great Depression. New models also played an important role in creating a rosier sales picture.

There was a new 1/2-ton truck called the T-14. Priced at $425 for the chassis with cowl and windshield, $525 for a chassis and cab, or $566 for GMC's very first 1/2-ton pickup, the T-14 series used a 126-in. wheelbase and weighed 2,210 lbs. in chassis-only format. It used the 213.3-cid 85-hp Oldsmobile engine and many Oldsmobile passenger-car components. The new model had a three-speed synchromesh transmission, torque-tube drive, and Huck-type hydraulic brakes. It accounted for 42 percent of total GMC production in 1936. In addition to the handsome pickup, the line offered GMC's first Carry-All Suburban.

Part of the 1/2-ton model's strong sales was based on an order for 187 GMC 1 1/2-ton trucks placed by the U.S. Army. A special military version of the T-14, with four-wheel drive, was produced under a government contract. While this was not an exceptionally large order at the time, the experience that GMC got in building four-wheel-drive trucks would help the company secure much larger military orders in future years.

The T-16L was also carried over in 1936. It had the Oldsmobile six and a 131-in. wheelbase. The T-18 and T-23 both got GMC-built "Buick–type" overhead-valve six-cylinder engines. In the former, GMC used the 238.90-cid version with a 3 5/16 x 4 5/8-in. bore and stroke, 81 hp at 3000 rpm and 170 lbs.-ft. of torque at 1,000 rpm. In the latter, the engine was a 257.5-cid version with a 3 7/16 x 4 5/8-in. bore and stroke, 87.5 hp at 2800 rpm and 190 lbs.-ft. of torque at 800 rpm. Other sixes offered in larger trucks were the 286.40-cid 90-hp version that developed 205 lbs.-ft. of torque at 1,000 rpm, the 331.40-cid 94-hp version good for 230 lbs.-ft. at 800 rpm, the 400-cid 110-hp version good for 296 lbs.-ft. at 800 rpm, and the 450-cid 150-hp version that produced 380 lbs.-ft. at 800 rpm. A total of 10 engines were offered and the largest trucks were powered by 525-, 616-, or 707-cid power plants.

The big GMC trucks ranged up to 12-tons in capacity. All GMCs were now available in a choice of 10 colors and in standard or deluxe versions. The list of factory options and accessories began to grow as well. In the middle of the year, General Motors President Alfred P. Sloan, Jr., paid a visit to GMC headquarters and gave a nod of approval to the design advancements incorporated in the new heavy-duty trucks.

Sloan's visit to Pontiac heralded other changes in truck and bus operations. On September 30, 1936, the General Motors Truck Corp. was dissolved. One day later, Yellow Truck & Coach Mfg. Co. became more than just a holding company when it assumed the manufacturing responsibilities for all GMC trucks, tractors, trailers, taxicabs, and Yellow Coach buses. On November 30, General Motors Truck Co., a Louisiana company, was dissolved. After December 1, 1936, sales responsibilities previously conducted by General Motors Truck Co. were transferred to General Motors Truck & Coach Div. of Yellow Truck & Coach Mfg. Co.

1937: Stream-Style and Dual-Tone

The 1937 GMC light- and medium-duty models featured a modernized front-end design with what the company called "built-in" styling. These were the first trucks to reflect the influence of the General Motors styling staff. The headlights were set in the fender valleys, new "dual-tone" color designs appeared and the radiator grille combined three sections of horizontal bars with a broad

center portion of horizontal fins. There were 12 dual-tone paint options with the wheels, radiator surround, and body beads done in contrasting color.

The Oldsmobile-sourced L-head engine used for the GMC light-duty models was enlarged to 3 7/8 x 4 1/8-in. bore and stroke. It now displaced 229.7 cu. in. and developed 86 hp at 3500 rpm and 172 lbs.-ft. of torque at 1,200 rpm. The 3/4-ton T-16L was carried over with the same styling changes seen on the T-14 and the same engine. Other trucks had the same engines as in 1936, except that the 450-cid six was gone.

GMC offered a variety of conventional and COE trucks in 1937. The lightest was the 1/2-ton T-14 and the heaviest conventional was the 12-ton T-61H. The F-16 was

GMC offered a variety of conventional and cab-over-engine trucks in 1937 and the lightest were the 1/2-ton T-14 models such as this pickup. (AL)

By 1937 GMC's pickup truck sales were taking off to a level far above what they had been in 1936. (RNS)

General Motors stylists working on the innovative GMC FC series cab-over-engine truck in 1937. This model featured a "stream style" appearance and exclusive "dual-tone" color design. (© General Motors Corp.)

A 1938 GMC 1/2-ton AF230 forward-control truck was used by the New York Public Library System's Extension Division in Richmond County (Staten Island) New York, the author's hometown. (© General Motors Corp.)

Right: 1937 GMC advertisement.

the lightest COE, while the heftiest was the 12-ton F-61H. Prices ranged from $395 to $3,985 for conventionals, and $635 to $4,355 for COEs, while GVWRs ranged from 4,400 to 36,000 lbs.

"The Truck of Value, GMC Cab-Over-Engine," said a 1937 advertisement showing a drawing of the front end of a 1 1/2-ton COE truck finished in bright yellow with red trim. "See GMC for extra value...for advances stream-style with exclusive 'dual-tone' color design...for half-ton trucks with either short or long wheelbases and the biggest bodies available...for either standard or cab-over-engine trucks ranging in capacity to 12 tons...for 'truck-built' trailers...for improvements and refinements that assure greater economy and improved performance...and for prices that are extremely low." The ad also pointed out that buyers could take advantage of "time payments through our own Y.M.A.C. (Yellow Manufacturing Acceptance Corp.) plan at lowest available rates."

The 1937 engine offerings were reduced by one, as the big 450.9-cid 150-hp six was canceled. The smallest Olds 213.3-cid six was bored out to 3 7/16 in., giving it 229.7 cid. Its compression ratio was raised from 6.00:1 to 6.10:1. Horsepower increased to 86 at 3500 rpm and maximum torque rose to 172 lbs.-ft. at 1200 rpm. Chilton manuals referred to this as the "Old type eng. 230" and indicate that it was used in the T-14 1/2-ton models with a three-speed transmission, as well as the heavier T-16A and T-16B 1 1/2- to 3-ton models and the T-16 1 1/2- to 3 1/2-ton models with a four-speed transmission.

Calendar-year sales of GMC trucks crested 50,000 for the first time and *Ward's 1942 Automotive Yearbook* estimated model-year production at 56,996 trucks. GMC was evolving into a major player in the manufacture of all classes of trucks and its growth brought new acquisitions. In April 1937, GMC purchased the Wilson Foundry and Machine Co. buildings on South Saginaw Street in Pontiac, Michigan. They were converted over for use in the manufacturing of engines for light-duty trucks.

1938: An Array of Models

The *1947 Branham Automobile Reference Book* shows an incredible array of 108 basic models and wheelbase variations for 1938 GMC trucks. The smaller 1938 GMC trucks featured new hood-mounted headlights and grilles with added bright work. No hood louvers were installed. This was the last year the light-duty models used single-piece windshields. The 1/2-ton line included the 112-in. wheelbase T-14A (chassis $410) and 126-in. wheelbase T-14B (chassis $445) models weighing 2,195 to 2300 lbs. The T-14 had a three-speed manual transmission. All other GMCs used four-speed gearboxes. Other standard equipment included a floor-mounted gearshift lever, hydraulic four-wheel brakes, pressed steel wheels, and heavy-duty shock absorbers.

Conventional trucks included the 1 1/2-ton T-16, the 1 1/2-ton T-18, the 2-ton T-23, the 2 1/2-ton T-33, the 3 1/2-ton T-46, the 4-ton T-61, and the 5-ton T-61H, each of which came on from two to five different wheelbases.

Three all-new models were offered: the 3/4-ton T-145, the 1-ton T-15, and the 1 1/4-ton T-155. COE trucks included the 1 1/2-ton F-16, the 1 1/2-ton F-18, the 2-ton F-23, the 2 1/2-ton F-33, the 3 1/2-ton F-46, the 4-ton F-61, and the 5-ton F-61H lines, each also offering multiple wheelbases. The medium- and heavy-duty models had all-new steel "helmet-top" cabs.

All engines used in 1937 were carried over for 1938, but one smaller new engine appeared on GMC specification charts this year only. It was actually a 1937 Pontiac 222.7-cid six with a 3 7/16 x 4-in. bore and stroke and 6.20:1 compression ratio. This engine was rated for 81 hp at 3400 rpm in T-145, T-15, and T-155 3/4-ton trucks, as well as in T-14 1/2-ton trucks with serial numbers T-14-34528 and up. It was used in small GMC-built trucks that wore Oldsmobile badges and were made for export to other countries. Some books have mistakenly identified it as an Oldsmobile engine.

After experiencing a great year in 1937, General Motors anticipated a need for additional GMC production facilities and started producing 1938 models in Chevrolet's Oakland, California, plant. As things turned out, an economic recession took place and GMC's output actually experienced a considerable drop. According to the *Encyclopedia of Commercial Vehicles*, calendar-year truck production was 20,640 units. *Ward's 1942 Automotive Yearbook* estimated model-year production of 1938 GMCs at 31,346 trucks. That included 4,929 2 1/2-ton six-wheel-drive (6 x 6) and 50 1 1/2-ton four-wheel-drive (4 x 4) military trucks manufactured in May and June

under a government contract. Late in the calendar year, GMC started production of 228-cid and 248-cid engines at plant four, on South Saginaw Street, for use in 1939 models. These replaced the Pontiac and Oldsmobile engines used in most light- and medium-duty GMC models.

1939: First Steps Toward the '40s

Totally new GMC models arrived in 1939. An AC prefix indicated conventionals and an AF designated the COE or forward-control trucks. There was also a new AF-230 parcel delivery model. As a hint of what was to come during the 1940s, GMC designed the ACKWX-353 6 x 6 military transport truck this year. Rumblings from conflicts throughout the world had prompted the U.S. Army to initiate a mobilization program through which General Motors would become, as chairman Alfred P. Sloan, Jr., once put it, "the world's largest private producer of military hardware."

Branham shows more 1939 model listings and wheelbase variations than in 1938. A study titled, *GMC Truck History 1900 to 1950*, compiled in 1956 by R.A. Crist, a GMC divisional historian at that time, lists 19 basic conventional models and 16 basic COE models. The offerings included a variety of wheelbases and 59 new 2- to 6-ton models with three-cylinder Detroit 3-71 or four-cylinder Detroit 4-71 diesel engines developed by General Motors' Detroit Diesel branch.

The 1939 conventionals were restyled with V-shaped, two-piece windshields. The grille remained high and narrow, but it had a more massive appearance with thicker and more sharply angled horizontal bars attached to a center vertical bar. The design seemed to be patterned after a fish skeleton. The uppermost bar carried the GMC logo. As in earlier years, the side hood bar on conventional trucks read "General Motor Truck," but its leading edge was more blunt than in 1938. The main change on COEs was that they got their own version of the "fish skeleton" grille.

Prices started at $460 for an AC-100 chassis. The pickup sold for $593, the panel for $669. That compared to $850 for the AC-300 panel. Larger series also offered

platform-, express-, and stake-truck models. The largest AF-850 sold for $5,420 and had a shipping weight of 8,810 lbs.

Seven gasoline-fueled six-cylinder engines were used in 1939 and the only carryover was the 229.7-cid L-head that GMC continued sourcing from Oldsmobile for use in the new F-230 parcel delivery van. The smallest engine was a new 228-cid inline six with 3 9/16 x 3 13/16-in. bore-and-stroke measurements used in all trucks up to those in the GMC 350 series. It developed 80 hp at 3000 rpm and 178 lbs.-ft. of torque at 1,000 rpm. The GMC 400/450-series trucks used a 248.5-cid six with 3 23/32 x 3 13/16-in. bore and stroke. It produced 88 hp at 3000 rpm and maximum torque was 195 lbs.-ft. at 1000 rpm.

The GMC 500/550 series had exclusive use of a 278.66-cid six with 3 5/8 x 4 1/2-in. bore and stroke in 1939. It produced 100 hp at 2900 rpm and 213 lbs.-ft. of torque at 1000 rpm. GMC 600/650 models shared a 308.23-cid motor with 3 13/16 x 4 1/2-in. bore and stroke that produced 110 hp at 2800 rpm and 239 lbs.-ft. of torque at 800 rpm. The 700 series trucks had a 360.83-cid motor with 4 1/8 x 4 1/2-in. bore and stroke that generated 122 hp at 2800 rpm and 265 lbs.-ft. of torque at 800 rpm. The GMC 800 series trucks had a 425.58-cid six with 4 1/4 x 5-in. bore and stroke that put out 145 hp at 2700 rpm and 322 lbs.-ft. at 1000 rpm. Finally, GMC 850s used a 450.9-cid six with 4 3/8 x 5-in. bore and stroke that was good for 146 hp at 2400 rpm and maximum torque of 350 lbs.-ft. at 1000 rpm.

This year, all GMCs offered synchromesh transmissions. With military orders included, total calendar-year production rose to 44,000 units. According to *Ward's 1942 Automotive Yearbook*, estimated model-year production rose to 34,265 trucks.

A restored 1937 GMC platform stake truck at the Iola Old Car Show. (KTA)

General Electric Co. fitted this 1938 GMC panel truck with a multitude of lights while conducting tests of sealed-beam headlamps. (GE/RE)

Left: This 1939 advertising illustration shows a GMC AC350 1 1/2-ton conventional truck being used to make wholesale meat deliveries. (© General Motors Corp.)

C h a p t e r   3

The Fighting '40s

1940-1949

Page 34 and 35: The perfect vehicle for a large family's picnics was the 1948 GMC FC100 Suburban Carryall. (© General Motors Corp.)

Right: A 1940 GMC conventional platform truck with a stake rack body. (CH)

This 1940 GMC sales brochure promoted the 450 3-ton range of trucks and depicted an AC450 grain box truck and an AF 450 COE tractor towing a trailer. (CTC)

1940: Built for the Duration

In 1940, GMC continued to produce the AC ("C" stood for conventional), AF ("F" stood for forward-control), and ADC/ADF ("D" diesel-powered) models. These would be the company's final civilian trucks before the Japanese attack on Pearl Harbor brought a sudden and total switch to military production for World War II. In many cases, these trucks were called upon to last the duration of the war, surviving longer and traveling further than ever anticipated by the engineers and designers who created them.

Truck-design changes for light-duty 1940 models were adaptations of 1940 Chevrolet truck sheet metal to the GMC chassis. New for these models were a "Quick-Vision" instrument panel, sealed-beam headlights, and front-fender-mounted parking lights.

GMC offered at least 47 series, sub-series, and models in 1940. Many variations were possible. For example, in its AC-450 3-ton range, GMC offered the AC-452 with a 133 3/4-in. wheelbase, the AC-453 with a 157 3/4-in. wheelbase, the AC-454 with a 175 3/4-in. wheelbase, and the AC-455 with a 193 3/4-in. stance. Each model could be had with a standard body or an optional range of body sizes. For instance, the normal AC-452 body was 9-ft. long, but the optional body range listed 7 1/2- to 9-ft. lengths. The AF-450 COE trucks had the same options, plus the 108-in. wheelbase AF-451.

"This GMC model is a 'truck-of-all-trades,'" the sales catalog said of the AC-450. "Cartage, Coal, Food Products, Brewery and Long Distance Hauling vocations, as well as

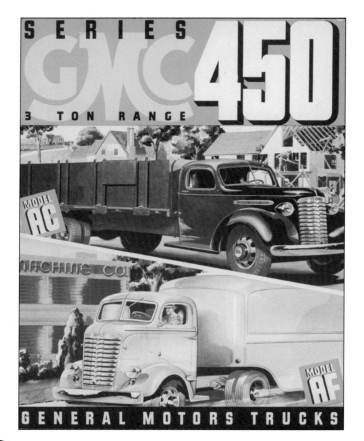

Municipalities, find the AC-450 an ideal truck for their work. When such bodies as Stakes, Vans, Dumps, High Racks and Tanks join forces with the AC-450, they make a profitable combination. The short wheelbase unit makes an ideal tractor, because it can handle trailers with practically any type body." The catalog listed general haulers, brewers, public utilities, and milk, steel, gas, oil, and food haulers as potential AF-450 users. Trucks in the GMC 450 series featured full-floating double-reduction rear axles, Hotchkiss drive with tubular-type propeller shafts, and vacuum-booster hydraulic brakes. The 3-ton models had a four-speed transmission, while 5-ton models substituted a five-speed gearbox.

The 228-cid 80-hp six was used in light-duty models up to the GMC 350 series, except Walk-In Delivery Vans, which had a 229.7-cid Olds side-valve motor. The GMC 450 series again used the 248.5-cid 88-hp six, while the GMC 500 series stuck with the 278.66-cid 100-hp engine. The remaining engine choices were identical to 1939, with the GMC 600s and 650s using the "308," the GMC 700s using the "361," the GMC 800s using the "426," and the GMC 850s employing the "451." Diesel models were also offered.

The ACE model—introduced for the first time in 1940—was designed for export to other countries in CKD (completely-knocked-down) form. This provided jobs for workers in other countries who were hired to assemble the pieces once they arrived at their destination. Also new was an ACS school bus aimed at the growing market niche for student-transportation vehicles. GMC trailer manufacturing ceased this year. Between 1931 and 1940, the company built a total of 8,283 trailers.

On May 23, 1940, Yellow Truck & Coach Mfg. Co. announced the purchase of additional buildings from Wilson Foundry & Machine Co. These had been leased for several years, but were christened as Plant 3 after the purchase was consummated in June 1940. The acquisition comprised six buildings and 339,000 sq. ft. of working

space. Extensive additions and improvements were also made to Plant 2 to allow increased production of military vehicles. In September, Plant 4 started cranking out the new Type 256 engine, as well as the Type 270 engine that was eventually used in thousands of 2 1/2-ton military cargo trucks and DUKW amphibious vehicles that "fought" in World War II. The "270" became known as GMC's "workhorse" engine.

Although General Motors Truck & Coach was still a division of Yellow Truck & Coach Mfg. Co., of Pontiac, Michigan, General Motors started recording production figures again in 1940. The calendar-year totals indicate that GMC held a 7.56 percent share of the U.S. truck market in 1940. GM's defense production totaled $75 million, but orders mounted rapidly. By the end of January 1941, defense contracts with the United States and allied governments totaled $683 million.

1941: 'CC' Riders

For 1941, GMC's Model AC and AF light- and medium-duty trucks became CCs and CFs. They came in model groups from 1/2-ton CC-100s up to 2 1/2-ton CC-490s. Heavy-duty tractors with short-wheelbases were introduced for the first time, along with a complete line of six-wheel-drive models and special dump trucks. Two models with the six-cylinder Detroit 6-71 diesel engine were put into production and a radically new AY series of 3 1/2- to 5-ton COEs with set-back front axles was brought out.

The headlights of smaller trucks, like the 1/2-ton CC-100 and 3/4-ton CC-150, were moved onto the fenders and now carried the parking lights. A new two-tier grille

arrangement, highlighted by horizontal bars, was adopted. The CC-101 line contained nine models on a longer 115-in. wheelbase. CC-102s shared a longer 125 1/4-in. wheelbase with 3/4-ton CC-150s. The CCV 1/2-ton Walk-in Delivery was carried over as the CCV-100 on a standard 113 1/2-in. wheelbase and a 115-in. option. A 115-in. wheelbase 1-ton CC-251 series was new.

Eight 1-ton CC-250/CC-252 trucks were offered on a new 134 1/2-in. wheelbase. Also new this year was a medium (125 1/4-in. wheelbase) 1-ton CCX-252 series with chassis models only. CC-262 1-ton trucks were virtually identical to CC-252s, except for having larger wheels and tires. The CCL-300 1-ton series duplicated the CC-262 line in models, wheelbase, engine, and (front) tire size, but these were "L" (light-duty) editions of the sturdier 1 1/2-ton CC-300 series and added larger, dual rear tires. Prices for most 1941 GMC civilian models increased $60-$65.

GMC built its first 2 1/2-ton 6-x-6 trucks with 270-cid engines for the U.S. Army during 1941. Two all-wheel-drive military models were released as the ACK350 (4 x 4) and ACKW350 (6 x 6). Military truck production eventually increased to 1,700 units per week.

By the end of 1941, America's car-and-truck makers would deliver $1.2 billion in arms to the nation's military forces and be working on another $5.1 billion worth of war goods orders. As early as January 9, the U.S. Army said that it was seeking 250,000 vehicles for its war motorization program. The step up in military production helped GM set sales records in all categories for April. Eight days later, GM averted a United Auto Workers' strike with a 10-cents-per-hour pay raise. On June 3, salaried employees

Left: This 1940 GMC sales brochure promoted the 500 series 3 1/2-ton range of trucks and depicted an AC500 tractor with a trailer and an AF500 cab-over-engine cargo truck. (CTC)

This 1941 GMC sales brochure for the 400 series 2 1/2-ton range of cab-over-engine trucks depicted a CF400 cargo van and CF400 tractor with a trailer. (GHC)

This streamlined 1941 GMC horse van is a custom cab-over-engine model with a 13,150-lb. GVWR and 8.25 x 20 tires. (OCWC)

Perhaps due to military production, the number of six-cylinder gas engines for GMC models grew to a dozen. The "228" was now offered in a 61-hp "economy" version and the 76-hp standard version. The drop from 1940's 80-hp rating was due to the adoption of a new system for all engines that listed what was called "certified net horsepower." This system measured the power of an engine as produced with standard equipment rather than the gross horsepower produced by a bare engine.

GMC 300 series trucks used a 3 5/8 x 3 13/16-in. bore-and-stroke engine that displaced 236.10 cid and generated 87 hp at 3000 rpm. Carryover engines included the "248" with 89.5 hp, the "278" with 85.5 hp, the "308" with 92.5 hp, the "426" with 126 hp, and the "451" with 146 hp under the new system. There were three new engines. The first had a 3 25/32 x 3 13/16-in. bore and stroke, 256.86 cid, and 91 hp at 3000 rpm; the second had a 3 25/32 x 4-in. bore and stroke, 269.52 cid, and 94 hp at 2800 rpm; and the third had a 4 1/2 x 5-in. bore and stroke, 477.13 cid, and 136.5 hp at 2400 rpm.

received raises of $15 and up per month. Yellow Truck employees received 10-cent pay raises on June 4. By the end of that month, government agencies had imposed production and price ceilings on the industry.

Restrictions on pig iron and tires went into effect during the summer of 1941. By September 10, GM had a contract to build medium and heavy tanks. Less than a month later, on November 5, the tank program was enlarged. Automakers were told to eliminate bright metal trim by the end of December. Japan raided Pearl Harbor on December 7, prompting the U.S. to declare war. By December 15, GM's truck plants adopted extended working hours.

GM had $400 million worth of defense work in 1941 and General Motors Truck and Coach Division of Yellow Truck and Coach Mfg. Co. was a major player in the war build-up effort. The company's share of calendar-year truck production in the U.S. rose to 10.18 percent. Irving B. Babcock continued as GMC's president in 1941. J.P. Little was again in charge of truck sales, but H.E. Listman headed coach (bus) sales. C.O. Ball was chief engineer, while H.J. Crichton was purchasing agent. GMC was the fifth-largest American-truck producer behind Chevrolet, Ford, Dodge, and International, in respective order. Yellow Truck & Coach Mfg. Co. won an armament award for building combat vehicles.

The 1941 GMC Model CCK 1/2-ton Suburban Carryall. (© General Motors Corp.)

1942: More Than Ever Before

GMC trucks for 1942 were unchanged in any significant way; the company simply built more of them than ever before. The two-tier grille arrangement highlighted by horizontal bars continued. The model lineup was virtually identical to the prior year. Prices dropped below 1940 levels, with a 1/2-ton CC-101 pickup listing for $648. The comparable panel was $790; the Suburban was $875. A heavy 1-ton CC-260 panel sold for $915. The CCl-300 Canopy Screen model was $992.

During the early part of the year, the available civilian-model trucks included 33 with four-wheel-drive, 34 six wheelers, 16 tractors, six heavy-duty dump trucks, and 10 school bus cowls. The capacities of 1942 GMC trucks ranged from 1/2 ton to 20 tons.

Mechanical specifications were also very similar to 1941, with only a few minor refinements. Engine choices were the same. The optional equipment list grew to include front and rear bumpers, a radio and antenna, heater and defroster, clock, cigar lighter, seat covers, heavy-duty oil-bath air cleaner, external oil filter, and whipcord upholstery.

On January 1, 1942, the United States Government issued its first "freeze" order covering the production and sale of civilian trucks. Assemblies of all civilian vehicles ceased by June. That didn't bring a sales drop, however, as military contracts came flooding in. In April, GM started work on the prototype of a 2 1/2-ton, 6-x-6 amphibious military vehicle, Model DUKW353, that was nicknamed the "Duck." The first of these was completed in only 36 days and by November 10, production versions were rolling off the assembly line.

According to *GM: The First 75 Years of Transportation Products*, GMC's combined truck-and-coach output for calendar-year 1942 zoomed to 150,506 units. This included 135,861 multi-drive vehicles. It had a 16.88 percent share of the U.S. truck market. GMC also became the largest producer of military vehicles for the war effort and won many additional government commendations.

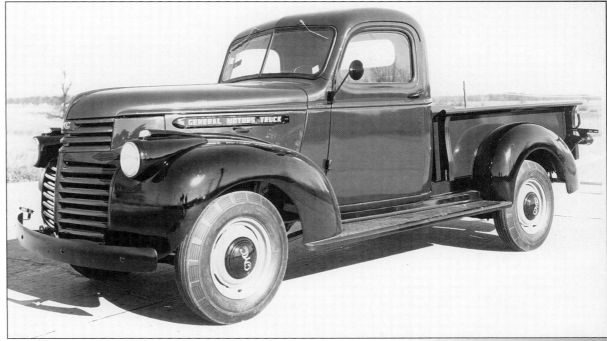

1943: 'Victory is Our Business'

By 1943, General Motors was building 16 different types of trucks for the military from a 1 1/2-ton Small Arms Repair truck to an 8-ton tractor-truck for use at military arsenals. Its contribution included the production of around 560,000 "deuce-and-a-half" (2 1/2-ton) army workhorses with 6-x-6 chassis, and about 20,000 copies of the famous DUKW "Duck," a 2 1/2-ton six-wheel-drive amphibious craft. Both of these models used the 94-hp "270" six-cylinder engine.

On July 14, 1943, General Motors management developed a plan to completely reorganize its truck and coach branch once again. Based on an agreement reached on July 14, 1943, the GMC Truck & Coach Division came into being on September 30, 1943, when General Motors finalized a purchase of the property and assets (except specified cash assets) of Yellow Truck & Coach Mfg. Co. This move represented a merger of GMC Truck Co. and Yellow Truck & Coach Mfg. Co. On October 1, 1943, the GMC

A 1942 GMC Model CC-100 1/2-ton pickup with World War II "blackout" trim. (OCWC)

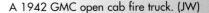

A 1942 GMC open cab fire truck. (JW)

GMC calendar-year truck production during the later war years averaged more than 130,000 units annually. As a corporation, GM produced $1.9 billion, $3.7 billion, and $3.8 billion of defense goods, respectively, over this period. In 1945, GMC still had a strong 15.71 percent share of the market.

1944: Award Winners

GMC resumed building civilian trucks under War Production Board (WPB) authorization in March 1944. These were called "Victory" or "interim" models. For their high achievement in the production of war equipment, the GMC Truck & Coach Division employees received an Army-Navy "E" award on June 2, 1944. On December 31, 1944, Irving B. Babcock resigned as vice president and general manager of the Truck & Coach Division. One day later, Morgan D. Douglas was appointed general manager. Douglas had previously worked at Chevrolet Motor Division.

1946: Back to Reality

After building nearly 584,000 all-wheel-drive trucks and "Ducks" for the World War II effort, GM Truck & Coach came back to reality in 1946. Even with pent-up civilian demand for new vehicles, production fell back to a far less hectic pace than during the conflict. Part of the drop was due to problems associated with the conversion of factories, equipment, and parts inventories from wartime to peacetime production and part was due to postwar labor unrest in the auto industry. As a result of such factors, the days of double-digit market-share figures were over for a while. For 1946, GMC held a 3.59 percent

Truck & Coach Division of General Motors Corp. was officially formed. Irving B. Babcock became general manager of GMC Truck & Coach and was subsequently elected a General Motors vice president. In an article titled "They Just Keep Trucking Along" in the GM 75th anniversary issue of *Automotive News* (September 16, 1983), author Jack Walsh quoted an unnamed GMC divisional historian as saying of this merger, "It was a great step forward, but it was made at the expense of a loss of a lot of morale among the people who were involved."

Above, below, and right: The engine, dash, and front view of a nicely restored 1946 GMC CC101 pickup truck. (GTVG)

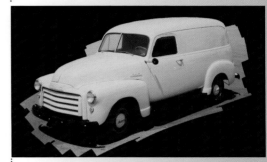

piece of the pie.

After the conclusion of a bitter four-month strike that started on November 21, 1945, the "Truck & Coach" workers resumed building civilian trucks on April 1, 1946, one month later than Chevrolet. They made 3,900 trucks that month. The postwar era was a time of labor conflicts, work stoppages, parts shortages, and other bottlenecks. The negative results of supplier strikes that throttled the auto industry are reflected in trade journals that show a mere 136 trucks leaving the Pontiac plant in May. Production was only 611 trucks in June, then rose to 5,133 in July, 4,883 in August, 2,846 in September, 5,718 in October, 6,590 in November, and 4,033 in December. Ward's shows the sum of 33,850 as calendar-year truck production. General Motors lists 36,289 GMC vehicles as its official calendar-year production total, which probably includes transit buses and parlor coaches.

GMC developed a peacetime lineup of 22 basic series. In the conventional CC series, there were seven lines from 1/2-ton to 2-ton with 30 models. The AC conventional line offered four series and 16 chassis models in the 2 1/2- to 5-ton ranges. Model ACR conventional tractors were available in four lines from 2-ton to 3 1/2-ton and a pair of CCS-300 1 1/2-ton school buses was offered. There were two six-cylinder diesel series, the ADC-900 with four 5-ton conventional trucks on two wheelbases, and the ACDR-900 series with two conventional tractor choices: the chassis or chassis-and-cab model. Cab-over-engine series were the CF-300 line with six 1 1/2-ton models, the AF-520 2-ton tractor line with four models, and the AFR-750 3 1/2-ton tractor line, also with four models.

The largest GMC truck was the 5-ton ADCW-974 conventional six-wheeler, dual-drive diesel, which cost $16,270 in chassis-and-cab form. It had a 218-in. wheelbase, 12,670-lb. curb weight, 55,000-lb. gross vehicle weight, and 425-cid Detroit 6-71 six-cylinder diesel engine with 154 net bhp.

All in all, there were 88 GMC chassis-and-body models. GMC still operated like a real truck company, so very few of its trucks came standard with factory bodies. The 1950 NADA Truck Reference Book indicates that 80 trucks came in chassis or chassis-and-cab models only. School buses were sold in chassis or chassis-and-cowl configurations. As for factory-bodied trucks, there was a pickup and panel (but no Suburban or canopy express) listed in the 115-in.-wheelbase CC-101 1/2-ton line. A pickup came in the 125 1/4-in.-wheelbase CC-102 1/2-ton line; a panel and a stake-bed were part of the CC-302 1 1/2-ton line, and a stake-bed also came in the long-wheelbase CC-303 1 1/2-ton line.

GMC historian Donald E. Meyer photographed this 1948 GMC Model AC890 5-ton dump truck when he worked for the truckmaker. (DEM)

A fleet of nine 1948 GMC trucks, including FC300, FC350 and FC450 models, was operated by Mr. Rexius, the owner of a fuel and sawdust retailer. (OCWC)

1947: Multiple Personalities

Buying parts for a 1947 GMC can be confusing. Three series of trucks show up in historical sources and parts books of the era. The first is the CC series, which was simply a continuation of the 1942-1946 models. This series had only seven lines in the 1/2-, 3/4-, 1-, 1 1/2-, and 2-ton ranges, with a total of 29 models. Prices climbed $100 on average.

The second-series 1947 trucks also had prewar styling on new EC models. In addition to the 1/2- through 1-ton models, there was EC-280, EC-300, EC-350, EC-370, EC-400, EC-450, and EC-470 models in the 1 1/2-ton to 2-ton ranges. Styling was basically unchanged from CC models, although there may have been some detail variations.

Along with these prewar-styled CC and EC conventional trucks, GMC offered a full range with about 15 different types of prewar-styled trucks and school buses with capacities from 1 ton to 5 tons. Models included the EF parcel delivery; EFP bakery delivery; AC medium-duty conventional; ACX conventional dump; ACR conventional tractor; ADC conventional diesel; ADCR conventional diesel tractor; CCS, ECS, and ACS school buses; AF, CF, and EF cab-over-engines; AFR cab-over-engine tractors; ADF and ADFR cab-over-engine diesel tractors; EY cab-over-engine with set-back front axle; ACT and ACW conventional six-wheelers; AFW cab-over-engine six-wheelers with dual drive; and ADCW conventional six-wheeler diesels with dual drive. The ADCW-970 chassis-and-cab model was the most expensive truck in the line, with its $16,311 price tag!

In July 1947, the GMC factory started building totally restyled light-duty trucks. It had General Motors' all-new postwar-only styling. The appearance was attractive, devoid of excess trim, smooth, and streamlined. Large GMC letters were seen at the top of a simple multi-tiered grille with broad horizontal bars. The headlights were mounted totally within the front fenders and small, circular-parking lights were positioned directly below the headlights. These trucks continued using the 228-cid, 93-hp overhead valve, inline six-cylinder engine. Even though the drive train was basically unchanged, drivers were quick to appreciate the GMC's improved cab ventilation, improved visibility, and revamped front-suspension system.

The 1946 trucks themselves were virtually identical to their prewar counterparts. The front grille was characterized by a horizontal bar scheme, with the GMC logo prominently displayed on the uppermost section. The headlights extended forward from the fenders and were crowned by torpedo-shaped parking lights. The side-hood section on conventional trucks had a chrome spear bearing "General Motors Truck" lettering.

Prices for 1/2-ton CC-101s began at $651 for a chassis. The pickup cost $805 and the panel would set you back $887. You could spend $5,896 to buy an AC-850 5-ton conventional, with a 196-in. wheelbase and dual rear wheels. The most expensive 1946 model was the ADCW-974, a diesel-powered conventional six-wheeler. It had a 218-in. stance, dual drive and a $12,670 price tag. An unusual offering was the West Coast Special, which had no front brakes and made extensive use of aluminum body panels to save weight.

GMC built an average of nearly 6,000 trucks per month from January to May 1947, then made only 2,507 in June. In July, production was 655 units, followed by 2,143 in August. From September to December, output averaged almost 6,800 a month. This reflects a build-out of prewar trucks after May and introduction of a new model in July. By August, production increased because buyers wanted the latest GMC truck.

Conventional trucks with the new postwar styling were called FC models. They came in 21 lines offering 79 models including trucks and school buses in the 1/2- to 2-ton ranges. The smallest FC-101 series included chassis, chassis-cab, pickup, panel, canopy express, and Suburban models, all on a 116-in. wheelbase, priced between $845 and $1,445. The largest FC Series truck was the FC-470 which had a 20,000-lb. GVWR and a body-and-payload rating of 13,600 lbs. No tonnage rating was given for the FC470 in GMC sales literature, but the 1950 *NADA Truck Reference Book* indicates it had a 2-ton rating.

All gasoline engines used in F Series trucks were built by GMC. The 228-cid inline six was used in the 100-280 series; the 248-cid inline six was used in 300, 350, and 400 models, and the war-proven 270-cid "workhorse" inline six was used in the 450 and 470 models.

While all of the trucks mentioned above were built and sold in 1947, as 1947 models, there are factory-issued "Truck Model Identification" sheets that clearly show the new FC Advance-Design trucks as the only 1947 models. They consider CC trucks to be 1941-1942-1945-1946 models and EC trucks to be 1946 models. As previously mentioned, this can cause confusion for historians and parts suppliers, but is easy to understand.

To GMC factory engineers, FCs were the new 1947 models, even though they did not arrive until midyear. However, no GMC dealer would sell a truck in May 1947 and tell a customer it was a 1946 model. You can bet that the dealer wanted that truck titled as a 1947 model. Still, the AC and AF Series heavy-duty models were carried over as part of the 1947 line.

In November 1947, the first signs of a postwar expansion of plant facilities at GMC Truck & Coach Division began to show up. The company moved its light-duty engine assembly lines from Plant 4 to a new engine plant

in Building 29 at Plant 2. In December, engine-manufacturing machine shops were moved from Plant 1 and Plant 4 into the same location. The final phase of this move did not come until February of 1948, when heavy-duty engine-assembly lines also moved to Plant 2's Building 29. By the end of 1947, a new civilian-truck-production record of 61,918 units had been achieved. It would not stand very long, however.

1948: A Model for Every Purpose

The postwar-styled conventional trucks that GMC introduced midway through 1947 continued to be marketed in 1948 in model ranges up to 1 1/2-ton. There were no new models or major changes announced. Larger conventional models on the market this year that fell into the 2- to 5-ton ranges were still a continuation of the classic prewar AC and AF Series trucks.

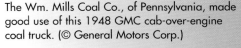

The Wm. Mills Coal Co., of Pennsylvania, made good use of this 1948 GMC cab-over-engine coal truck. (© General Motors Corp.)

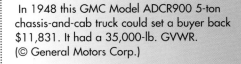

In 1948 this GMC Model ADCR900 5-ton chassis-and-cab truck could set a buyer back $11,831. It had a 35,000-lb. GVWR. (© General Motors Corp.)

This 1948 GMC 1/2-ton Deluxe pickup sports a chrome radiator grille and hubcaps. (BF)

A 1949 Model 100 1/2–ton pickup with standard painted grille and caps. (© General Motors Corp.)

GMC literally built a truck, school bus, or coach for every purpose in 1948 and the full line encompassed 347 different body-and-chassis models in 78 different lines. All of this added up to the company's best peacetime year in history with 92,677 units built. The cheapest 1/2-ton chassis cost under $1,000 and the monstrous ADCW-974 six-wheeler, with a diesel engine and dual drive, went out the door at $16,336 in chassis-and-cab format, without a body.

There were two series of postwar cab-over-engine trucks in the 16,000-lbs. GVW class. They were the FF-350, offering 10 models with wheelbases from 122 in. to 197 in. on a 1 1/2-ton chassis and the FF-450, which was a heavier version of the same line with a lager, more powerful 104-hp version of the GMC 270 six-cylinder engine. These classic COE models have a heavy following among GMC collectors. It seems as if they were heavily promoted in 1948, since they appear in many of the "factory photos" that GMC issued for that year. They were available with optional Deluxe cabs that included stainless-steel trim and rear-quarter cab windows. A four-speed synchromesh transmission replaced the previous sliding-gear type and solenoid starter motors and spare-tire carriers were standard equipment.

The gas tank on pickups was mounted under the frame, though an inside-the-cab tank was optional. The Model EF delivery vans had new 102-in. and 132-in. wheelbases. Prices on a model-by-model basis climbed in the $70 range.

A new peacetime record high for GMC production was established in 1948 when the company turned out 92,677 units.

1949: Big Year!

In 1949, General Motors Corporation kept M.D. Douglas, the general manager of GMC Truck & Coach Division in Pontiac, Michigan, pretty busy. The corporation achieved an all-time record in motor-vehicle production. A total volume of 2,678,874 cars, trucks and buses were built that year, eclipsing the previous record of 2,252,695 set in 1941. The factories cranked out more than 600,000 more vehicles than the previous year.

In July of 1949, it was statistically determined that GMC was the fifth all-time most-popular brand of truck in America. Of the estimated 7,087,120 trucks in operation on America's roads at that date, some 399,205 were GMCs. As a point of interest, the total included 39,132 of the latest 1949 models, as well as the following "survival" figures.

During calendar year 1949, GMC built 83,840 trucks and nearly 75 percent of them were models that fell into the smaller-gross-vehicle-weight category. For the 5,000-lb.-and-less-GVW category, GMC produced 38,729 units. Another 20,937 GMC trucks fell into the 5,001-lb.-to-10,000-lb.-GVW class. This included the smaller models up to about the FC-253 medium-duty series (1-ton range), all of which were basically unchanged from 1948.

Also carried over with practically no changes were the 1 1/2-ton trucks in the FC-300 and FC-350 ranges, which had GVWs between 14,000 and 16,000 lbs. GMC built 8,606 trucks in the 10,001-lb.-to-14,000-lb.-GVW class and 8,040 in the 14,001-lb.-to-16,000-lb.-GVW class, though not all of them were these models.

The remaining 7,500 or so trucks made by GMC in 1949 were the bigger models and there were some changes in this category. In the heavy-medium truck category, the prewar-styled AC-450s were replaced with new FC-450s with 19,000-lb. GVWs. These came in 10 models on five different wheelbases from 137-in. to 197-in.

The last of the AC/AF Series heavy-duty trucks were built in March and the first of a new postwar-style HC type of heavy conventional went into production in June of 1949. HCs were COE models in the 2-ton to 5-ton ranges. They came in dump, school bus, diesel, and diesel-tractor versions. Models from the HC-520 up were introduced progressively throughout the year. There were 12 HC series, five HCR tractor series, five HDC diesel series, and three HDCR diesel-tractor series. Together they included 67 different chassis models.

With record corporate sales and production and a vastly modernized and enlarged range of heavy-duty trucks, GMC was able to lift its share of the 1949 U.S. truck market to 7.41 percent, which was a significant gain on International Harvester, the fourth-largest manufacturer. In fact, by 1950, GMC would pass IH for the first time since the war and capture the number-four slot. There's no doubt that the popularity of the 1949 models contributed to that improvement.

By the end of the year, GMC was billing its products as "America's finest all-star truck line." In all, there were 75

This 1949 GMC FC152 3/4-ton pickup has a painted grille, headlamp doors, and wheel-trim rings. (© General Motors Corp.)

basic model series, 224 different types of bodies and chassis, nine engine displacements, and a large variety of special-equipment options. The division's full postwar conversion program was deemed completed with the release of the last H series model. On October 1, Roger M. Keyes was appointed assistant general manager of GMC Truck & Coach Division.

Richfield Oil Co. used this 1949 GMC HDF750 tractor and tank trailer. It was in the 3 1/2-ton range and had a 33,000-lb. GVWR. (DEM)

Chapter 4

The Fabulous '50s

1950-1959

Page 46 and 47: Bringing back memories of a creative presentation that GM executive Bob Lutz once made at the Chicago Auto Show, this scene shows professional truckers admiring a 1957 GMC 860 Series tractor parked at their favorite diner.

A man loads lumber onto a 1950 GMC FC350 platform truck. (© General Motors Corp.)

Parked outside a construction site near Detroit is a 1950 GMC HCW400 6 x 4 truck with a dump body. The rectangular building in the upper right corner is the Fisher Building, an old GM facility. (© General Motors Corp.)

1950: Catching the 'Corn Binders'

Due to their proud agricultural heritage, the trucks made by International Harvester Co. (IHC) were affectionately known as "corn binders." For many years, IHC trucks outsold GMC trucks. The huge demand for military trucks and the vast production facilities of General Motors combined to make GMC the fourth-largest truck producer during World War II. When peace returned, IHC pulled ahead again. However, GMC came close to taking the fourth sales rank in calendar year 1949, when it sold 7.41 percent of America's new trucks (83,840 units) and IHC sold 9.77 percent (110,558 units).

This trend continued in the first year of the new decade and the big news in 1950 was that GMC out-produced IHC by more than 4,000 trucks (110,528 GMCs to 106,418 IHCs). GMC also carved out an 8.22 percent market share compared to 7.92 percent for International Harvester. While the two companies would change positions again, the narrowing of the gap between them was a symbol of GMC's growing postwar success as a full-range truck maker.

In 1950, GMC's real strength was in the 5,000-lb.-and-less-GVW class, where it clearly was the fourth largest truck builder and where it assembled 47,936 trucks to IHC's 26,350. For 1950, GMC advertised 20 improved models, including pickups. It also added seven new models in all series for the year. The output of the overhead-valve 228-cid inline six used in light-duty models was increased to 96 net bhp. New airplane-type shock absorbers were introduced. In addition, improvements were made to the electrical system and the availability of some options and accessories was changed. In the popular 1/2-ton FC-101 series, the pickup truck sold for $1,265, the panel was

This 1950 GMC ADC640, which had a 4-110 diesel engine, was used as a Mobile Diesel Training unit. It traveled to GMC dealers and truck and bus fleet operators to educate mechanics about new diesel technology. (© General Motors Corp.)

$1,445, the canopy express was $1,495, and the Suburban cost $1,675.

GMC continued to make a full assortment of models including conventional trucks and cab-over-engine models for the light-, medium-, and heavy-duty ranges. In addition to basic flatbeds, stakes, and delivery models, they included highway tractors, dump trucks, and school buses. New models of larger trucks included the medium-duty HC-470 and HF-470, the HCW-400 and HCW-620 six-wheelers, and the HDCR-640 and HDCR-650 diesels.

Roger M. Kyes became general manager of GMC Truck and Coach Division, as well as a GM vice president on April 1, 1950, upon the retirement of Morgan D. Douglas. When the Korean War broke out that year, Kyes remembered the fuel shortages of World War II and started putting more emphasis on diesel engines. GMC built 3,991 diesel trucks in 1950, which was an increase from the 521 made in 1947, the 1,001 made in 1948, and the 1,332 produced in 1949. At mid-year, the company experimented with a new 6-110 six-cylinder diesel engine with 275 hp.

GMC's earlier Detroit Diesel had 71 cubic inches per cylinder and came with various numbers of cylinders. A well-known version used in both trucks and buses was the six-cylinder 6-71 model, which gained 35 hp in 1950 and now carried a 200-hp rating. Each cylinder of the new 6-110 engine displaced 110 cubic inches. The new heavy-duty diesel also featured an efficient, gear-driven centrifugal blower with an aluminum impeller. Pacific Intermountain Express (PIE), a famous trucking company, took delivery of the first three experimental units that GMC built. However, the 6-110 engine was never released for production in GMC trucks.

By the end of the year, GMC's two new lightweight highway tractors—Models HDCR-640 and HDCR-650—appeared in the line. These were 55,000-lb. GCW trucks with 4-71 diesel engines designed for inter-state or intra-state hauling. There was room for sleeper cabs and other special long-distance equipment.

Most of the trucks parked at this Torrence Oil Co. Mobil Oil terminal are 1950 GMC FC450 models with 4-compartment tanker bodies. (© General Motors Corp.)

A 1951 GMC 300-24 1 1/2-ton platform truck with a high-rack stake side body makes a perfect vehicle for hauling Christmas trees. (© General Motors Corp.)

All civilian production records were broken in December of 1950, when GMC built its 100,000th truck of the year, an HDCR-650 diesel. The production of coaches other than school buses also rose slightly to 2,251 units.

1951: On Target!

General Motors Truck & Coach Division entered the 1951 model year with two primary goals: The first was to achieve a 10-percent share of the overall truck market and the second was to become America's largest seller of diesel-powered trucks. By the end of the year, GMC general manager Roger M. Keyes could boast of having met both targets. Total new-truck registrations in the United States that year were 1,003,850 and 100,285 of them went to GMC. That included the 5,565 diesels shipped from the GMC facilities in Pontiac, Michigan, giving the division 40 percent of the total diesel market. The company's diesel-truck sales were greatly enhanced by a "whole-fleet" replacement order from McLean Trucking Co., of Winston-Salem, N.C. It called for the delivery of 278 Model HDCR-650 tractors with 133-hp 4-71 diesel engines.

Both of these goals were achieved by GMC in a year during which the American truck industry was plagued with problems and National Production Agency (NPA) restrictions aimed at conserving raw materials for government defense contracts. For instance, GMC's NPA percentage allocation limited it to 7.65 percent of light-duty, 7.0 percent of medium-duty, and 12.6 percent of heavy-duty truck production. It was only through product innovations, aggressive planning, and bold sales campaigns that J.E. Johnson, truck sales general manager, was able to meet GMC's marketing plan.

August 1951 brought the virtually indestructible "Million Miler" Detroit diesels to GMC dealerships to keep the factory assembly lines rolling. Neither of the diesel engines—the 4-71 or the 6-71—were entirely new, but they had been improved over the years with features such as aluminum blocks, heads, and bell housings. Such refinements brought them to the point where they seemed to run a million miles without major problems. The larger 6-71, which produced 165 hp immediately after World War II, was upped to 200 hp in 1950 and 225 hp in 1951.

Another big change was that the "71" series diesels

became standard equipment in larger trucks, rather than a special order item. The 283-cid 4-71 was standard in 650, 740, and 750 models and the 425-cid 6-71 was standard in the 900 and 950 trucks. With the development of a new fuel modulator, GMC was also able to offer a 3-71 two-stroke engine that was very well suited for very economical, low-speed operation in cities. The Million Miler engine also eliminated cylinder head gaskets and used synthetic rubber rings and strip gaskets to seal fluid passages. A special long-duration camshaft promoted better breathing and scavenging of exhaust fumes. According to factory literature, governed top speed was increased from 2000 to 2100 rpm to increase performance.

Many articles written today will talk about "the GMC factory," but the division's Pontiac headquarters actually encompassed four factories by 1951. They covered 600

A 1951 GMC 100-22 1/2-ton pickup truck. (© General Motors Corp.)

P.I.E. was the first to take delivery of the experimental 6-110 diesel engines. (© General Motors Corp.)

This man gives perspective to the experimental 275-hp six-cylinder 6-110 diesel engine under the hood of a 1951 GMC HDCK W950 tractor used by Pacific Intermountain Express. (© General Motors Corp.)

Right: The General Motors Technical Center Fire Department used this 1951 GMC 630 fire truck with red fenders and a white body. (© General Motors Corp.)

acres and provided 5,000,000 square feet of floor space. More than 1,500,000 square feet of this space, including the dynamometer laboratory, an ultra-modern engine plant, and a coach assembly unit, had been added since the end of World War II. About 77 percent of GMC's production took place in Pontiac, with the balance sourced from other facilities in St. Louis, Missouri, and Oakland, California. On August 7, 1951, General Motors announced that it was acquiring a 255-acre site in Arlington, Texas, where it planned to construct a "dual-purpose" plant for Buick, Oldsmobile, and Pontiac car production and GMC truck production.

General styling of the 1951 GMC light-duty models was unchanged from 1950. Ventipanes were added and the door windows grew smaller as a consequence. The seats had a new adjusting mechanism. Front-suspension-stabilizer bars on 1/2-ton models were redesigned. Braking improvements were also made. The output of the GMC 228-cid six-cylinder engine was increased to 100 hp.

In 1951, GMC also devoted more energy than ever before toward making and selling larger trucks. More than 47 percent of the division's overall production efforts were focused on models in the more-than-14,000-lb.-GVW category, which was up from 26 percent in 1950. At the year's Chicago Automobile Show, GMC exhibited a new HDCRW-953 diesel-powered highway tractor that had a 200-hp engine and a GCW rating of 70,000 lbs.

In September 1951, military truck production for the Korean War got underway. Defense work initiated in 1951 included orders for tank trucks and 6-x-6 military-cargo

trucks, as well as regular commercial trucks and passenger coaches for military use. GMC's M-211 was released in a new M-135 version. Both were equipped with a new 302-cid six-cylinder engine that produced 130 hp at 3400 rpm according to U.S. Army specifications. It was hooked to a four-speed Hydra-Matic transmission and two-speed transfer case and had a top speed of 58 mph when carrying a 10,000-lb. load. The truck also had automatic front-drive engagement for extra traction. The rear-axle springs were assisted by secondary springs of higher load capacity and controlled-ride clearance. The 24-volt electrical system was dustproof, waterproof, fungus-proof, and suppressed against radio interference.

Other M-211-derived military models included the M-215 dump truck, the M-221 semi-tractor, the M-220 "hard-top" version of the cargo truck with special equipment, the M-222 water tanker, and the M-217 gasoline tanker. The U.S. army bought a total of 9,000 trucks of the M-211 family during the Korean War.

By the end of 1951, GMC held a 9.03 percent share of the U.S. truck market based on calendar-year production and was once again America's fifth-largest producer of trucks. As of July 1951, there were 526,367 GMC trucks of all years and types registered in the U.S.

1952: A New Man Takes Charge

In 1952, Phillip J. Monaghan took over as general manager of GMC Truck & Coach Division. At age 40, Monaghan—a former football hero—was GM's youngest vice president and had many youthful ideas for product innovations. He had previously been the company's manufacturing manager and his promotion reflected the good job he had done using factory-parts inventories to maintain GMC's production at 10 percent of total industry while GMC was limited to 8 percent of allocated raw materials by NPA guidelines due to Korean War materials restrictions.

Production of coaches, which totaled 2,466 for the year, was an important factor in GMC's health in early 1952, while truck output strengthened late in the year. The fact that coach bodies were made of aluminum played a role in

keeping the bus-building lines running after a steel shortage shut down truck production in July.

GMC heavily publicized the fact that it became the first motor-vehicle producer to build motor trucks with automatic transmissions late in 1951, by installing Hydra-Matic Drive at extra cost in some 1952-model commercial panel delivery trucks. In states that used a calendar-year dating system, some of these trucks were registered as 1951 models. Company literature noted that "1951 and after, trucks with an 'M' designation without letter prefix in the 150, 250, 350, 400, 450, and 470 ranges have Hydra-Matic Drive."

The appearance of GMC light-duty trucks was unchanged from 1951. The Suburban model saw its sales

increase to 2,823 units. There were some technical refinements, including cooling-system improvements. The availability of an optional chrome-plated front bumper was temporarily discontinued due to Korean War material restrictions. By this time, prices for the 1/2-ton models (now designated 100-22s) were up to $1,385 for a pickup, $1,566 for a panel, $1,617 for a canopy express, and $1,826 for a Suburban.

GMC's P series parcel-delivery vans came in a variety of sizes and featured a wide-track I-beam front axle and hypoid rear axle. Dual-range Hydra-Matic Drive was first made available in these trucks—in the P150-22 model—in 1952. Toward the end of the year, the P150-22 was advertised as "America's most beautiful delivery truck." It had a wrap-around design that extended up to the two-piece curved windshield. Wide whitewall tires were pictured in the advertisement.

Medium- and heavy-duty GMC models made more news this year with the introduction of new lines including three diesel models, one of which was a six-wheeler. By focusing on weight reduction to conserve precious materials, GMC engineers were able to slice as much as 865 lbs. from some of these trucks.

There was a 2 1/2-ton medium-duty conventional called the Model D450-37. Its three-cylinder 110-hp 3-71 diesel engine was a smaller version of the famous GMC 4-71 and 6-71 diesels used in larger trucks. All "71" series engines had interchangeable cylinder liners, pistons, piston rings, connecting rods, main and connecting rod bearings, valves, and fuel injectors. The D450-37 also featured an electrically controlled two-speed rear axle. It was rated for 19,500-lb. GVW and offered a choice of five wheelbases for truck and highway-tractor models. Later in the year, the similar D470-37, DW450-37, and DW620-47 models were offered with GVWs up to 21,000 lbs.

In the coach-building field, GMC introduced a radical new type of body suspension in a new GMC coach model that employed an air bellows in place of leaf springs.

A junior fire chief pedals past a 1952 GMC HC620 fire truck that belonged to the Moonachie, New Jersey Fire Department. (© General Motors Corp.)

Ward Bakery Co. of Detroit, Michigan, purchased this 1950-1953-style GMC P250-22 forward-control truck. (© General Motors Corp.)

Catsman Co. was another fan of GMC products which operated these 1952 HCW720 trucks with Redi-Mix Concrete bodies. (© General Motors Corp.)

GMC was among the first truck manufacturers to offer automatic transmissions. These 1953 GMC PM250-22 forward-control models with Hydra-Matic transmissions were used as Hydra-Matic Service Training Vans. (© General Motors Corp.)

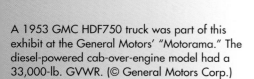

A 1953 GMC HDF750 truck was part of this exhibit at the General Motors' "Motorama." The diesel-powered cab-over-engine model had a 33,000-lb. GVWR. (© General Motors Corp.)

1953: Trucking Re-Defined

There were no important alterations in the appearance of GMC trucks for 1953. The big news was the availability of the famous four-speed Hydra-Matic Drive as a small-truck option. Models with automatic transmissions carried Hydra-Matic identification plates on their side-hood panels. Other new extras were tinted glass and side-mounted spare-tire carriers.

The basic light-duty models were again in the 1/2-ton Series 101-22, with a 116-in. wheelbase. They included the pickup for $1,385, the panel for $1,566, the canopy express for $1,617, and the Suburban for $1,834. The 102-22 line was also rated for 1/2-ton, but had a 125 1/4-in. wheelbase (the same as the 150-22 3/4-ton trucks). These lines offered chassis, pickup, and stake rack models for a bit more money. The Series 253-22 offered seven 1-ton models on a 137-in. wheelbase. They included the pickup for $1,641, the panel for $1,831, the stake rack for $1,725, and the canopy express for $1,907.

The 302-cid gasoline engine that was first used in the M-211/M-135 military 6-x-6 trucks was quickly made available in 450-30 and 470-30 civilian trucks built late in 1952 as 1953 models. It claimed the best power-to-weight ratio in the truck-building field. The engine weighed only 545 lbs. and produced up to 145 hp in civilian trucks.

Engine suffixes for 1953 were again abbreviated to 22 for the 228-cid six, 24 for a newly introduced 248, 30 for the 302, 36 for the 360, 42 for the 426, and 50 for the 503. The new 248-cid engine was standard in a 125-hp version, but an optional 115-hp powerplant with a carburetor set up for better fuel economy was available. The diesel engines were again coded 37 for the 3-71, 47 for the 4-71, and 67 for the 6-71. The heaviest GMC truck was the DW980-67, which was formerly called the HDCW-980. This giant was rated at 63,000-lb. GVW and 100,000-lb. GCW. It rode on 12.00x24 tires.

Hydra-Matic was now standard equipment in some GMC models. In the others, it was optional at extra cost, but truck buyers were willing to pay for the convenience. In fact, when the General Motors Hydra-Matic factory in Livonia, Michigan, had a devastating fire on August 12, it showed up in GMC's monthly production figures. Its output from July through December was 37 percent lower than the previous year's total.

On March 13, GMC introduced a new 130-hp 270-cid engine in the Model 400-27 truck. On April 30, the company hit its peak 1953 monthly volume of 12,882 vehicles. May 9 marked the top work week of the year with 3,199 units produced. On November 24, the company introduced a line of new 1954 models. On December 7, the Truck & Coach Division built its 30,000th diesel-powered unit. Also leaving GMC production facilities were 2,531 buses. Total production declined 4.3 percent from 1952, but GMC still held a 9.48 percent market share. That put it ahead of Dodge for the year and made it America's fourth-largest truck builder again. It was noted that divisional personnel director E.A. Maxwell and comptroller V.P. Blair were responsible for a $51-million payroll in 1953.

1954: Straight Forward

GMC light- and medium-duty trucks were given their most extensive styling revisions since 1948. The familiar GMC grille format was continued, but the sidebars were wider and flared at the bottom, where they extended out to serve as large, chrome parking-light housings. Even the front fenders were changed to incorporate rectangular depressions that accommodated the parking lights. One-piece windshields replaced two-piece designs.

Chrome grilles and bumpers returned, as Korean War material restrictions were eased. The chrome trim was optional and cost extra, so most trucks featured these parts painted. A unique rear bumper (unlike the 1947-1953 type) was designed with a center dip to show the license plate. Also found on 1954 light-duty models was a one-piece windshield. The pickup's cargo box was redesigned, too. Its side and front panels, as well as the tailgate, were 18 1/2 in. high. The top rail was changed to a flat (not sloping) style. Taillights were square, instead of round. Chrome hubcaps returned, but the GMC letters stamped into them were painted white. This was the first year GMC trucks featured color-coordinated interiors.

Recognizing the market value of automatic transmissions in trucks, GMC started offering Hydra-Matic Drive in its medium- and heavy-duty lines in 1953. "GMC's family of Hydra-Matic trucks creates the modern form of hauling," read one of the company's advertisements. It claimed that automatic transmission outmoded conventional equipment by offering superior efficiency and many new economies.

"In Truck Hydra-Matic Drive, GMC presents the answer for all classes of trucks from half-ton pickups to over-the-road haulers," said the ad. "It brings benefits so great, advances so notable, that trucking's new form has won a new name: Hydra-Matic Hauling." The copywriters noted that automatic shifting ended harmful engine lugging, as well as the practice of "shock loading" the engine,

drive line, and rear axle, and also eliminated clutch repairs and fuel-robbing shifting lags. "And it means freeing the driver of all gear-shifting chores to keep him fresher, more alert to cope with road hazards," the ad said. "Small wonder, then, that Hydra-Matic Hauling is redefining trucking."

Since GMC operated like a truck company, rather than a car company, all of its trucks were merchandised in a very straightforward manner. Sales catalogs were printed in black, white, gray, and one color and featured line drawings and shaded illustrations depicting the trucks at work, the engine and transmission offerings, the vehicle measurements, and seating arrangements.

Rather than using model names like "Jimmy" or "Sierra," the catalogs showed each truck's numerical designation, which indicated series and engine. For example, the cover of the "Gasoline Powered Trucks" brochure for the GMC 100-24 Suburban shows line drawings of this model at a train depot, an excavation site, a school

The Civil Defense emblem, which was commonly seen in the early 1950s, decorates this 1954 GMC HC620 open-cab pumper. (© General Motors Corp.)

Renderings of a 1954 GMC tractor used by General Motors' Electromotive Div. to transport a 500-KW Highway Generating Trailer called the Electro-Mobile Power Van. (WGC)

A 1954 GMC 620-series gas engine COE tractor pulling a 500-KW Highway Generating Trailer. (WGC)

A beautifully-restored 1954 GMC 100-24 1/2-ton Deluxe pickup truck. (RJE)

A 1954 GMC F660-50 tractor illustration with trailer and tarp top. This cab-over-engine model utilized the 503-cid gasoline engine. (© General Motors Corp.)

Right: This 1954 GMC trade-show exhibit included a 100-24 1/2-ton Deluxe pickup, a 100-24 Deluxe Suburban, a forward-control delivery van and a GMC bus. (© General Motors Corp.)

(dropping off kids), and a home-construction site. In the center is a larger illustration of a Suburban in a farm setting with two-tone orange shading. The truck illustrated has a chrome grille, but it wears black sidewall "truck" tires and lacks even an outside rear view mirror. The "100" part of the model designation indicates the 1/2-ton series and the "24" indicates use of the GMC-built 248-cid overhead-valve six-cylinder engine.

The 1954 engine was 20 percent more powerful than the 1953 version, thanks to a 7.5:1 extra-high-compression head that produced 125 hp on regular gasoline. GMC described it as a long-life, low-maintenance engine with a Tocco-hardened crankshaft, Moraine M-400 main and connecting rod bearings, full-pressure lubrication, and other heavy-duty features. This engine came as standard equipment attached to a GMC-built SM-318 three-speed synchromesh transmission with steering-column gearshift.

The Suburban catalog also shows a cut away of the extra-cost Dual-Range Truck Hydra-Matic and illustrates that Suburban buyers had a choice of lift and tailgate construction or double doors for interior access at the rear of the truck. On the back of the four-page brochure are bird's-eye drawings of six different seating arrangements, from eight-passenger to two-passenger seating.

Suburbans featured a two-passenger driver's bench seat on the left, a single-passenger front auxiliary seat on the right, an "intermediate" two-passenger bench in the center (toward the left), and a full three-passenger rear seat. For different hauling needs, the owner could remove all but the driver's seat. This arrangement permitted eight-, six-, four-, and two-passenger seating configurations, as well as two five-passenger options.

The back of the catalog also shows the Suburban's specifications and lists miscellaneous standard equipment

including the front and rear spring-type bumpers; illuminated instrument panel; ammeter and gauges for oil pressure, fuel level, and water temperature; oil-wetted air cleaner; foot throttle, hand-throttle, and choke controls; a key-locked ignition switch; an electric air-tone horn; a spare wheel, spare tire, and tire carrier; the seats described above; and a jack and wheel-nut wrench. Major options listed are also fairly straight forward and consist of two oil-bath air cleaners, an economy carburetor, an AC oil filter type L-1, E-Z-Eye tinted glass, a velocity-type governor, and a selection of two transmissions—the SM-420 four-speed synchromesh or Hydra-Matic.

In June 1954, GMC announced the development of a new Twin Hydra-Matic multiple-speed automatic transmission for heavy-duty trucks in the up-to-45,000-lb.-GWC class. By August, power steering was offered on all trucks in the 100- to 450-model ranges.

In January 1954, GMC general manager Phillip J. Monaghan announced that the GMC Truck & Coach Division produced approximately 750,000 vehicles since the end of World War II. Unfortunately, that same month, defense contracts were slashed and the U.S. Government told GMC that orders for 6-x-6 military trucks would end in the middle of the year. On February 22, power steering was offered for medium- and heavy-duty models. On March 28, the "Super Duck" amphibious military truck was announced, but no orders for this vehicle were ever received.

On May 17, 1954, GMC expanded the availability of Hydra-Matic Drive to all lines. This represented a truck-building industry first. In selected heavy-duty models, seven-speed "Twin Hydra-Matic" transmissions were made available. A GMC-built two-speed "reduction box" auxiliary transmission was available with Hydra-Matic transmissions in medium- and heavy-duty trucks.

On July 14, coach general sales manager E.P. Crenshaw got a new product to sell when the first GMC Scenicruiser bus rolled off the assembly line. The Golden Chariot 47-passenger parlor coach was introduced September 15. On December 4, GMC set up a Fleet Division for low-end truck sales. Calendar-year output for GMC was 76,243 trucks or 7.45 percent of industry. That gave GMC the fifth rank in sales again.

1955 First Series & Blue Chip

All General Motors cars and trucks were due for changeover in model year 1955, but GM had trouble getting so many product revisions completed by new-model-introduction time in the fall of 1954. Therefore, it decided to postpone the release of all new 1955 GMC trucks until the spring of 1955. The 1954 series was continued as a 1955 "First Series" line with revisions to styling, finish, and engineering that were relatively minor, but important to GMC truck collectors today.

The 1955 First Series models had the same basic appearance as the previous models. Some small revisions took place. The circular fender impressions in the new-for-1954 pickup bed were changed to make flat inner walls. The battery was moved from under the passenger side floorboard to below the hood. Through 1954, the postwar models all had a single tubular propeller shaft enclosed in a torque tube with an enclosed universal joint at the front, but the 1955 First Series trucks switched to an open drive shaft.

In an advertisement aimed at attracting new GMC dealers, general manager Phillip J. Monaghan described his all-new 1955 models—which were unveiled on March 17—as "Blue-Chip" models. Monaghan noted that the growth rate of truck sales over the preceding 25 years had been three times that of car sales—and this may explain why the new 128-model lineup was double the number of 1954's offering.

"Blue-Chip GMCs give our dealers many competitive advantages," Monaghan pointed out. "They are the new generation of trucks: designed to haul more payload farther, faster, for less money, with greater driver comfort, less traffic trouble, in greater safety, and in better style than ever before." The public agreed in 1955 and gave GMC the best peace-time year in its history.

GMC introduced bold new styling in mid-1955, when completely redesigned light- and medium-duty models were announced. The most dramatic appearance changes that came out of William F. Lange's GMC Truck & Coach styling studio were passenger-car like in nature. The front end featured a two-bar grille format suggesting the grille of the 1954 Oldsmobile. The GMC grilles carried numbers like 100 (1/2 ton), 150 (3/4 ton), and 250 (1 ton) to indicate the series. Hooded headlights and a bumper with protruding circular guards reflected styling themes that had earlier been associated with Cadillac. No hood ornament was fitted. Traditional GMC lettering, more stylized than ever, was mounted on the lower hood surface in an oblong cove with a grid-work background.

The use of a panoramic windshield and backlight substantially increased the glass area of GMC pickups. The higher front fender line extended back through the full length of the cab. Joining the GMC truck line was a stylish new model, originally called the Town & Country Pickup that was later re-christened the Suburban Pickup.

RISS Express Service operated this 1955 GMC DF860-67 6 x 2 tractor with 6-71 diesel engine and 10-speed Road Ranger and "dead pusher" rear axle. This truck was part of a large fleet order. (© General Motors Corp.)

Left and Below: The first ads for the 1955 GMC "Cameo" style pickups called them the "Town & Country Runabout." The next series of ads called them the "Suburban Runabout." Later they became "Suburban Pickups." (Bud Juneau)

This fancy truck had flush outer-fender panels made of fiberglass and a $2,023 base price.

The Town & Country Pickup was GMC's version of a Chevrolet design that stylist Charles M. "Chuck" Jordan created after being inspired by the futuristic Nike guided-missile carriers that he saw while serving in the U.S. Air Force. In April of 1954, Jordan was given the responsibility of supervising an experimental styling group within Luther W. Stier's Chevrolet Truck styling studio where Jordan was assistant chief designer. In addition to the Town and Country Pickup, Jordan was also in charge of designing a unique GMC experimental show truck named the L'Universelle.

Chrysler advised GMC that it had already used the Town & Country name on its station wagons and the new model became the Suburban Pickup. It was 4.5 in. longer than the Chevrolet model and weighed 130 lbs. more, at 3,645 lbs. Base engine was the 248.5-cid overhead-valve inline six with 125 hp. A 287.2-cid Pontiac V-8 rated at 155 hp was available at extra cost. Some historians say 300 Suburban pickups were built in 1955 and some say it was 326.

Major styling changes were also apparent on the trucks in GMC's medium- and heavy-duty model ranges. The 550 and 650 models, with GCWs up to 55,000 lbs., featured a new 96-in. bbc (bumper-to-back-of-cab) design that combined the cab accessibility of conventional trucks with the payload and maneuverability of cab-over-engine models. During the latter part of 1955, the 3- through 4 1/2-ton GMC "Blue-Chip" trucks captured 38.2 percent of new-truck registrations in that category.

The GMC power-plant options included a half dozen GMC-built six-cylinder engines with outputs ranging from 125 hp in the 248 to 225 hp in a 503-cid engine (compared to 125 hp to 200 hp in 1954). In addition, GMC offered two brand new overhead-valve V-8s, a 287.2-cid Pontiac-built model with 155 hp, and a 324-cid Olds engine with 175 hp. For big trucks, three diesel engines were available. All three had higher 18.0:1 compression ratios, which resulted in a five-horsepower increase for the largest, a 230-hp diesel. A 12-volt electrical system replaced the previous 6-volt system.

Forty-four percent of GMC's 1955 models were powered by V-8s, compared to none a year before. The 287.2-cid V-8 was the same engine that was introduced in Pontiac passenger cars in 1955. It had a 3 3/4 x 3 1/4-in. bore and stroke and a two-barrel carburetor. Sixty-five percent of GMC trucks used Hydra-Matic Drive, up from 13 percent in 1954. In total, the "Blue-Chip" GMCs were said to incorporate 500 major refinements.

On August 12, 1954, GMC announced a new forward-control (COE) truck as part of its 1955 line. This DF model was styled under the supervision of General Motors design director Harley Earl. Its new appearance was characterized by a snub-nosed look and rounded-feature lines. Truckers nicknamed it the "cannonball." As with prewar COE models, the DF came in two-tone color schemes, with 12 different colors available in five combinations. It featured a new "Stripway" system designed for COE trucks with 5-ton-and-up GVWS. This allowed quicker access by service personnel to the engine, transmission, and other components through the use of counter-balanced seats that slid up to the ceiling. This permitted engineers to incorporate fold-back floorboards and side doors that swung open on each side of the large hood.

With the carryover of the 1954 models as First Series 1955s early in the year, GMC's assembly lines were moving slowly. In February, only 995 of the old-style trucks

were built, but truck general sales manager R.C. Woodhouse had his sales teams ready to go immediately after the new models arrived. By early spring, general manufacturing manager T.E. Wilson had the assembly lines "tuned up" to hit an all-time record of 13,162 trucks built in May. Strong yields became normal during the remainder of the year. GMC raised its market share a full point to 8.4 percent of the total industry and held 8.9 percent of the new-truck registrations in the U.S. Deliveries rose 23.3 percent over 1954 and registrations increased 23 percent.

Helping business at GMC in 1955 was the July 12 signing of a $10,500,000 defense contract for 6-x-6 tactical vehicles. Less than a month later, on August 10, GMC secured a $5,600,000 military contract for 2 1/2-ton stake trucks. All in all, 1955 turned out to be the best peacetime year ever for the company.

1956: Top Success Story

"The better you know GMC—the better the truck business looks," a 1956 advertisement designed by the Kudner Agency advised those in the business of selling new trucks. The copy noted that GMC-registration figures for 1955 were 127.4 percent higher than those of 1954 and that "Blue-Chip" GMC trucks were moving faster than any other full line of trucks. "It was the top success story of the past year," said the advertisement. "Early '56 reports indicate this momentum is still growing. And as the stream of GMC advances continue to open the doors on vast new markets, it's little wonder the GM franchise has become the most coveted in all trucking."

It was no lie! W.L. Vandewater was doing a great job making the men and women who sold GMCs more successful than the year before. Vandewater served as executive assistant to general manager Phillip Monaghan and

was also in charge of dealer relations. That made his job easy. The dealers were happy, too, because annual new-truck registrations of GMCs accounted for 9.2 percent of the industry total, compared to 8.9 percent the previous year. The company was one of few truck makers to increase its portion of the new-truck market in the tough 1956 marketplace.

On January 13, 1956, GMC's chief engineer C.V. "Davy" Crockett had his designers ready to unveil a prototype of the first air-suspension truck. A production version would arrive just a little more than a year later. On April 6, coach general sales manager E.P. Crenshaw announced that GMC's coach-making branch had developed a safer and

Sam Braen Rockland Materials Co., of Mahwah, New Jersey, owned this 1956 GMC Model 662 tractor fitted with a cement mixer body. (DEM)

A Ward Baking Co. dealer-servicing salesman visited Tom's Market, in southwest Michigan, in this 1956 GMC PM 250 forward-control chassis with bread van body. (© General Motors Corp.)

Right: This 1956 GMC K100 four-wheel-drive 1/2-ton Suburban may have been a prototype unit. (© General Motors Corp.)

simpler-to-operate 72-passenger school bus with forward control. The division's total coach production climbed to 2,912 units in calendar 1956, a gain of 29 buses.

After the dramatic changes of 1955, the new GMC light- and medium-duty trucks introduced on March 7, 1956, were virtually unchanged in appearance. As in 1955, the grille carried 100 (1/2 ton), 150 (3/4 ton) or 250 (1 ton) numbers to indicate the series. The 100 Series model line-up included the Suburban Pickup with deluxe trim and special "flush-side" fiberglass outer-fender panels. Almost all the other 1955 trucks returned, too. Tubeless tires became new standard equipment on light-duty trucks.

Mechanical revisions were highlighted by the use of larger six-cylinder and V-8 engines with displacements of 270 and 316.6 cid, respectively. The latter engine was the same one used in 1956 Pontiac cars, but with a different 156-hp rating in the heavier GMCs. Trucks with a V-8 were no longer listed as a separate series, since the V-8 engines became optional. GMC also widened its engine options for medium-duty trucks.

On May 1, GMC brought out an expanded line of heavy-duty trucks. New models were the FW-550 dual-purpose tandem-axle tractor and the tandem-axle W670. The former used the V-8 engine introduced in 1956 with improvements upping output to 210 hp. The W670, with its 59,000-lb. GVW, used a 503-cid 190-net bhp six and a gearbox with a five-speed main transmission. A three- or four-speed auxiliary transmission was optional. GMC also introduced an inter-axle differential that could be used to lock out the rear-tandem axle for off-road operation and connect it for highway use. A special Model 630 was available for fire-truck service that also used the big 503-cid gas engine.

On June 18, four-wheel drive was made available as a regular factory-installed option for pickups in the 100, 150, and 250 series. Six basic 4-x-4 models were offered with ratings from 1/2 to 1 ton. Previously, four-wheel drive had only been offered as an aftermarket conversion.

Sage Green finish was used on the 1957 Series 6-71 Detroit Diesel engine that powered many GMC trucks. (© General Motors Corp.)

1957: The Money Makers

"When your business is selling trucks…of any size…of any type…for any job…there's nothing like selling the Money-Makers," said a GMC advertisement showing a variety of new 1957 models working at a construction site. The copy described the trucks as, "The GMC Blue Chip Money-Maker Line."

GMC's light- and medium-duty "money-makers" for 1957 were introduced on November 3, 1956. Styling changes were highlighted by a new grille design. Replacing the twin-bar arrangement was an insert with a center divider and horizontal bars. A model designation plaque was placed in the left section. The plaque carried 100 (1/2 ton), 150 (3/4 ton) or 250 (1 ton) numbers to indicate the series. The secondary grille mesh, which served as a backdrop for the GMC logo on the 1955 and 1956 models, was eliminated. The small-truck model line up was largely unchanged. Directional signals were now standard equipment.

GMC prices were beginning to show an upward movement and the 1/2-ton Series 101 panel truck cracked the $2,000 price barrier for the first time in 1957 with its $2,147 window sticker. The Suburban, which had hit $2,150 back in 1954, was now up to $2,498. The pickup was still a bit cheaper at $1,846, but more than likely, taxes and extra-cost accessories pushed most sales into the $2,000 bracket. In the Series 252 3/4-ton range, the larger pickup with a 123 1/4-in. wheelbase and 7 1/2-ft. bed cost $2,042. The Series 253 1-ton line offered a 9-ft. pickup on a 135-in. wheelbase for $2,191 and the 9-ft. panel, for $2,519, was the priciest light-duty model.

On March 18, GMC introduced new heavy-duty trucks with the industry's first air suspension. Ten basic models in the 50,000- to 65,000-lb. gross-combination-weight class were offered and attracted lots of attention from dealers. Their unique air-suspension system consisted of rubberized cushions of air that absorbed heavy road jolts and high-frequency vibrations before they could reach the frame. Other models in the heavy-duty bracket ranged from 22,000-lb. to 59,000-lb. GVWs and 38,000-lb. to 90,000-lb. GCWs. Eight engines were offered from 150 hp to 236 gross hp, gasoline and diesel.

In October 1957, GMC announced that it was embarking on a far-reaching engineering-development program, which wound up being promoted as "Operation High Gear." It was designed to bring "super trucks" to America's superhighways of the future. The engineering department, which was still under the direction of C.V. Crockett, was expanded by 22 percent to become one of the largest in General Motors Corp.

A 1957 GMC Series 550 tractor pulls a Fruehauf semi-trailer past a scenic-looking, snow-capped mountain range. (© General Motors Corp.)

Looking almost too nice to haul the furniture being carried behind it is a 1957 GMC 100 Deluxe 1/2-ton pickup.
(© General Motors Corp.)

This is most likely a 1957-vintage GMC 271-cid inline six-cylinder engine. Red was the base color used for this power plant.
(© General Motors Corp.)

Right: The "butcher" theme appears in several GMC ads from the 1930s through late 1950s. This 1957 350 Series refrigerated van was perfect for meat deliveries. (© General Motors Corp.)

During 1957, the Truck & Coach division opened two new zone offices and warehousing installations. The 68,000 sq.-ft. warehouse in Elizabeth, New Jersey, and the 50,000 sq.-ft. building in Pittsburgh, Pennsylvania, kept personnel director E.A. Maxwell busy hiring managers and workers to staff the new facilities. But if employment was rising, sales were going the other way as the nation slipped toward another economic pullback. New-truck registrations of GMC models for the year totaled 62,165 units as compared to 82,266 in 1956 and market penetration dropped to 7.2 percent, from 9.2 percent in the same period. Part of the reason behind the decline was that General Motors Corp. sales of defense products dropped to 5 percent of total business, down from 7 percent in 1955.

1958: America's Ablest Trucks

GMC advertised its 1958 Money-Maker models as "America's ablest trucks." The company again offered a full range of models from 1/2 ton to 45 tons. There was a new package-delivery truck and a new diesel tractor. In the light-duty line, a new wideside pickup body looked like the Suburban Pickup, but featured all-steel construction in place of fiberglass outer-rear-fender skins.

Dual headlights and a restyled grille also highlighted the exterior appearance of the smaller GMC trucks. The grille again carried 100 (1/2 ton), 150 (3/4 ton) or 250 (1 ton) numbers to indicate the series. A broad, creased-body feature line on the wideside models was suggestive of a similar styling treatment used by Cadillac in 1956. The front-hood GMC logo was slimmed down and series numeral identification was placed in the center of the grille. Also found on 1958 models were new hubcaps that looked less ornate than those used from 1955 to 1957.

Cruising through the Southwestern setting is a 1957 GMC 100 Series 1/2-ton pickup with a 336-cid V-8 below its hood.
(© General Motors Corp.)

On November 8, 1957, the 1958 light- and medium-duty trucks were introduced. Annual model-year changes included a new V-8 engine, a stronger chassis, and a new automatic transmission for some models. The new gasoline engine of 336-cid and 200 gross bhp headed a group of nine gas and diesel engines used throughout the GMC line. A heavier, stronger front-frame cross member was provided on many GMCs for greater rigidity. One new model was a 16,000-lb. GVW package-delivery chassis. Other package-delivery models were in the 7,000- and 10,000-lb. categories. Early in 1958, GMC presented a new 30,000-lb. GVW tractor with a 190-hp diesel engine for lighter weight, economical hauling.

A head-on look at the 1958 Suburban Pickup reveals its dual headlights. This model was replaced by the all-steel Wideside Pickup late in the year. (© General Motors Corp.)

For trucks in the 32,000- to 55,000-lb. weight range, GMC offered its new Torqmatic Drive, an automatic transmission made by General Motors' Allison Division. Torqmatic succeeded Hydra-Matic for these models, with Hydra-Matic remaining on the 1/2- through 2-ton models. Torqmatic provided six forward speeds and four forward-driving ranges to eliminate the need for reduction units or wide-range axles. Another new Torqmatic feature available from GMC was a hydraulic retarder that multiplied engine braking up to six times the normal amount.

By this time, GMC was selling many Model DF-860 "cannonball" highway tractors into major freight-hauling fleets. These steel COE tractors were powered by the dependable Detroit 6-71SE economy-diesel engine.

GMC Division accounted for 7.1 percent of total U.S. truck output in calendar year 1958, while turning out 61,768 trucks. This compared to output of 69,675 units in 1957 that captured 6.4 percent of the industry total. In addition, 2,405 coaches were produced in 1958, compared to 3,108 in 1957. That was probably a disappointment for C.S. Dick, who replaced E.P. Crenshaw as coach general sales manager this year.

The year 1958 brought another big change for GMC when its advertising account was transferred to McCann-Erickson, Inc. It had previously been with the Kudner Agency, which started in 1935 when Art Kudner broke away from Erwin Wasey's New York company and started his own agency with Buick, Goodyear, and General Motors as clients.

The Kudner Agency was "fired" by Buick general sales manager Edward Kennard in 1957 after an incident involving a televised championship-boxing match sponsored by Buick. The cameras cut to a commercial at a crucial moment in the match. Viewers who missed the knockout punch became incensed with Buick and Buick got mad at Kennard. He then fired the ad agency in an emotional reaction. Shortly thereafter, Kudner lost all of its other GM accounts, including GMC Truck & Coach.

Sporting the standard painted grille is another 1958 GMC 350 platform truck with stake rack body. (JMSC)

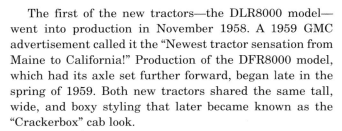

GMC enthusiast and collector, James M. Semon of Westlake, Ohio, restored this 1959 GMC DF860 "Cannonball" to use in his hobby business S & S Enterprises. In addition to real GMCs, Jim has a massive collection of company literature and photos of GMC trucks. (JMSC)

Two carpenters get ready to depart a jobsite in their two-tone 1958 GMC 100 Series Suburban Carryall. This truck used the 336-cid V-8 engine. (© General Motors Corp.)

1959: Operation 'High Gear'

Back in October of 1957, GMC stepped up its engineering development program 22 percent with the aim of creating "super trucks" for America's forthcoming superhighways. A 1959 advertisement heralded the first results of this move with a bold headline reading, "Watch Operation 'High Gear' at GMC." The ad showed six GMC trucks, from a 1/2-ton Suburban to a 45-ton conventional tractor-trailer sweeping through a curve at the GM Proving Ground in Milford, Michigan. It promised, "The biggest engineering, design, and quality-control program the industry has ever known brings you the greatest money-making, money-saving advances in trucks today!"

Outwardly, the 1959 GMCs were still "Blue-Chip" models, which were in their last year on the market. The regular pickups had a more functional straight-line bumper without pod-style automobile-type bumper guards. A totally different mesh-type grille and "guardrail"-type bumper was seen on the entry-level Fleet models, which also had less overall body trim and more-spartan interiors.

As 1959 got under way, GMC was preparing to market a pair of innovative tilt-cab highway tractors. GMC said that these trucks offered the "extreme flexibility of 48-in. bbc." The "bbc" abbreviation meant that the tractor bodies measured only four feet long from (front) bumper to back of cab. They were made of aluminum. The shorter length of the new tractor cabs permitted the use of maximum-length trailers in all states, which allowed truckers to convey heavier loads to more locations. In addition, the lighter weight of the aluminum cabs helped the trucks carry more freight without exceeding road-weight limits. The new "true" tilt-cab design allowed the cab to be tilted forward manually because the aluminum cab's weight was counter balanced by torsion bar-type springs.

The first of the new tractors—the DLR8000 model—went into production in November 1958. A 1959 GMC advertisement called it the "Newest tractor sensation from Maine to California!" Production of the DFR8000 model, which had its axle set further forward, began late in the spring of 1959. Both new tractors shared the same tall, wide, and boxy styling that later became known as the "Crackerbox" cab look.

The DLR8000 had its front axle set back 50 in. This moved the front fenders rearward and allowed room ahead of them for a running board and cab-entry step plate. The DLR8000 was designed to carry up to 1,824 lbs. more than other trucks in the 61,000-lb. GCW range. Its road-ready weight with 100 gallons of fuel and a driver was "only" 9,987 lbs. Weight distribution was 7,164 lbs. front and 2,823 lbs. rear.

The DFR8000 model had the same cab with only a 28-in. front-axle setback. Due to moving the wheels 22 in. forward, the running boards and step plates required to enter the cab were designed to go behind the front fenders. This type of design made the tractor adaptable to loads ranging up to 76,000-lbs. GCW.

Both trucks utilized "stabilized" air ride, independent front wheel suspension, fabricated frames, and aluminum tilt-cabs to achieve major breakthroughs in lightweight and safety design. Both of the new heavy-duty trucks were powered by the same 6-71SE two-cycle diesel engines used in D860 GMCs. They featured a new fabricated frame that was 300 lbs. lighter than a conventional type. It had very deep, welded I-beam construction and utilized 3/16-in.-wide top flanges continuously welded to light-steel webs. The air-suspension systems for the front and rear of both trucks were re-designed into a single convolution-type air cylinder that eliminated the need for an added air reservoir. The front suspension was rated at 11,000 lbs.

Illustrating a "Fleet" grille option that commercial customers could order to get a buyer's credit is the front-end treatment on this 1958 GMC 350 Series platform truck with stake rack body. Note the old gasoline pumps, which would be collector items today. (© General Motors Corp.)

Although this photo was taken in conjunction with the 1964-1965 New York World's Fair "Futurama" exhibit, the tractor pulling the trailer owned by Oldsmobile Div. is a 1959 GMC 550 Series model with a 370-cid Oldsmobile gas V-8. (© General Motors Corp.)

GMC produced nearly 14,000 more trucks in its Pontiac, Michigan, and Oakland, California, factories in 1959 than it had in 1958. During the calendar year, 74,411 trucks were made at GMC factories in Pontiac and 7,033 on the West Coast, but some of these units were Chevrolets.

Calendar-year production was 75,411 units. By GVW class, this total broke down as: (up to 6,000 lbs.) 24,659; (6001-10,000 lb) 10,482; (10,001-14,000 lbs.) 150; (14,001-16,000 lbs.) 6,711; (16,001-19,500 lbs.) 15,911; (19,501-26,000 lbs.) 9,652; (26,001-33,000 lbs.) 6,037; and (33,001 lbs. and higher) 1,809 units. In terms of industry output, GMC's 1959 production total accounted for 6.62 percent of all U.S. truck sales. With the release of the new tilt cabs, the division's share of the diesel-truck market leaped to 14.1 percent, from 7.2 percent the year before. GMC was now America's fourth-ranked maker of diesels.

After the Kudner Agency's falling out with General Motors in 1957-58, GMC's advertising account was transferred to McCann-Erickson, Inc. This change led to a heavy advertising campaign in 1960, with colorful multi-page ads telling the story of how GMC's Operation "High Gear" led to many truck-making breakthroughs. The ads also reflected the fact that truck designs were modernizing quickly as the 1950s came to an end and that GMC was in high gear for the 1960s.

GMC Historian Donald E. Meyer was at the Chicago Auto Show in the winter of 1958 to serve as an announcement guide for this 1959 GMC DLR8000 tilt-cab tractor with air suspension. The all-new 2 1/2-ton COE model had a short BBC (bumper to back of cab) measurement to allow truckers to haul longer trailers without increasing the overall length of the tractor-trailer combination. The trucks in the background are 1958 models. (© General Motors Corp.)

It looks like this one-of-a-kind 1951 GMC HDCW 950 was color-coordinated to match Pacific Intermountain Express headquarters. This rig carried a 6-110 diesel test engine that produced 275 hp.(© General Motors Corp.)

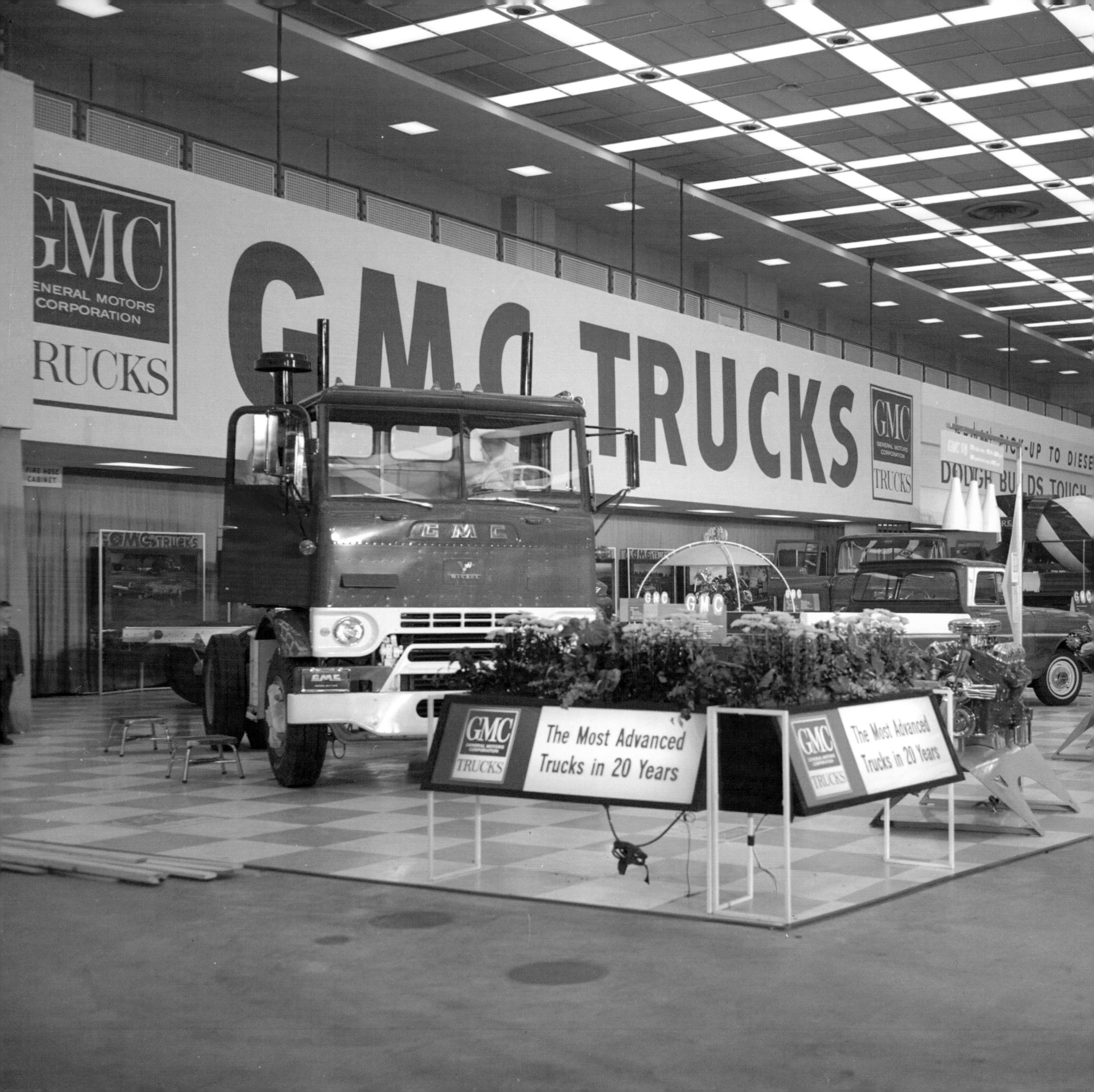

Chapter 5

The '60s

1960-1969

Page 64 & 65: "Most Advanced Truck in 20 Years" was the slogan used to promote sales of the 1962 GMC DF7000 model in an auto show. This unit used an 8V-71 diesel engine. (© General Motors Corp.)

Ralph O. Weaver Oil Co., of Allentown, Pennsylvania, employed this 1960 GMC L6000 tilt-cab truck with a tanker body to deliver Gulf Solar Heating Oil. (DEM)

The rear view of a 1960 GMC Series 100 1/2-ton Wideside pickup illustrates the decade's brand new truck styling. (© General Motors Corp.)

1960: The Big GMC Breakthrough

The start of a new decade brought changes at the top of the GMC corporate ladder and a completely new line of trucks for 1960. During the year, Calvin J. Werner took over as general manager with the departure of P.J. Monaghan. Also gone from the organizational chart was the name of W.L. VandeWater, who had served as executive assistant to Mr. Monaghan, as well as the person in charge of dealer relations. The rest of the executive team remained in place.

The new trucks arrived with a bang! "Announcing from Operation 'High Gear'—for 1960: The Big GMC Breakthrough in Truck Engineering!" heralded a two-page announcement that GMC's new advertising agency, McCann-Erickson, placed in national magazines like *The Saturday Evening Post*. By this time, GMC's model selection was unsurpassed anywhere in the world. There were 48 models in the 1000, 1500, 2500, 3000, 3500, 4000, 5,000, 5500, 6000, 7000, 7100, 860, 8000, 8100, and 9000 series. They ranged from 1/2 ton up to 60 tons.

The line included 15 light-duty and pickup conventional-gasoline models. These trucks had a completely new appearance combining a modern cab with lower overall height. A "pinched-in-waist" feature line ran along the hood and doors of all models and the rear quarters of panels, Suburbans, and Wide-Side pickups. The massive, full-width hood had "jet-pod" styling. A screen-like grille filled the upper front end with rectangular parking lamps on grilles inside the pods at each end. The lower grille bars had a "barbell" look with GMC letters in the center and dual headlamps at each end.

On August 10, 1959, GMC announced an entirely new line of V-6 gasoline truck engines for its 1960 models. These power plants were the first of their kind ever

"Cracker Box" was the nickname given to trucks like this 1960 GMC DF 7000 tilt-cab tractor. They were designed to allow truckers to haul larger loads. (© General Motors Corp.)

developed. They were designed to operate on regular-grade gasoline and promised better fuel economy, greater performance, and a high degree of parts interchangeability. The engines could develop maximum torque at moderate engine speeds, which meant more power with less wear. The family included 305-, 351-, and 401-cid V-6s and a 702-cid V-12 called the "Twin-Six." The body trim on 1960 GMC trucks included a circular medallion on the fender sides, behind the headlamps, with a "V" through the circle to indicate a V-type engine.

The roof of the 1960 GMC truck cab had an overhang at the rear. Up front, there was a wraparound windshield with rear-slanting upper windshield-door pillars. Deluxe and Custom cabs were available. A side-trim molding option was available. The molding ran across the cowl side and doors of all models and the rear quarters of the flush-fender Wide-Side pickups. Along with a new easy-riding torsion-bar front-suspension system, the GMC light-duty trucks had stronger, more rigid, yet lighter, frames. The division said that greater product reliability was assured by the fact that it was making "over one thousand separate quality-control inspections" on its trucks.

A 1/2-ton Fender-Side pickup on the standard 115-in. wheelbase sold for $2,072, including torsion-bar independent-front suspension, double-wall cab construction, foam-rubber seats, a hardwood-body floor, and four protective coats of finish. The slab-sided Wide-Side version was $21 additional. The new Suburban had more room and more comfort. It could seat eight passengers with all three seats installed or carry truck-size loads in its 175 cu. ft. cargo area with the auxiliary seats removed. It rode on the same 115-in. wheelbase as the standard pickup and had two doors up front. The rear of the body was available with two additional doors or with a lift-gate combination. Ads said that it was "ideal for sportsmen" and described it as being "truck-built" with the car-like comfort and handling ease provided by independent front suspension and coil rear springs. The window sticker showed a $2,821 price for all of this.

Four-wheel drive was a $650 option on 1/2-ton trucks and $700 extra on 3/4-ton models. This season GMC switched from a four-wheel-drive system, made by an outside supplier named NAPCO, to its own four-wheel-drive system. According to advertisements, this resulted in "4-Wheel Drives with a new, low look!" The copywriters said the trucks were "designed from tires to top as 4-wheel-drive trucks—not conversions—they have extra-strong frames, axles, suspensions." GMC said that these rugged workhorses could "claw their way up a 60% grade or walk through hub-high mud."

As a replacement for the inline six-cylinder engine in light-duty trucks, GMC offered the new family of V-6s. They featured a completely new design with 33 percent more cooling area around valves and cylinders. This allowed the engines to circulate up to 176 gallons of coolant per minute. As a result, cooling temperatures varied less than four degrees throughout the engine, thereby eliminating hot spots.

The short new V-6 blocks with extra-strong inner ribbing, staggered cylinders, and deep-block construction were extremely rigid. Their short, stiff crankshafts were said to be twice as husky as those in contemporary V-8s. According to GMC, the M-400 bearings used in the V-6s could outlast others by seven to one. The engines' rugged GMC-built aluminum pistons had cast-in-steel rings to control expansion.

The gasoline V-6s were offered in three displacements and five horsepower ratings. The GMC-305A (it actually

White sidewall tires add to the good looks of this 1960 GMC Series 100 1/2-ton Suburban. (DEM)

had 304.7 cu. in.) V-6 used in light-duty models had a 4.25 x 3.58-in. bore and stroke, a 7.75:1 compression ratio, and a one-barrel Holley carburetor. It produced 150 gross bhp at 3600 rpm and 260 lbs.-ft. of gross torque at 1600-2000 rpm. Also available in larger trucks were the 351- and 401-cid V-6s and the 275-hp Twin-Six (V-12) 702-cid gasoline engine. Transmissions available in light-duty models included three- and four-speed manual gearboxes, as well as a four-speed Hydra-Matic.

Ads claimed that the new gasoline V-6s, with proper maintenance, had the potential to go 200,000 miles without a major overhaul. According to GMC historian Donald E. Meyer, who worked for the company as a sales engineer, many trucks with the V-6s did achieve such mileage. Ed Snyder, an expert on 1960s GMC trucks, states, "History has proven that 400,000 to 500,000 miles without an overhaul is actually achievable."

A new 1/2-ton van was called the Model PV1000 Junior Delivery Van. It was constructed on a short 98-in. wheelbase and designed for multi-stop delivery service. The forward-control design and short 18-ft. turning radius made it perfect for package-delivery work. Selling for only $2,658, it was the only light-duty truck that did not use the new V-6. Instead, it had a thrifty 269.5-cid inline six that produced 133 hp at 3600 rpm. The larger 3/4-ton and 1-ton walk-in delivery vans were still available.

Other technical changes included improved front and rear suspensions. Torsion bars were used at the front of light- and medium-duty trucks instead of conventional springs to give a car-like ride. The torsion-bar springs could better absorb road jolts and high-frequency vibrations. They also eliminated wheel tramping and shimmying. Coil springs or a "Vari-Rate" spring suspension were used at the rear. The new three-inch-wide Vari-Rate rear springs brought new ride comfort to the heavier trucks, because the variable-deflection system gave a soft ride whether the truck was empty or loaded. These springs were also lighter in weight.

This 1960 GMC 4000 Series truck had a stake rack body, tarp cover and 351-cid V-6 engine. (© General Motors Corp.)

Left: 1960 GMC advertisement

In addition to its light-duty models, GMC offered 20 Model B 90-in. bbc conventionals, 16 tilt-cab (90-in. bbc) gasoline models, two forward-control models, seven school-bus chassis, 10 Model B conventional diesels, five 48-in. bbc tilt-cab diesels, and eight 72-in. bbc tilt-cab diesels. GMC advertising stressed the big breakthroughs in engine, chassis, and cab engineering that could drastically reduce a trucker's costs. According to GMC, lighter-truck weights and other improvements led to engines lasting two to three times longer. New fabrication methods made frames 28 times more rigid, and the aluminum cabs would last twice as long because they would not rust.

Nine different engines were available in the heavier trucks including a gasoline-fueled inline six, the five gasoline V-6s, the Twin-Six, an inline six-cylinder diesel, and new V-6 and V-8 diesels with up to 240 hp. The latter was the Detroit 8V-71, offered for the first time in GMC Models DF7100, DFW7100, and DF8100. The 702-cid Twin-Six was standard in the Model BW9000. The latter truck served well pulling double-trailer gravel, steel, and tank trains in Michigan, with gross-train weights of up to 157,000 lbs.

And speaking of big trucks, military work that carried into 1960 included a contract for researching and developing a highway tractor and two carriages to haul Minuteman inter-continental ballistic missiles. A second contract was for a series of tactical military trucks.

GMC ranked fifth in U.S. truck production for calendar year 1960 and realized a 33.3-percent gain in output over 1959. Knowledgeable sources attributed a large measure of the gain to the new V-6 engines and the expansion of the model line up. In 1960, GMC installed 95,000 V-6s in its trucks, 4,000 inline sixes, 1,000 Twin-Six V-12s, and 200 diesel V-8s. "Nobody has more to sell than GMC truck dealers," read an advertisement aimed at those who might have been thinking of selling the new 1960 GMC trucks.

1961: Truck Triumph of the '60s

McCann-Erickson certainly had a bold, colorful way of promoting GMC models and boldly described them as the "Truck Triumph of the '60s." One 1961 ad showed a coloring-book-style illustration of a V-6-powered pickup in a for-advertising-purposes-only two-tone yellow-and-purple color scheme with a red-orange interior. The copy emphasized that "more revolutionary advancements than the industry has seen in 20 years" made the 1960 trucks less prone to wear and tear.

In reality, GMC trucks were not produced on a model-year-change basis at this point in history. Production of the 1960 designs simply continued into the 1961 model year, with some refinements and expansion of the variety of models. Many people would have to see a title to tell the 1961 trucks apart from 1960 models and even that could

be confusing, as GMC did not report its serial numbers to industry sources. In some states, the trucks were simply titled in the year sold, so that units built and sold in December 1960 with "1961" features could be titled as 1960 models in one state and 1961s in another.

Modifications made in late-1960 that were carried over to 1961 included revisions in heaters that increased cab temperatures by up to 10 degrees. The 1961 light-duty models actually had a lower and narrower floor tunnel for greater foot room and leg room. They also offered new options including two-speed windshield wipers and foam-rubber seats. Ads stressed that even 1/2-ton trucks had reinforced double-wall cabs that lasted longer than average and that GMC sprayed on four coats of its tough, diamond-bright 777 Super Enamel finish, not just two or three coats. No-rust hardwood-body floors and the use of steel moldings around door windows to reduce chipping and breaking were promoted as "extra value at no extra cost!"

By the late 1950s, the camping and outdoor-recreation movement was growing in America and nearly all automotive magazines published features about aftermarket pickup-truck camping units. GMC made it easier to get such equipment in 1961 by introducing a new Sports-Cab combination aimed at sportsmen like hunters, fishers, and campers. The spacious slide-in camper unit could be installed in a pickup bed in a few minutes and included adjustable windows, two interior lights, a full-length clothes hanger, and a cab-wide storage shelf as standard equipment.

Three all-new four-wheel-drive models were added to the line. These 127-in. wheelbase 1/2-ton trucks were available in chassis-and-cab, Wide-Side, and conventional pickups rated from 4,900 to 5,600 lbs. GVW. The lockout-type hubs on four-wheel-drive models were redesigned so that they could tolerate more torque.

GMC offered a new crankcase-ventilation system on conventional light- and medium-duty trucks with six-cylinder engines. The system ducted unburned hydrocarbons from the crankcase to the intake manifold and funneled them into the combustion chamber, where they were burned off with the fuel mixture. There was also a rugged new 305D V-6.

During 1961, GMC launched a new quality-control system in which the trucks were scientifically road tested without leaving the factory grounds. In the tests, medium- and heavy-duty trucks were operated on an electrically driven dynamometer that was designed to simulate road travel and gauge the performance of the vehicles under "actual driving conditions." The company said that it was the only testing system of its kind.

The GMC 90-in. conventional was innovative in that it could haul a 40-ft. trailer within 50 ft. overall. "You can't pick the road, load, or laws," GMC advertised to tractor-trailer operators in 1961, "But you can pick a GMC truck." The 90-in. conventional had an exclusive swing-away grille that made servicing faster and easier. New features for medium- and heavy-duty trucks included improved air-compressor assemblies for air-hydraulic and full air-brake systems that resulted in greater braking efficiency.

An impressive array of models, from 1/2-ton to 60-ton, was available in the GMC line. It included a complete range of cabs from the 48-in. aluminum tilt-cab with set-back front axle that could haul 2,000 lbs. extra payload per trip to versatile 105-in. conventional-cab trucks. There were numerous cab-and-chassis combinations from 72-in. steel tilt cabs to 90-in. conventionals. From the options list, you could pick a tractor that could haul extra legal payload and choose an engine from six long-life gas V-6s, plus a Twin-Six or three different diesels. In one weight range alone—the 4000 series—buyers had a choice of 34 different axle-transmission-engine combinations, as well as GVWs from 19,500 to 23,000 lbs.

On the corporate front, GMC added another production point during 1961, building 2,042 trucks in a General Motors plant in Bloomfield, New Jersey. The bulk of production—some 62,541 trucks—were made in Pontiac and 7,505 units were produced in Oakland, California. In April 1961, GMC also opened a new factory branch in Dearborn, Michigan, and established a new defense-products position manned by former chief engineer C.V. Crockett. Appointed as GMC's new chief engineer was H.O. "Hal" Flynn. Another change in executive positions was the appointment of J.A. Castle to the post of public relations director after B.W. Crandell's departure. With a recession in effect, GMC had a 6.69 percent share of market in 1961.

Above & Below: This expertly restored 1962 GMC 1-ton pickup has the trusty 305-cid V-6 under its hood. (JM)

Left: A great vehicle to take on fishing excursions was the 1962 GMC 100 1/2-ton Suburban Carryall. (© General Motors Corp.)

Camping and recreational-vehicle use were on the rise in 1962 when this GMC 1000 1/2-ton Wide-Side pickup was used to carry a slide-in camper shell. (© General Motors Corp.)

Ranchers and farmers found the 1962 GMC V3000 1 1/2-ton platform truck great for hauling hay. (© General Motors Corp.)

Right: This sales catalog for GMC's 1963 Series 5000 trucks featured a dump truck, a tanker and a beverage truck on its cover. (OCWC)

1962: Only GMC has it!

The big news in 1962 was the announcement of a more powerful Model 305D V-6 engine as standard equipment for all of GMC's light- and medium-duty trucks. GMC advertising stressed that "Only GMC has it!" when it came to V-6 power. While the bore-and-stroke and compression ratio were unchanged, GMC made other improvements, such as switching from a Holley one-barrel carburetor to a Bendix-Stromberg model WW 381031 two-barrel carburetor. The result was an increase to 165 gross bhp at 3800 rpm (up from 150 at 3600 rpm) and 280 lbs.-ft. of gross torque at 1600 rpm (up from 260 lbs.-ft. at 1600-2000 rpm). As a result of the engine upgrades and other advances, GMC sales jumped 35 percent over 1961 and the company built its 250,000th V-6 engine in late November.

In October 1961, GMC announced an important styling improvement for all of its 1962 conventional-cab trucks. This covered all light trucks, as well as heavier models having 105-in. bbc cabs. The hood was lowered and rounded off in front to improve the driver's view of the road ahead. The new design carried the upper-body-side-feature line horizontally around the front of the trucks, eliminating the upper grille. Twin air slots were seen between the parking lamps on the front face of the hood. The parking lamps had clear lenses. The lower grille was similar to before. Emblems on the hood sides had a 6 inside an oval inside a "V." This gave them a piece-of-pie shape when viewed from far away. The emblems were raised to the forward hood side, just behind the parking lamps. New hubcaps with a dark-colored, round center medallion had a white circle and GMC lettering on them.

Standard equipment on the 1000 series 1/2-ton trucks included a fuel filter, oil bath air filter, painted front bumper, electric windshield wipers, fuel filter, left-hand outside rearview mirror, left-hand inside sun visor, and five 7.10 x 15 four-ply black-sidewall tubeless tires. Series 1500 3/4-ton trucks included fuel filter, painted front bumper, electric wipers, left-hand outside rearview mirror, left-hand interior sun visor, and four 7 x 17.5 six-ply black sidewall tubeless tires.

A new series of versatile heavy-duty trucks powered by an advanced V-6 gasoline engine was announced on

January 4, 1962. The new 478-cid power plant developed 235 gross bhp at 3200 rpm and reputedly had the highest torque of any comparably sized gas engine in the industry. In April, the division added a "tri-axle" model to its heavy-duty truck offerings. This air-suspended "tag" axle, mounted behind the regular tandem-drive rear axles, was a factory-installed special-equipment option. The extra rear axle allowed added vehicle weight to be transferred from the front axle to the rear tandems for greater off-road traction and floatation. The setup permitted GMC dump trucks to haul eight yards of transit-mix concrete in Michigan and Ohio and nine yards in Indiana. Previously, seven-yard loads were the maximum in those states.

Late in May, GMC brought out two new DFI-7000 and DFWI-7000 heavy-duty models with inline six-cylinder diesel engines to meet the needs of operators who used other trucks with inline engines and required interchangeability. Single and tandem rear-axle units were available on all 7000-series trucks, regardless of the engine used.

GMC's calendar-year production rose 19.7 percent, making 1962 the third-best peacetime year in company history behind 1955 and 1960. The combined total of truck-and-coach production was good for an increased 7.16 percent market share. Ninety-three percent of all GMC vehicles made had V-6 engines. Factory output included 77,256 units made in Pontiac, 11,189 made in Oakland, and 1,344 units made in Bloomfield, New Jersey. On the division's organizational chart, J.D. "Jack" Mintline replaced R.L. Ganter as the company's comptroller and went right to work counting the money that was rolling in.

1963: 'Job Tailored'

The 1963 trucks line of GMC trucks went on sale on October 11, 1962. They were basically the same in appearance as the 1962 models, since GMC continued its policy of ignoring annual model-year changes. Technical advances in these trucks included refinements to the V-6, suspension changes, and important mechanical and electrical improvements.

GMC sold a quarter million V-6s since 1960 and said in a 1963 advertisement that "many owners report durability records that were previously expected only from diesel engines." At the same time, the company had enough customer feedback on fuel economy and other typical problems to make significant enhancements for 1963. To begin with, a new economy-engine version of the 305E V-6 became standard in all light-duty models. On top of that, all GMC 305E V-6s were redesigned to provide twice the oil flow by utilizing an oil pump that had twice the capacity of those used in comparable engines. The two-speed Pow-R-Flo (GMC's name for the Chevrolet Powerglide) transmission replaced the old four-speed Hydra-Matic in the light-duty trucks.

Suspension system changes to the light- and medium-duty GMC trucks eliminated the once-heavily-promoted torsion-bar front springs. The light duty trucks now had a coil-spring independent-front suspension combined with a leaf-spring rear suspension. On the medium-duty models, an I-beam front axle was employed with Vari-Rate leaf springs.

The electrical systems of 1963 GMC trucks were improved through the use of Mylar printed circuits and a new Delcotron diode-rectified AC generator that maintained a charge even at low-idling speeds. The new "alternator" was said to extend battery life and rarely need maintenance. A running design innovation during the year was the introduction of a narrow-cab model called the GMC Journeyman, which was designed specifically for

plumbers and pipe fitters who needed to haul long pipes to a jobsite. Another running change during the 1963 model year was the use of amber parking-lamp lenses required by the federal government.

The Junior Delivery Van was dropped, while a 102-in. wheelbase forward-control utility truck was new. It featured a 153-cid overhead-valve four-cylinder engine that had a 3.875 x 3.25-in. bore and stroke and 8.5:1 compression ratio. The engine produced 90 hp at 4000 rpm and 152 lbs.-ft. of torque at 2400 rpm.

In the 3500-4000 medium-duty truck series, which were used for many fuel-oil tankers, straight trucks, and semi tractors with GVWs from 10,500 to 24,000 lbs., GMC offered conventional-cab trucks with styling resembling that of the light-duty models and a 105-in. bbc; the B

Caught in the paint booth before the completion of final finishing was this new 1963 GMC Handi-Van model. (© General Motors Corp.)

The American Fire Apparatus Co., of Battle Creek, Michigan, built this 1963 GMC 4000 tanker for the Glen Burnie, Maryland, Fire Department. (OCWC)

It's not very likely that a large number of professional gardeners opted for the Custom Trim package when they ordered a 1964 GMC 1000 1/2-ton pickup like this one. (© General Motors Corp.)

A 1964 GMC 1000 Series 1/2-ton Suburban Carryall at a plant nursery. (© General Motors Corp.)

Right: The sales catalog for GMC's 1964 Series 3500/4000 trucks used the same art as the 1963 edition, reflecting the minimal amount of annual product changes. (OCWC)

range of short conventionals with a 93 1/4-in. bbc cab, and the L range with 72-in. bbc steel-tilt cabs. The medium-duty model lineup included 3500 and B3500 models with 11,000-lb. rear axles; 4000, B4000, and L4000 models with 15,000-lb. rear axles, and H4000, BH4000, and LH4000 models with 17,000-lb. rear axles. These models were available with dozens of engine, transmission, axle, and dimensional options in each weight class, not to mention a choice of Deluxe or Custom Cab interior trims.

The 305E economy V-6 engine was standard in the 3500 series and the 305C V-6 was standard in the 4000 series. The 305C included all features of the 305E, plus a 1-qt. oil-bath air cleaner, a velocity-type governor, a 2-qt. full-flow oil filter, a drop-forged crankshaft, cast-in-steel inserts for the upper piston rings, sodium-cooled exhaust valves, and exhaust valve seat inserts. The 351-cid V-6 was optional in all 4000 series trucks. The standard transmission was a GMC four-speed synchromesh with a five-speed synchromesh unit optional at extra cost on 4000 and H4000 series models.

Conventional B- and L-style trucks were also marketed in the 5000 series and H5000 "heavy" series, which were commonly used for large dump trucks, beverage trucks, and tractors for tankers. The trucks came with GVWs ranging between 18,500 and 26,000 lbs. for 5000s, and up to 27,000 lbs. with H5000s. In these hefty lines, the 351-cid V-6 was the standard engine in all 5000s and the 401-cid version was used in H5000 models. These lines used different five-speed synchromesh transmissions—the one employed in H5000s was heftier. Buyers also had a choice of single- or dual-speed spiral-bevel rear axles.

GMC saw a large increase in sales of heavy-duty

models in 1963 and this was partly due to new products, which included some "job-tailored" trucks built specifically for individual customers. For example, large fleets of model DFW7100 tractors with 8V-71 diesel engines were sold to gravel haulers for pulling double trailer trains in Michigan and Ohio. GMC also built specially designed tractors for the U.S. Air Force to use in transporting Minuteman missiles. They had very-low-profile cabs mounted forward of twin-steering front axles and tandem or triple rear axles. Powering them was a 702-cid Twin-Six gas engine.

During 1963, truck general sales manager R.C. "Dick" Woodhouse and coach general sales manager C.F. Dick supervised a realignment of the division's marketing force designed to provide customers with more personal service because the truck marketplace was becoming more specialized in terms of product requirements. To facilitate this new broader approach to product marketing, as well as better parts sourcing, GMC constructed or modernized factory outlets in Chicago, Illinois; Detroit, Michigan; Los Angeles, California; Houston, Texas; and Salt Lake City, Utah.

In terms of both production and sales, 1963 was a banner year for GMC. Counting both trucks and coaches, the division hit an eight-year peak and increased its overall production by 13.2 percent. More than 90 percent of production, including all manufacturing of coaches, was done at Pontiac, Michigan, where the assembly lines rolled out an estimated 94,234 vehicles. Added to that were some 6,000 units built in Oakland, California, and some 1,000 made in Bloomfield, New Jersey.

1964: Breakthrough Engineering

An important new truck line was the G Series of small, forward-control Handi-Vans marking GMC's entry into the light van market. The Handi-Van had a short 90-in. wheelbase, but could handle loads up to 2,100 lbs. It combined high-cube load capacity and integral-body-frame construction in a light-duty model. The base engine was the 153-cid 90-hp four-cylinder, but an inline six-cylinder engine was an extra-cost option. Factory-installed camper versions of the Handi-Van arrived late in the year.

On conventional 1964 light-duty models, GMC made some extensive changes to the "greenhouse" section of the truck cab. The wraparound windshield of 1960-1963 was replaced with a non-wraparound one-piece curved glass that was much flatter. This changed the slant of the windshield and front-door pillar from forward slanting to rear slanting. Ventipanes (vent windows) also had an entirely new triangular shape.

A low, beveled, rounded-in-front hood still carried the upper-body side-feature line horizontally around the front of the trucks. A larger air slot was located between the parking lamps on the front face of the hood. The lower grille had the same barbell shape and same horizontal dual headlamp arrangement. Emblems on the hood sides still had the piece-of-pie shape. New hubcaps with rotor-shaped center embossments flanking a dark, round GMC center medallion were seen.

Standard equipment on 1000-Series trucks included a fuel filter, oil-bath air filter, painted front bumper, electric

windshield wipers, fuel filter, left-hand outside-rearview mirror, left-hand inside sun visor, and five 7.10 x 15 four-ply black sidewall tubeless tires. The V-6 was still standard, but a new option for 1000-Series models was a Chevrolet-built inline six-cylinder engine. The 1000 models with this motor were $16 less expensive. Since light-duty trucks with the new motor technically constituted a different series, GMC could advertise that it offered a choice of 40 pickup trucks for 1964!

The pickups received a major promotional push in 1964 as the McCann-Erickson advertising agency continued its colorful "coloring-book" style full-page advertisements in national magazines. "GMC breakthrough engineering in action," they read. "V-6 engine turns in amazing records. Many owners report 100,000 miles, 125,000 miles, 150,000 miles, and more of rough, grueling work...and still no major engine overhaul! V-6...only GMC trucks have it!"

But, not every truck owner wanted a V-6 and the new inline six was an appealing option to these buyers for various reasons. This was the first Chevrolet-built engine used in a GMC truck. It had an overhead-valve design with a cast-iron block. It had 3.875-in. x 3.25-in. bore and stroke and displaced 230 cid. With an 8.5:1 compression ratio and Rochester downdraft carburetor, it produced 120 net bhp at 3600 rpm and 205 lbs.-ft. of net torque at 1600 rpm. A 1964 pickup advertisement promoting this engine stressed its new budget price, GMC quality and durability, and thriftiness. "Skimps on gas, but not durability," it said. "Perfect for the budget buyer who insists on GMC Truck quality."

Another 1964 GMC advertisement featured the Handi-Van model. (OCWC)

This 1964 GMC advertising art was used to promote sales of the company's tractor-trailer trucks. (OCWC)

Left: Colorful illustrations like this one helped find buyers for the 1964 GMC Wide-Side pickup. (OCWC)

What's new?
This one's made by GMC.
Built, sold and serviced by truck people.
But it's priced right down there
with the others.

So the van to get is GMC's Handi-Van.
Right? GMC

The 1965 GMC Handi-Van came in models from 1/2-ton to 1-ton and with a choice of a 90-hp four-cylinder engine or a 140-hp six-cylinder engine. (OCWC)

Series 1500 3/4-ton trucks were equipped with a fuel filter, a painted front bumper, electric windshield wipers, a left-hand outside-rearview mirror, a left-hand interior sun visor, and four 7 x 17.5 six-ply black sidewall tubeless tires. While V-6 power was standard, the 3/4-ton trucks could also be had as I-1500s with the inline six. One-ton trucks were also offered as I-2500s. The four-wheel-drive option was not offered for inline six-cylinder-powered trucks.

Another 1964 innovation was a Toro-Flow V-6 diesel engine for medium-tonnage trucks. This engine was based on the gasoline V-6 engine, which meant a great deal to truckers in terms of parts interchangeability and service ease. For years, GM had been the sole manufacturer of two-cycle diesels, but the Toro-Flow engine was a four-cycle job that came in 150- and 170-hp options. It had the highest horsepower-to-weight ratio of any medium-tonnage diesel-truck engine in its class, as well as the lowest fuel consumption. With twice the cooling capacity and 20 percent greater oil flow than comparable diesels, the Toro-Flow promised GMC buyers maximum durability. GMC advertised that its medium-tonnage diesel trucks would start, steer, and shift virtually the same as their gas-powered counterparts.

In 1964, GMC advertised that it had the widest selection of medium-tonnage trucks in the industry. The full conventionals with Toro-Flow V-6 power brought new economy to a wide variety of truck applications in the 15,000-27000-lb. GVW and 35,000-45,000-lb. GCW ranges. City pickup and delivery services, bottlers, furniture companies, and meat and poultry providers were typical users of full conventionals. Short conventionals were typically employed as trucks and tractors in beverage, utility, and farm vocations requiring trucks in the 15,000-27,000-lb. GVW and 35,000-45,000-lb. GCW range.

GMC steel tilts with Toro-Flow power offered the advantages of maximum front-axle loading, ideal weight distribution, and good maneuverability. They were often seen being used in the petroleum and lumber industries and other applications requiring trucks in the 15,000-27,000-lb. GVW and 35,000-45,000-lb. GCW class. Tandem conventional models were used as dump trucks, transit cement mixers, and fuel oil-delivery tankers, plus other applications in the 37,000-39,000-lb. GVW and 45,000-lb. GCW range.

Information on GMC's 3500, B3500, 400, B4000, L4000, H4000, BH4000, and LH 4000 trucks and tractors was the same as 1963 and the sales catalogs for the two years were virtually identical, save for some air brake model notations and a weird change in the dashboard wiring description. Receiving only the most minor changes were the 5000, B5000, L5000, H5000, BH5000, and LH5000 models. The B55000, L55000, 6000, B6000, and L6000 trucks were much like those in the 5000 series, but with the big 210-net bhp GMC 401 V-6 as their engine. This engine developed 377 lbs.-ft. of torque at 1400 rpm, which was needed, as the GVW range for these trucks was 25,500 lbs. to 32,000 lbs.

The Toro-Flow that was introduced in January 1964 proved very popular with truckers. Within just eight months, it had accounted for 37 percent of industry-wide factory sales of trucks up to 5-ton capacity with diesel power. It was a major contributor to a 9.2-percent increase in GMC production, which came despite a strike that prevented GMC from building another 10,000 trucks. In 1964, GMC trucks were built at a record eight different General Motors Corp. plants. The bulk of the vehicles, some 95,255 units in the calendar year, were made at Pontiac, Michigan. About 1,392 additional trucks were built at a Norwood, Ohio, assembly plant; about 139 were made in St. Louis, Missouri; 11,539 were made in Fremont, California; 1,392 were made at Bloomfield, New Jersey; 125 were made at Baltimore, Maryland; 514 were built at Tarrytown, New York, and 128 were made in Atlanta, Georgia. When the strike ended, the Pontiac and Fremont assembly plants were called on to produce 12,893 vehicles in the final month of 1964.

1965: A Truck for Almost All

A cute advertisement that GMC used in 1965 to sell its products to the trade illustrated front views of six trucks: a compact Handi-Van, a pickup, a full conventional, a steel tilt-cab tractor, a short conventional, and an aluminum-tilt cab. "All truck owners are potential GMC customers...," said the headline below the drawings. Then came a drawing of a young boy playing with a toy GMC truck, then the tag line, "...well, almost all!" It was a great way to promote the GMC "family" of 1/2- to 60-ton trucks.

Still avoiding model-year changes for the sake of change, GMC continued the 1964 series for another industry model year. Sometime in 1965 or 1966, the grille emblem "GMC" was modestly changed with squarer-shaped letters. In the 90-in. wheelbase forward-control van series, there was a new windowed model called a Handi-Bus with a $2,330 list price. The regular panel van model was only $2,080.

Prices for 1965 pickup trucks started as low as $2,025 for a 1/2-ton Wide-Side model on the standard 115-in. wheelbase with an inline six. The V-6-powered version of the same truck was $2,141. Both of these could be had as 1/2-ton 8-ft.-bed models sharing a 127-in. wheelbase with the 3/4-ton Wide-Side pickup, which was base priced at $2,210 with a straight six and $2,328 with a V-6. The 1-ton pickups came only in the Fender-Side style with a 9-ft. bed and sold for $2,367 with the inline engine or $2,486 with the V-6.

McCann-Erickson ran a series of advertisements during 1965 stressing the fine points of the pickups and their low suggested retail prices. They showed photos of the truck and chassis in top, bottom, normal, and cut-away views with call-outs for each selling feature. A typical sales message said, "From top to bottom, this GMC pickup looks like it costs a lot of money. Don't let it fool you. Its price is only $49 more than others."

The range of trucks available with the popular Toro-Flow diesel was increased for 1965 with a new series of school buses powered by GMC's D478 and DH478 engines. These raised the number of available Toro-Flow models to 19. By late 1965, in the Toro-Flow engine's 18th month in the marketplace, GMC built the 10,000th unit and announced that the Toro-Flow accounted for 50 percent of sales in the up to 5-ton weight class.

GMC introduced an L3500 steel cab for gasoline-powered vehicles in the lighter end of its heavier-trucks range. In the two-cycle diesel offerings, a 5500-Series model was added. It featured the Detroit 6V-53N engine that produced 185 net bhp. Also new for 1965 was a P3500 2-ton forward-control chassis designed for large package-delivery-van bodies. It was powered by a 140-hp version of the 230-cid inline six and a 292-cid 170-hp engine was optional. The 702-cid V-12 option was replaced by a new 637-cid V-8 that was essentially a 478-cid V-6 with two extra cylinders. An unusual feature of this engine was its use of balance shafts to correct a firing impulse imbalance resulting from the fact that it was a 60-degree V-8. Only 90-degree V-8s fire evenly.

In 1966, GMC continued to run advertisements that called out the features of its products. This one promotes the 1/2-ton Fenderside pickup truck. (OCWC)

Left: This 1965 advertisement showed a GMC 1/2-ton Wide-Side pickup cut in half to illustrate its selling features. (OCWC)

The 1966 GMC Handi-Van offered double doors on the passenger side and at the rear, which made it a truly handy cargo carrier to small businessmen. (OCWC)

Right: The 1966 GMC Series G1000 1/2-ton Handi-Van was based priced at $2,116. It had a 90-inch wheelbase and a new 194-cid inline six-cylinder base engine. (OCWC)

During 1965, GMC promoted W.W. "Wally" Edwards from director of reliability to director of purchasing and production control. Another executive-level change moved N.F. "Norm" Trost from the position of general parts manager to director of reliability, and the company's new truck-sales manager was Robert C. "Bob" Stelter, who previously served as truck-wholesale manager.

During this time, GMC Truck & Coach and other divisions, such as Detroit Diesel Engine, took on projects for America's new defense program and space activities. GMC manufactured transporter-erector units for the nation's Minuteman-guided missile program. Sheldon G. Little was appointed to the new post of director of defense products, which would take on even more significance as U.S. military advisor activities in Southeast Asia led to the nation becoming more deeply involved in a treacherous war in tiny Vietnam.

GMC set sales and production records in 1965. The calendar-year output of 136,696 trucks and buses included 119,914 with gasoline engines and 16,782 with diesel power. That was a 23.7-percent gain over the 1964 strike-year figures. Retail sales rose 17.8 percent to 123,925 vehicles. This year, all of the trucks were made in two factories, with Pontiac, Michigan, producing 124,144, and 12,561 additional units rolling out of the Fremont, California, assembly plant.

1966: 'Truck Talk'

By 1966, General Motors was already planning to combine the production of light-duty GMC and Chevrolet trucks in 1967. After that, GMC would build all of the corporation's medium- and heavy-duty trucks. Due to this change, in 1966 GMC began to stress its mastery of what it called "truck talk." Said one announcement, "We've been interpreting 'truck talk' for a long time. Trucks take up our entire working hours. (If you made trucks for all vocations, from 1/4 to 60 tons, you'd hardly have time for anything else, either) This, we humbly believe, makes us best qualified to deliver the best truck that best answers your problems. Best see your GMC dealer first. He's listed in the Yellow Pages."

All in all, a much larger line of gasoline and diesel GMC trucks was introduced for 1966. There were 102 basic models that further divided into models with many different wheelbases from a 1/4-ton delivery van to giant highway tractors.

For the light-duty trucks, this was the last year of the styling cycle that started back in 1964. No design changes were made. The Handi-Bus with windows was made available with 3/4-ton and 1-ton payload ratings. The base engine for 1/2-ton and 3/4-ton Handi-Vans and 1/2-ton Package-Delivery models was switched from the 153-cid four-cylinder to a 194-cid inline six. A new 250-cid inline six was standard in larger Package Delivery trucks.

The V-6 that was standard in conventional trucks up to 1 ton now had 170 hp. The 230-cid inline six was no longer available. Standard equipment was the same. The 220-hp 351E V-6 was introduced as an option in the light-duty trucks at the beginning of the 1966 model year. Although

the two-speed Pow-R-Flow transmission continued as an option, the three-speed AT-400 Turbo-Hydra-Matic transmission was introduced as an additional option at midyear. Seat belts also became available.

In the medium- and heavy-duty lines, there was a series of new 92-in. bbc trucks that shared an aerodynamic design with new 114-in. bbc models. The "92" came with the choice of a forward-tilting hood or a side-opening "butterfly" hood, while the "114" was only available with the forward-tilting hood. Both included extra driver-comfort features and added safety equipment.

Engine choices expanded with the release of several new engines. The first was a family of "Magnum" V-6 gasoline engines, with advances in performance and operating economy. These were introduced as replacements for the Twin-Six, which was dropped. These new engines came in three sizes—351-, 401-, and 478-cid—and generated up to 225-hp. There was also a new diesel V-8 that came in D637 and DH637 versions. These were basically the 478 and D478 V-6 diesel engines with two additional cylinders.

The 1966 calendar year started off with the first five months topping the previous year's record output for the same period, but the 12-month figures wound up declining by 6.8 percent. However, 1966 model-year production was the highest in GMC peacetime history at 134,735, a 6-percent gain from the 1965 model-year's 127,710 units. All buses and 89.8 percent of the trucks were made in Pontiac, Michigan. The balance of truck production went to other assembly plants: 10,4888 at Freemont, California; 468 at

The 1966 GMC Series 1000 1/2-ton Wide-Side pickup listed for $2,199 and weighed 3,735 lbs. Four-wheel drive was a $665 option. (GC)

Baltimore, Maryland; 468 at Atlanta, Georgia; 468 at Tarrytown, New York; and 600 at Bloomfield, New Jersey. In March of 1966, GMC achieved a major milestone by building its 500,000th V-6-powered truck.

Martin J. Caserio became GMC general manager. He was a native of Laurium, Michigan, and graduated from Michigan College of Mining and Technology in 1936 with a degree in metallurgical engineering. He took his first job at AC Spark Plug and spent 21 years there, becoming chief engineer in 1953. While a student at the GM Institute, Caserio had a run-in with GM founder "Billy" Durant at the bowling alley that Durant operated in Flint, Michigan. Upset about a pin boy dropping his new bowling ball, Caserio went to the owner of the alley to complain. "Charge it to my account" Durant told him. Caserio never did, but recognized Durant's name and always remembered meeting him.

Caserio moved from AC to Delco Radio Division in 1958. He became general manager of Delco and learned some advanced ideas. For example, in 1961, he used a "Dick Tracy"-style wrist radio to activate a remote-controlled bulldozer to break ground for a semiconductor-manufacturing building in Kokomo. Caserio returned to Flint in 1964, as general manager of AC Spark Plug Division. He became vice president of GM's Electrical Component Group and a member of the corporation's administration committee. He got his chance for a chief executive-officer role when Calvin J. Werner left GMC to become general manager of Cadillac. During his tenure at GMC, Caserio lived in Bloomfield Hills, Michigan. His GMC achievements would eventually earn him the top job at Pontiac in 1973.

Left: A head-on view of the 1966 GMC 1/2-ton pickup was presented in this advertisement. This was the last year of the styling cycle that began in 1964. (OCWC)

This 1967 GMC HM7670 fire engine was built for the Greenville Fire Department of Kentucky. It was powered by a 401-cid engine. (OCWC)

The American Fire Apparatus Company built the body on this 1967 GMC B7011 fire truck for the fire department in Marshall's Creek, Pennsylvania. It had a 702-cid engine. (OCWC)

Robert C. Stelter became GMC's general-sales manager when R.C. Woodhouse retired and E.F. Lewis got a new title that made him sales manager for both trucks and coaches. George A. Brundrett also took over as director of reliability.

1967: Pretty Much Alike

A series of 1967 GMC ads said that all trucks weren't "pretty much alike" and suggested that GMCs were different, but the division's all-new light-duty models were very much like Chevrolet trucks of the same year. This was because General Motors started producing Chevrolet and GMC light-duty models on the same lines to cut the costs involved in making and marketing two lines of trucks.

With new styling and numerous technical refinements, the 1967 GMCs were outstanding trucks. They were more like their Chevrolet counterparts, except for having different grilles, different exterior and interior trim, and the 305-cid V-6 as an engine option. GMCs also shared inline six-cylinder engines with Chevy trucks. A Chevy 292-cid inline six producing 170 hp was introduced at the beginning of the year. In addition, a "new" 283-cid Chevrolet small-block V-8 that came in 175- and 220-hp versions was available.

Replacing the angular-shaped pickup, panel, and Suburban bodies used since 1960 were new bodies with rounded edges, smooth surfaces, and chrome accents along the lower feature line. The GMC grille was very neat, with a crossbar design. The wide horizontal bar had GMC lettering at its center and carried dual headlamps in bright metal housings at each end. A short vertical bar divided the radiator opening in the center. The thin, rectangular parking lights were positioned horizontally below the headlights.

Numerous safety features were standard on the 1967 models including an energy-absorbing instrument panel and steering column, padded sun visors, seat belts, and four-way hazard-flashing lights. They also had a dual master cylinder braking system with self-adjusting brake shoes.

The Handi-Van line featured new models with longer bodies built on a 108-in. wheelbase. They came in Handi-Van and Handi-Bus styles and in both 1/2- and 3/4-ton capacities. In addition to base trim, the Handi-Bus offered optional deluxe and custom appointments.

The new 1/2-ton pickups were designated C1500 models, the 3/4-ton were C2500 models, and the 1-ton were C3500s. A 115-in. wheelbase was used again for the regular 1/2-ton versions and a 127-in. wheelbase was optional. A 127-in. stance was the sole choice in the 3/4-ton range. The 1/2-ton line offered a Fender-Side Pickup, a Wide-Side pickup, a panel, and a Suburban. The Suburbans moved from two doors with a 115-in. wheelbase to three doors with a 127-in. wheelbase. The extra door was added to the curb side for easier, safer rear seat access. The 3/4-ton series added a chassis-and-cab and a stake bed to the mix. The 1-ton trucks included a chassis-and-cab, a pickup, and

The American Fire Apparatus Company built the body on this 1968 GMC 8500 fire truck for the fire department in Pottsville, Pennsylvania. (OCWC)

1968: The Difference a Name Makes

"We're the truck people from General Motors," boasted GMC Truck & Coach Division advertisements for 1968 models. Many ads showed cut-away views of GMC pickups with cab or engine features numbered to match the descriptions under the photos.

The new GMC light-duty trucks were restyled with cleaner exterior lines. The cross-bar grille arrangement was retained, but instead of having "GMC" letters stamped in the center of the horizontal bar, there were chrome GMC letters on the front lip of the hood. GMCs also featured more attractive interior appointments in a wider selection of colors. A broader line of seven engines was offered throughout the line. A new Chevrolet-built 307-cid V-8 replaced the 283-cid small-block and a Chevrolet 396-cid big-block V-8 was optional. The horse-power ratings for these were 200 hp at 4600 rpm and 310 hp at 4800 rpm.

Standard equipment now included a full range of safe-ty features such as push-button seat belts, a padded dash-board, a dual-master-cylinder brake system, a thick lami-nated windshield, and dual-speed windshield wipers. Bucket seats with a folding center-auxiliary seat, a center console, and full carpeting were available at extra cost. Interiors came in 14 different selections with colors keyed to the exterior finish. "A truck doesn't have to look or ride like a buckboard," said one bit of promotional copy.

GMC was still promoting its V-6 as the engine that went 150,000 miles without a major overhaul. Also avail-able in the division's seven-engine line up was a pair of inline sixes, the 230 and the 292. As things turned out, 54.1 percent of all 1968 GMCs had six-cylinder engines, 37.5 percent had V-8s, and 8.4 percent had diesel engines.

There weren't many changes in the medium- or heavy-duty models for 1968, but GMC added a plastic gas tank, which it had first announced in 1967, to many more

Left: Sporting the same basic "C/K" styling introduced on 1967 models, this 1968 GMC C1500 1/2-ton Wide-Side long bed pickup had a 127-in. wheelbase and $2,541 base price. (OCWC)

The American Fire Apparatus Company built the apparatus body for this 1968 GMC 8500 fire truck that was delivered to the Oakland Fire Department. (OCWC)

The price of optional four-wheel drive for the 1968 GMC Wide-Side pickup averaged about $700. When so equipped, the trucks became K1500 models. (OCWC)

a stake truck all on a 133-in. wheelbase. Four-wheel drive was a $680 option on the 1/2- and 3/4-ton lines and 4-x-4 trucks were called K1500s or K2500s.

In exchange for giving up the design and engineering of distinctive light-duty trucks, GMC Truck & Coach became General Motors' sole manufacturer of medium- and heavy-duty trucks, whether they had GMC or Chevrolet badges. H-series conventional-cab trucks were added to the Chevrolet model line up, but some mechanics must have been surprised when they opened the hood and found a GMC V-6 inside the engine bay. There was also a new series "E" model that extended the 92-in. bbc larger cab into the 1 1/2- to 3 1/4-ton weight classes. For Vietnam War duty, GMC continued its stellar tradition of national service and built thousands of special rear-engine ambu-lances, aircraft fuel trucks, and missile carriers.

GMC's 1967 calendar-year production rose 2.6 percent over 1966, but sales of 118,170 trucks and buses were down 2.9 percent from the 121,676 sold in 1966 and 4.7 percent from 1965's total of 123,981. GMC workers built 165,252 trucks and buses in Pontiac, but only 116,639 were GMCs. The rest were Chevrolets. GMC trucks only were also built in five other assembly plants as follows: 1,408 units at Flint, Michigan; 284 units at St. Louis, Missouri; 11,551 units at Fremont, California; 354 units at Baltimore, Maryland; and 423 units at Tarrytown, New York.

The utilitarian-looking 1969 GMC Fender-Side pickups were a little less expensive than Wide-Side models. This C1500 1/2-ton version listed for $2,370, a savings of about $40. (FHC)

all-time record. GMC sold 139,140 trucks and buses, a 17.7 percent jump over 1967. New faces joining Caserio's management team at GMC headquarters included B.T. Olson, who became general-manufacturing manager, and M.D. "Skip" Walker, who took over as director of purchasing. The home plant in Pontiac produced 68.3 percent of all 1968 GMC models.

1969: The Truck People from GM

"The Truck People from General Motors" was the new sales slogan that GMC adopted in 1969. It was designed to stress the name association between the company's larger models and its light-duty models and to convince the public that the smaller GMCs were more than clones of similar Chevrolets.

There were no significant styling changes to 1969 GMC light-duty trucks, but they came with many new options. The extras included an interior-convenience group with special seat trim, roof trim, sunshades, door trim, and color-coordinated floor mats. The Custom trim package included custom seat trim, sunshades, and a headliner; a cigar lighter; chrome hubcaps; a horn-blow ring; coat hooks; and a full-width rear window. The Custom Appearance group included a chrome grille, extra chrome moldings, a cab trim panel, a custom steering wheel with bright horn ring, and bright windshield moldings. The Custom Comfort & Convenience group included foam seat cushions, nylon upholstery, a cigar lighter, door armrests, door locks, sunshades, and extra-cab insulation. There were new engine choices. Inline sixes came in 230- and 250-cid options. The V-6 was continued, but then dropped

trucks. The plastic tank was 30 to 50 percent more resistant to impacts than conventional fuel tanks, although it was 21 lbs. lighter. In crashes, the new tanks usually bent inward and then returned to the original shape, making them less prone to being punctured when sharp objects hit them.

Martin J. Caserio continued running the GMC Truck & Coach Division in 1968, steering it to a banner season. Calendar-year production climbed 13.6 percent to set an

Ordering four-wheel drive for a 1969 1500 Series 1/2-ton pickup like this one added about $700 to its price. (FHC)

from the light-duty trucks midway through the model year. Available V-8s included the 307-cid and 350-cid Chevrolet engines. These had lower horsepower ratings, indicating a reaction to fuel-economy and air-pollution concerns.

Notable this year was that the base price of the 1/2-ton Suburban cracked the $3,000 barrier by $59. The 1/2-ton panel truck was $2,823. Both of these models came only on a longer 127-in. wheelbase. C1500 1/2-ton pickup trucks still offered a choice of 115- or 127-in. wheelbases and Fender-Side or Wide-Side bodies with list prices from $2,370 to $2,463. Four-wheel drive was an average of $700 extra. The C2500 models included all of these pickup-body styles on the 127-in. wheelbase, plus a Wide-Side pickup with an 8.5-ft. "long" bed. This new Custom-Camper model was especially designed to accommodate slide-in camper units that didn't fit well in the normal 8-ft. long-bed trucks. CS3500 1-ton models were chassis and pickups only on a 133-in. wheelbase.

The five-main-bearing 307-cid V-8 offered in light-duty models was a small-block engine sourced from Chevrolet. It had a 9.0:1 compression ratio and a Rochester four-barrel carburetor. Rated horsepower was 200 at 4600 rpm. The 350-cid also came from a Chevrolet engine plant. It had the same 9.0:1 compression ratio and a similar Rochester carburetor and put out 255 hp at 4800 rpm.

Four new medium-duty 96-in. bbc models were released as 1969 models. Three were single-rear-axle trucks and one had tandem-rear axles that gave it a GCW rating of 60,000 lbs. These trucks offered a choice of 200-, 235-, and 260-hp versions of the gasoline V-8s.

GMC also introduced a new Astro 95 series of heavy-duty models that featured aluminum tilt-cabs in regular and sleeper versions. These had GCWs up to 76,800 lbs. and diesel-engine options from 195 to 198 hp. The Astro 95 series replaced the "Crackerbox" aluminum tilt-cab models and offered big improvements in comfort, visibility, and appearance.

General Manager Martin J. Caserio continued to build and change his management team and returned to the system of having separate sales managers for coaches and trucks. E.R. "Ed" Stokel handled the bus sales and T.L. "Tom" Harris took care of moving the trucks. R.G. Courtier stepped into the comptroller position when J.D. Mintline left and F. Cronin took J.A. Castle's place as public-relations director.

Business remained strong in 1969 and GMC achieved its second consecutive year of record-high production and sales. Calendar-year output rose another 1.2 percent and sales shot up 8 percent to 150,319 trucks and buses. More than 52 percent of the company's products now had V-8 engines, which was a 41-percent increase over 1968. Six-cylinder engine installations were down 30 percent to 38 percent of the total and diesels were used in the remaining 10 percent of the trucks and buses built. Notably, only 39.2 percent of GMC assemblies took place at the home plant in Pontiac, which built 58,920 GMCs, but almost twice as many (116,179) Chevrolets.

The production of GMCs at other assembly plants was increased to 16,903 units at Flint, Michigan; 31,650 at St. Louis, Missouri; 21,270 at Fremont, California; 2,300 at Lakewood, Georgia; 958 at Janesville, Wisconsin; 10,213 at Baltimore, Maryland; and 7,965 at Tarrytown, New York. By co-producing GMCs and Chevrolets at plants around the country, General Motors was able to provide faster filling of customer orders and cut its transportation costs at the same time.

GMC

Chapter 6

The '70s

1970-1979

Page 82 & 83: Making a splash with buyers in 1976 was GMC's four-wheel-drive K1500 1/2-ton Jimmy. (KCC)

Right: With recreational vehicle use on the rise again in the early 1970s, it's not surprising to see this 1970 GMC CE2500 Suburban with custom trim pulling an Airstream trailer. (© General Motors Corp.)

Right: This 1970 GMC Astro 95 fitted with a Turbine D9500 was a test truck created by GMC Truck & Coach to evaluate operation of the gas turbine engine. (© General Motors Corp.)

1970: Trucks for Every Job

"GMC builds a line of trucks for every job. Trucks for people, for freight, for fun," said a 1970 GMC advertisement showing a Handi-Van and a wideside pickup with an Astro 95 tilt-cab tractor and a Series 9500 conventional truck. "GMC. From coast to coast, a symbol of quality and leadership in the truck industry."

But despite producing products for every purse and purpose, production dropped 18.8 percent this year, but only due to the effects of a drawn-out UAW strike. GMC dealers retailed 125,208 trucks. While that was 15.7 percent off the previous year, it was the third-best total in company history and would have been higher, had there been more trucks to sell.

Joining the 1970 GMC line introduced on October 16, 1969 was the new "Jimmy" model. Available in either two- or four-wheel drive and with a removable fiberglass hardtop, the Jimmy was GMC's entry into the expanding off-road recreational-vehicle market. It was named after the famous 6-x-6 military truck used in World War II. With a standard six-cylinder engine and two-wheel drive, its starting price was $2,377.

Light-duty conventional models like pickups, panels, and Suburbans featured new body colors and interior trims, as well as a wider selection of engines. The front styling was modified in that the body-color radiator grille surround became the vertical grille divider. A bright metal horizontal bar, similar in appearance to the 1969 style, extended out from it to each of the twin headlight units in bright-metal, rectangular housings.

Cummins diesel engines were added to heavy-duty conventional-cab models during 1970 and gas-turbine engines were being tested in Astro 95 models.

On February 9, GMC announced that it was building a new medium-duty truck-assembly plant starting in the spring. Construction of the 1.6-million sq.-ft. plant

actually began in the summer. It was scheduled to be completed in two years and was called the company's largest-ever expansion. It was part of a plan to modernize the three existing chassis lines at Plant 2 in Pontiac for heavy-duty truck manufacturing and then transfer all assemblies of GMC and Chevy medium-duty models to the new facility.

In March, ground was broken for a new GMC Master Service Parts Center. The one-million sq.-ft. structure sat alongside Willow Run Airport, in Ypsilanti, Michigan. GMC also expanded and modernized its coach-building facility starting this year.

In the heavy-duty market niche, the flagship of the line, aluminum tilt-cab Astro 95, was offered with nine basic diesels ranging up to 335 hp, plus a 475-hp V-12 diesel engine. In all, GMC made 15,317 trucks and buses with diesel-power plants.

People on the move at GMC in 1970 included R.J. Sullivan, who moved to near the top of the corporate ladder as director of systems data processing. R.W. Podlesak took the post of general-manufacturing manager. W.W. Edwards went from director of purchasing and production control to chief engineer. A new title, director of production, material control, and material handling was given to W.D. "Walt" Noon.

The perfect truck for hauling a horse trailer was this 1971 GMC KE1550 Jimmy four-wheel-drive sport utility vehicle with custom trim. (© General Motors Corp.)

1971: Back Up to Speed

An improved U.S. economy and General Motors strike-recovery program helped to make 1971 the best year in history for GMC production and sales. Calendar-year assemblies rose 41 percent, while sales of 150,026 trucks and buses topped the previous high of 148,741 set in 1969.

The big news for 1971 at GMC was the introduction of the Sprint. Based on the Chevrolet El Camino, this was a sedan-pickup that combined passenger-car sheet metal with a pickup box. The first Sprint had a two-tier grille and double-horizontal slot-front parking lamps as visual characteristics. Its base sticker price was $2,988. The idea behind this example of GM badge engineering was to achieve more sales of the El Camino-type model by making it available at GM dealerships.

No major appearance changes were introduced on the 1971 GMC conventional trucks. They were highlighted by the use of new blacked-out grille sections and a new two-tone color scheme for Wide-Side pickups. Disc brakes replaced drum-type brakes on the front of light-duty models.

Added to the GMC lineup in May 1970 were new Vandura and Rallywagon vans with extended hoods for easier service, sliding side doors, and longer 110- and 125-in. wheelbases. They had completely different styling than the Handi-Vans and Handi-Buses they replaced, with single headlamps and grilles sporting narrow horizontal bars. Other new features included a "girder-beam" coil-spring independent-front suspension and a choice of six-cylinder or V-8 engines. Chevrolet sold these as 1971 models, but because GMC did not produce on a yearly model-change basis, the first of these vans may have been titled as 1970 GMCs.

The division's medium-duty truck line was beefed up with the addition of two new, low-cost three-speed automatic transmissions for trucks and school buses. Some heavy-duty models got a GMC-designed air-suspension system. Larger engines were offered for the 92- and 114-in bbc conventional-cab trucks. The Astro 95 aluminum-tilt cab was available with options to reduce weight by up to 500 lbs.

GMC's massive modernization program stayed on track and the truck-assembly plant expansion in Pontiac neared its completion. The Ypsilanti Master Parts center went fully operational in the spring and the work on the bus factory was also completed.

Following the trend of the past few years, GMC trucks and buses were assembled throughout the country, with 47,805 made at Pontiac, Michigan; 24,180 at Flint, Michigan; 15,831 at Fremont California; 1,826 at Van Nuys, California; 8,504 at Lakewood, Georgia; 13.707 at Baltimore, Maryland.; 28,707 at St. Louis, Missouri; 3,151 at Leeds, Missouri; 2,834 at Tarrytown, New York; 16,131 at Lordstown, Ohio; and 1,038 at Janesville, Wisconsin. Of the Pontiac units, 1,870 were coaches.

Trucks were getting a little fancier and more were being sold "fully loaded" with options. According to combined GMC-Chevrolet records covering light-duty models, 46 percent had V-8s, 49 percent had automatic transmission, 18 percent had air conditioning, 38 percent had power steering, 52 percent had power brakes, and 0.9 percent featured an AM/FM radio.

New names on the GMC organizational chart this year included Glenn R. Fitzgerald as director of purchasing and B.M. "Ben" Wilton as product-planning manager. Martin J. Caserio stayed at the helm of the division.

A 1971 GMC GE2500 "Dyna Van" with retro-fitted camper top. (© General Motors Corp.)

From the early days of its history, GMC took photos of its medium- and heavy-duty trucks pulling tanker trailers. Doing the up-front work here is a 1971 JH9500 6 x 4 tractor. (© General Motors Corp.)

This 1972 GMC Model 53380 1/2-ton Sprint pickup came in many trim variations. This one has a black vinyl top, a 350-cid V-8 and an un-striped hood with locking pins. The Sprint's "brother" was the popular Chevrolet El Camino. (DR)

Right: A 1971 GMC CE2500 3/4-ton pickup with custom trim and a slide-in piggyback camper. (© General Motors Corp.)

1972: The Right Truck

For 1972, GMC Truck & Coach Division offered a complete range of 59 basic models designed to meet any job or need. They started with the Sprint pickup with its 4,500-5,300-lb. GVWR and ranged up to conventional and aluminum tilt-cab models with 50,500-76,800-lb. GVWRs. GMC told truck owners, "The right truck, kept right, is your surest way to cut costs." The lineup included go-anywhere four-wheel-drive Jimmys; sleek new GMC Sprints; Vandura vans, and Rally Van wagons with sliding doors; pickup and panel trucks; Suburbans; stake-bed; medium- and heavy-duty conventional-cab models; and tilt-cab over-the-road trucks. The flagship of the line was the Astro 95 highway hauler with available Astro-Aire suspension.

With the completion of the new service parts center in Ypsilanti, GMC was stressing both kinds of owner support with what it came to call its "Sudden Service System." Advertisements urged buyers to call direct to the factory with questions about parts or service, providing a toll-free 800 number to "talk directly to truck people." Also being promoted was GMC's nationwide network of service centers and specialized-truck technicians and the availability of an electronic-parts service that used a computerized network to help find parts and get them delivered quickly.

Light-duty conventionals were unchanged in any significant way from 1971. Front-disc brakes and rear drum brakes featuring finned brake drums for extra cooling were now standard. Sprints had a new three-tier grille, with two thin chrome horizontal moldings running full width across the center of each tier. The tiers in the grille were separated by thicker, full-width, chrome, horizontal

moldings. There was GMC lettering in the middle of the grille. The front parking lamps were larger, one-piece lenses, more or less square, but angled to wrap around the front-body corners to do double duty as side-marker lights. The GMC vans looked much like 1971 except for a change to double-slot side-marker lights.

There were several new engines available in light-duty models in addition to the 250- and 292-cid inline sixes, and the 307- and 350-cid "Invader" V-8s. A Chevrolet 402-cid 240-net bhp V-8 (300 gross bhp) was offered for many models. It had an 8.5:1-compression ratio and a Rochester four-barrel carburetor. The Sprint's option list included the Chevrolet 454-cid "big-block" V-8 with 270 net bhp at 4000 rpm and 390 lbs.-ft. of torque at 3200 rpm. Only 29,527 GMC trucks had sixes this year, while 147,146 had V-8s. Diesels were used in 11.5 percent of all trucks built by the division.

The use of automatic transmission in medium-duty trucks was extended and heavy-duty trucks featured an air-suspension system for some models. The largest GMC truck was the Astro 95 COE tractor, which was cloned by Chevrolet as the Bison. The H and J Series models were among the largest conventional GMC trucks at this time and were produced in both the 7500 and 9500 series. The 7500 was often powered by a 6V-53N Detroit Diesel engine, while the 9500 usually had the more powerful engine options such as six-cylinder and V-8 Cummins diesels, as well as six-, eight-, and 12-cylinder Detroit Diesel engines with hefty horsepower ratings.

GMC had its best year ever during 1972. Calendar-year production was 195,332 units compared to 171,955 in 1971. Of these, 1,795 were buses built in Pontiac. Of the trucks, 94,469 were in the 6,000-lb. GVW and less bracket, while 45,937 were in the 6,001 to 10,000-lb. GVW class. In other GVW classes, the totals were: (14,001 to 16,000 lbs.) 76 trucks; (16,001 to 19,500 lbs.) 2,267 trucks; (19,501 to 26,000 lbs.) 27,019; (26,001 to 33,000 lbs.) 10,568 trucks; (33,001 and up lbs.) 15,140 trucks.

It was Martin J. Caserio's last year at GMC and he was promoted to general manager of Pontiac Motor Division. McCann-Erickson continued to serve as GMC's advertising agency.

1973: Luxury with Truck Durability

All-new light- and medium-duty trucks made the headlines at the Truck and Coach Division this year. GMC said they had "automotive luxury with truck durability." Innovations included a 3+3 six-man crew cab for pickups, two new engines, and automatic transmissions for medium- and heavy-duty models. By year's end, the division would register its fifth consecutive year of record sales. Combined truck and bus production for the calendar year was also a record of 244,780. Another change was a new general manager, Alex C. Mair.

Mair had a dynamic personality and 33 years of experience in Chevrolet's engineering department. His GM history traced back to 1939, when he began as a student at the GM Institute. The Navy veteran had returned to Chevrolet's drafting department after World War II and steadily moved up the ladder. In 1954, he was appointed staff engineer. He became Chevrolet's engineering director 12 years later. Mair was a dapper-looking medium-sized man with an engaging smile combined with the assertiveness to get things done his way. Mair liked to be involved in engineering and often visited the design areas. According to automotive advertising executive Jim Wangers, Mair took many pointers from his son Steve to help keep the products he was responsible for fresh and appealing to youthful buyers. He would have several good years at GMC before moving on to head Pontiac Motor Division.

The GMC Sprint had some youthful new styling that was in the hopper before Mair's arrival. Its full-width grille was topped off with a heavier molding that dropped down the sides of the grille insert and extended horizontally under the headlamps. The insert had a fine mesh of thin vertical and horizontal moldings. There was a small GMC badge in the center and Sprint lettering at the lower left-hand side. Square headlamps were sunk into rectangular housings ahead of square-like "bulges" that flared into the hood and fender lines for a classic look. There were rectangular parking lights in the full-width bumper. A High Sierra trim option with wood-grain body side and tailgate paneling was available for the Sprint Custom.

The Jimmy had new front-end styling in 1973. It was similar to that of conventional cab trucks. The wheelbase grew from 104 in. to 106 1/2 in. The basic model was again an open-bodied utility vehicle. A High Sierra trim package was available for those who wanted to go off-roading in style.

The 1973 vans seemed externally unchanged from 1973 in any appreciable way. On the dash, the heater-control panel retained its rectangular shape, but switched from a vertical to horizontal mounting in the dash. Vandura, Rally, and Rally STX trim levels were offered. All were offered on a standard 110-in. wheelbase or "stretched" 125-in. wheelbase with extra-length bodies.

Also available in 1/2-, 3/4-, and 1-ton models were commercial Value Vans designed for package-delivery work. The appearances of these were unchanged. They had single round headlamps, rectangular parking lamps, a grille with two narrow, full-width rectangular openings, and GMC lettering. Steel or aluminum bodies were offered. A 250-cid inline six was the entry-level engine in these, but V-8s were standard in larger sizes. Wheelbases ranged from 102 in. for P1500 1/2 tons up to as long as 157 in. for P3500 1 tons.

New styling appeared on conventional cab trucks. The 1/2-ton C1500 series came with a choice of longer 117 1/2 or 131 1/2-in. wheelbases. The 3/4-ton C2500s and 1-ton C3500s shared 131 1/2 to 164 1/2-in. wheelbases. The bodies were proportionally larger and wider and had 19 percent more glass area. Single headlamps in square housings were seen. The front had three large square openings with a dark cross-hatched grille work in the background and GMC lettering in the center. Large rectangular parking lamps were positioned below the headlamps.

Left: A hardworking 1973 GMC Sierra Grande 1/2-ton Wideside pickup truck with a 454-cid V-8. (FHC)

In 1973, GMC used the term 3+3 to describe the crew cab version of its Sierra Grande 1-ton pickup. This one has a 350-cid V-8 under the hood. (FHC)

1974 GMC Astro 95 with dual vertical exhaust pipes. (GDMC)

A six-cylinder powered example of the four-wheel-drive 1973 GMC K2500 3/4-ton Suburban with Sierra Grand trim. (FHC)

Options included two-tone color schemes and wood-grain trim for the sides of the body and tailgate. A fancy Sierra trim package included a sedan-like interior. The flagship Sierra Grande was like a luxury sedan inside.

Innovations for 1973 included suspension improvements, radio-antenna wires imbedded in the windshield, the addition of an energy-absorbing steering column as standard equipment, the use of new Lexan resin taillight lenses said to be "virtually unbreakable," a new easy-to-open tailgate handle, and the relocation of the ignition switch to the steering column to incorporate an interlock mechanism.

Prices for Sprints now started at just below $3,000. Entry-level vans were just a tad less expensive than that, but a fancy Rally STX model was about $3,800. The 117 1/2-in. wheelbase C1500 1/2-ton Wide-Side pickup listed for $2,882 and up. The 1/2-ton Suburban had a base price close to $4,000. The 3-+-3 six-man crew-cab models were completely new and available in the C2500 and C3500 series. Dual-rear wheels were available on nominally rated 1-ton models. This model was designed for hauling crews and cargo, but could handle a slide-in camper or travel trailer when properly equipped.

There were five engines available for series 1500-2500-3500 pickups, Suburbans, and cab-and-chassis models. They included the 250-cid 100-net bhp inline six, the 292-cid 120-net bhp inline six, the 307-cid "Invader" V-8 with 115 or 130 net bhp (none of these were available on 1/2-ton or 3/4-ton Suburbans), the 350-cid Invader V-8 with 155 net bhp and the big-block 454-cid Invader V-8 rated at 240 net bhp. Three different-diameter clutches, three automatic transmissions, and a choice of rear-axle ratios were offered. New full-floating Sailsbury-type rear axles were standard on 2500 and 3500 series models.

During 1973, GMC's new 1.6-million-sq.-ft. truck assembly plant in Pontiac became operational and started building medium-duty trucks. GMC-built 379- and 432-cid V-6 gasoline engines replaced the 351- and 401-cid V-6s.

This appears to be the first year that GMC mentioned a model year in sales catalogs. As a result of this change, GMC was now able to track the installation rates of optional equipment in light-duty models separately, rather than combined with Chevrolet. Its model-year production was 179,116 trucks. Of these, 90.8 percent had a V-8 engine, 69 percent had automatic transmission, 51.1 percent had power brakes, 70.8 percent had power steering, 42.1 percent had interior and exterior trim packages, and 6.4 percent had dual-rear wheels. Only 5.3 percent had an AM/FM radio. GMC also started building an innovative motorhome this year. This aspect of the company's operations is covered elsewhere in this book.

1974: Another Great Year

The year 1974 was another feather in Alex C. Mair's cap as general manager of GMC Truck & Coach Division. Both bus and truck production climbed in calendar year 1974, setting new all-time records in both categories. Sales were the second best in the company's long history and totaled 194,325 units compared to the previous year's 222,054. Production fell, however, with the drop due mostly to the energy crisis that unfolded in the fall of 1973, due to an embargo of oil shipments by Arab countries.

The oil crisis followed one of the industry's best Octobers on record. To make matters worse, in December 1973, GM idled 15 factories for a week to adjust inventories downward. This took place just before an unanticipated boom in demand for trucks by customers trying to make their purchases before price hikes took affect in 1975. The "production vacuum" cost GMC some sales.

The Sprint coupe-pickup had a wide "neo-classic" style grille with three separate horizontal tiers, a thin, vertical center molding and GMC lettering in its center. The square headlamps were sunk into rectangular housings ahead of "squarish" bulges that flared into the hood and fender lines for a classic look. There were rectangular parking lights below the main bar. A body-colored panel

showed through below the middle of the front bumper. There was a High Sierra trim option with wood grain body side and tailgate paneling.

The Jimmy kept the same new styling as 1973 and the 1974 vans were also unchanged in any appreciable way. Last year's new styling continued on the light-duty conventional trucks. Single headlamps in square housings were seen. The front had three large square openings with a dark cross-hatched grille work and GMC lettering in the center. The Sprint could be ordered with 350-, 400-, or 454-cid V-8s. The other trucks offered the same engines as last year with modest horsepower adjustments.

Medium-duty conventional-cab trucks had a 97-in. bbc design. Heavy-duty trucks came in 93-in. conventional-cab models; 93- and 114-in. conventional-cab 6-x-4 models with tandem rear axles; 72-in. steel-tilt cabs (4 x 2s and 6 x 4s) and 54-in. aluminum-tilt cabs (4 x 2s and 4 x 6s). There were also school-bus and motor-home models. Eleven engines were available, including inline six and V-8 gasoline power plants, Cummins inline six-cylinder diesels and a choice of five Detroit Diesel Engine Division diesels with inline six-cylinder, V-6, V-8, and V-12 configurations. Production included 17,467 trucks with DDED engines, 2,104 with Cummins diesels, and 357 with GMC diesels.

1975: Truxell Takes Over

After Elliott M. "Pete" Estes became president of General Motors in October 1974, he wanted to move Alex Mair, whom he had worked with at Chevrolet, into the top position at Pontiac Motor Division, because of his strong leadership qualities. This finally took place on October 1, 1975, when Martin Caserio left Pontiac to become vice president of a new electrical-components group at GM that combined the AC Spark Plug, Delco Radio, and Packard Cable divisions. Robert W. Truxell then replaced Mair as the head of GMC.

Overall, the automobile and truck industries were in turmoil, in 1975, due to an economic recession and struggles to satisfy new government mandates in the areas of safety and anti-pollution equipment. For example, starting in the 1975 model year, light-duty trucks with GVWs up to 6,000 lbs. were required to have catalytic converters

A 1974 GMC 9500 Series conventional tractor is ready to pull the attached trailer down America's highways. (KCC)

and other emissions hardware. Another negative factor was the public's increasing concern with fuel economy following the Arab oil embargo. Prices on cars leaped a then-hefty $400 on average, but the window sticker on GMC's entry-level edition of the car-based Sprint went up to $3,828 and that was a $709 gain! Prices on a basic van rose $205, while the least-expensive GMC pickup truck's price was $3,609, a gain of $492.

In the early part of 1975, red ink flowed. Detroit introduced up-to-$300 cash rebates to promote sales of small vehicles and rebalance inventories toward the production of additional small cars. General Motors ended its rebates February 28, then cut prices, by deleting standard equipment, and initiated production cutbacks. In March, the company announced that it had secured outside financing and borrowed $600 million so that it could revamp its entire line, by 1980, to meet the challenges of inflation, energy, safety, and clean air. By June, demand for cars and light-duty trucks started to improve. However, although it looked like a positive sign on paper, a 24 percent increase in demand for trucks in the 0-to-6,000-lb GVW class was actually problematic for American companies like GMC, since it reflected increasing sales of imported mini-pickup trucks.

In some cases, truck makers had a little more flexibility in meeting government rules than carmakers. For example, up-rating some heavy light-duty trucks to the just-over-6,000-lb. GVW class made it possible for them to be built and sold without catalytic converters. Nevertheless, the medium- and heavy-duty truck business would soon be suffering through a sales drought that lasted 14 months. At GMC, this contributed to a

Left: Fishing enthusiasts and hunters were typical buyers of the four-wheel-drive K2500 3/4-ton Wideside pickup. This one features High Sierra trim and a 350-cid V-8. (OCWC)

The four-wheel-drive 1976 GMC K1500 1/2-ton Suburban. (KCC)

Right: American families were doing more and more camping in 1975, and this four-wheel-drive GMC Jimmy was the perfect way to get their pop-up trailers to their favorite campsites. (OCWC)

10-percent decline in calendar-year production, although the division's share of the overall market rose from 8.12 percent to 8.72 percent.

GMC's 1975 Sprint had a new grille pattern with bright vertical division bars creating 10 segments with a cross-hatch insert. Square headlamps were used again and the front retained its "classic" appearance. A High Sierra option with wood-grain body side and tailgate paneling was added.

On Jimmys, a revamped grille had two full-width, narrow-horizontal slots. Each was divided into three sections. GMC letters were on the horizontal division bar between the two grille slots. GMC built 10,861 Jimmys in the model year and 92 percent had four-wheel-drive. Ninety-eight percent had V-8s and seven percent had a 400-cid version.

The GMC Vandura, Rally, and Rally STX vans continued to be popular. A Magnavan delivery van was added. Some sources also show a new 1-ton Vandura Special model on the stretched 146-in. wheelbase, which does not appear in normal 1975 Vandura-sales literature. Model-year output included 12,320 Vanduras, but only 2,677 Rally vans.

Conventional trucks continued to share front sheet metal with the Jimmy. This included the new grille with horizontal slots divided into three sections and GMC letters on the horizontal division bar. Single headlamps in square housings were seen. Options included two-tone color schemes and wood-grained body side trim. High Sierra, Sierra Grande, and Sierra Classic trim packages were offered. Model-year production included 56,704 in the 1/2-ton range, 30,934 in the 3/4-ton range, and 11,385 of the 1-ton models. The big 454 was used in only 9.8 percent of the 1/2-ton C1500s, but 20.2 percent of 3/4-ton C2500s and 26.2 percent of the 1-ton C3500s. Four-wheel-drive was added to 15.3 percent of the C1500s and 33.3 percent of the C2500s.

The Value-Vans were unchanged. They had single

round headlamps, rectangular parking lamps, grille with two narrow, full-width rectangular openings and GMC letters between the two grille sections. Steel and aluminum bodies came on a variety of wheelbases.

Larger medium- and heavy-duty trucks also had modest grille and trim changes. The same lineup of medium- and heavy-duty models was offered, but engine choices were down one selection to 10 options and several were new. Both gas and diesel GMC V-6s were gone, as well as the inline six-cylinder Cummins diesel and the Detroit Diesel 6V71. New options included a 6V-92 diesel and an 8V-92 diesel. The big Astro 95 highway tractor had a new Dragfoiler option. This was a roof-mounted air drag reduction device that improved its aerodynamics 35 percent to achieve a 9 percent fuel-efficiency gain.

Big truck manufacturers, including GMC, struggled to conform to a strict new Federal Motor Vehicle Safety Standard, called FMVSS-121, that established improved performance requirements for air-braked trucks, buses, and trailers to shorten stopping distances and improve lateral stability. Numerous exemptions and amendments had to be issued during 1975-1976 to help the manufacturers keep production lines rolling.

1976: A 'General' Success

In America, both car making and truck making rebounded during 1976. Overall business bounced back about 18 percent. Three of four trucks sold were light-duty models. Pickup truck and van sales were very strong. Large, American-made pickups enjoyed a 23 percent sales increase and vans were getting extremely popular. These smaller trucks were said to be taking sales away from cars because they were well suited to America's passion for suburban living and multi-vehicle ownership.

Heavy-duty truck sales were still stalled. This was due to the new government anti-skid safety standard (FMVSS 121) and to a weak economy causing a slump in capital spending. Nevertheless, in August 1976, GMC introduced a truck that it called, "The first really new heavy-duty conventional in years." This new General model replaced the M Series "long-nose" conventionals. The husky General

had a huge square grille, four square headlight housings, and a square-cornered aluminum cab made by the Budd Company. The tilting hood and fenders were also light-weight and made of fiberglass. Engines offered included the 6V-71 and 8V-71 Detroit Diesels and Cummins diesels.

Sales of light-, medium-, and heavy-duty GMC trucks combined rose 57 percent over the 1975 model-year total. The figures reflected the growing popularity of small, personal-use trucks and included 161,227 light-duty conventionals, 31,612 vans, 13,624 Jimmys, and 9,226 Suburbans. GMC sold only 5,436 Sprints, as compared to Chevrolets' 45,595 El Caminos, but this was probably due to GMC's image as the corporation's "real" truck branch. For larger vehicles, the sales numbers were 20,842 medium-duty trucks, 11,531 heavy-duty models, and around 1,900 buses. During 1976, GMC started a multi-million-dollar modernization program at Pontiac to increase the number of medium- and heavy-duty trucks it could build.

Product-wise, the 1976 Sprint had a new full-width grille with a fine mesh-pattern. The headlamps were changed to two squares stacked on top of each other. It came in base and Classic lines, with SP (Sport) and Sierra Madre Del Sur trim options. The "bulges" sculpted into the hood and fender lines looked great with the new grille.

Jimmys had no major styling changes. The grille again had two horizontal slots. Each was divided into three sections. A High-Sierra option was offered. The GMC Vandura, Rally, and Rally STX vans also remained the same. No new models were listed.

Conventional trucks continued to share front sheet metal with the Jimmy. This included the 1975-style grille. High Sierra, Sierra Grande, and Sierra Classic trim packages were available. New Bonus-Cab 1-ton models were added to the line.

Value-Vans were unchanged. The package delivery trucks had single, round headlamps, rectangular parking lamps, a grille with two narrow full-width rectangular openings, and GMC lettering between the two grille sections. Steel and aluminum bodies by various independent contractors came on a variety of wheelbases.

In the medium- and heavy-duty line, the 72-in. bbc steel tilt-cab tandem was gone. Engine choices now included 3200 Caterpillar diesel V-8 for the 7500 medium-duty models. All 7500 and 9500 heavy-duty conventional trucks had new bolted frames in place of the previous riveted type.

1977: 75th Anniversary

General Motors Truck & Coach Division celebrated 75 years of design, engineering, and production innovation with its "Diamond" anniversary in 1977. Max Grabowsky sold his first Rapid truck three quarters of a century earlier and sired GMC. Since that time, the employees of the company had earned an enviable reputation as "the truck people" within General Motors and for quality and leadership in the trucking industry. The current line of models from 1/2-ton to 3 1/2 tons offered "trucks for people, trucks for freight, trucks for fun," said a 1977 advertisement.

"Get Truckin'," said another 1977 GMC ad; and that's exactly what Americans were doing. "Underscoring their importance in the U.S. new-motor-vehicle market, trucks, in 1977, accounted for a larger share of the combined new car-truck market, including imports, than any other year since WWII," reported *Ward's Automotive Yearbook*. "Domestic and import trucks accounted for 24.5 percent of new-vehicle sales compared to just 15.4 percent ten years ago in 1967. The last time trucks topped 20 percent of the market was back in 1947 and 1948 when they accounted for some 22 percent."

Light-duty trucks held 89.2 percent of total U.S. truck sales by all manufacturers and led truck manufacturers to a record year with total sales of nearly $3.5 million, up 15 percent from 1976. Trucks with GVWs between 6,001 and 7,500 lbs. were the big gainers and this was largely due to the fact that they were not required to have the same emissions equipment and catalytic converters as 6,000-lb. and under models. With a 6.6 percent share of the total

The 1977 GMC Sprint Sierra Madre del Sur model featured two-tone finish with bright moldings and "exemplary coachwork." (KCC)

Left: The Vandura, Rally and Rally RTX vans adopted an ice-cube-tray grille in 1977, as seen on this 15 Series Gypsy Van. Note the sliding side door. (KCC)

Chope Stevens Paper Co., of Detroit, Michigan, made deliveries with this 1977 GMC Series 6000-6500 72-in. BBC steel tilt cab truck fitted with a cube van body. (KCC)

GMC celebrated 75 years of design, engineering, and production innovation with its "Diamond Anniversary" in 1977, the year that this C1500 Sierra Classic Wideside pickup was built. (KCC)

market, GMC was now America's fourth-largest light-duty truck maker behind Ford, Chevrolet, and Dodge, in order.

As far as product changes went, since it was the last year of the current style of the Sprint, it made sense that the sedan-pickup had no changes to speak of. Base and Classic trim lines were seen again.

GMC light-duty conventional models wore a new "ice-cube tray" grille. It could make 10 giant ice-cubes in the segments formed by four vertical dividers and a broad horizontal bar with GMC lettering in the center. High Sierra, Sierra Grande, and Sierra Classic options were marketed. Jimmys had the same new grille. They came with High Sierra trim as an option.

The Vandura, Rally, and Rally RTX vans also adopted the ice-cube-tray grille look. New Gypsy Van and Gaucho Van packages appeared. Value-Van package-delivery trucks once again saw little change.

It's interesting to check the trends of light-duty truck price changes every few years, as might be expected with the exceptionally high demand in 1977, prices were on the upswing again. Prices for the basic G-Series Vandura van now began at $4,112, but a fancy Rally RTX version would set a buyer back $5,634. This was the first year that entry-level prices for light-duty conventionals cracked $4,000, even for the chassis-and-cab version, priced at $4,206. To get a Suburban you had to spend a minimum of $5,279.

GMC's light-duty trucks were not the only models that gained new customers in 1977. The division sold 25,577 medium-duty trucks during the model year, which was a strong 22.7 percent increase. Heavy-duty truck sales leaped to 15,889, representing an even heftier 37.9 percent gain. Also up were the sales of diesel engines in the giant models in the 19,501- to 26,000-lbs. GVW category.

There were a few changes in the medium- and heavy-duty lines. The aluminum conventional-cab General model came in 108-in. and 116-in. bbc options. Engine options grew from 12 to 14 and the new ones, both for the Astro 95, were a Cummins KT-450 diesel with 434 net bhp and a Caterpillar 3406-DIT diesel. A special version of the Astro was available with a larger grille and radiator.

"Glider" kits for Astro 95s and Generals were first offered this year. They consisted of a cab and frame with a front axle, but no engine or drive train. Truck owners could re-use the engines, transmissions, and rear axles from their other trucks and rebuild them as an Astro 95.

For the total model year, GMC Truck & Coach Division hit an all-time record with model-year sales of 290,262 light-, medium-, and heavy-duty trucks and motor homes.

1978: Nothin' Like a GMC

Record sales and record production of trucks continued in 1978. The entire truck market grew 11.8 percent, with trucks representing 26.6 percent of all new-vehicle sales in America. More than 4.1 million trucks were produced and 89.3 percent of those were light-duty models with GVW ratings up to 10,000 lbs. GMC beat the industry average, with its overall sales rising 17.27 percent and model-year sales of light-duty trucks rising 18.03 percent.

Part of its better-than-average performance was the continuation of buyer interest in what was called Class 2 trucks. These were models in the 6,001- to 10,000-lb. GVW category that were not required to have catalytic converters. They accounted for 52.1 percent of all sales, compared to 37.2 percent for Class 1 trucks, including mini-pickups, with GVWs of 6,000 lbs. or less.

The most important product news from GMC was the

Record sales and record production of GMC trucks continued in 1978 and the offering of a 5.7-liter diesel V-8 in this C1500 1/2-ton High Sierra Wideside pickup was one reason for this. (KCC)

new Caballero Class 1 pickup. It replaced the Sprint as GMC's entry in the sports-pickup field. The Caballero was more efficient in design. It was nearly a foot shorter than the Sprint in overall length and nearly 600 lbs. lighter, although it possessed equal cargo-carrying capacity. The Caballero also had a new 231-cid V-6 engine as its base power plant.

The new Caballero styling included a completely new roofline, small side-quarter windows, and a wraparound rear window. The front featured single rectangular headlights. The spare tire was carried under the pickup box floor and was accessible from the vehicle's interior. Although the Caballero was shorter on the outside, it had greater interior roominess in all length and height dimensions. The pickup box length at the floor was virtually the same as before and longer at the top of the box. The truck still came in two series, which were renamed Pickup and Diablo Pickup. There was a Laredo option group. Caballero sales rose 12.5 percent over Sprint sales—to 6,700 units.

Jimmys, conventional-cab trucks, and Suburbans stuck with the ice-cube-tray grille that had been introduced in 1977. A new Street Coupe equipment package was released as an option for the C1500. GMC "Indy Hauler" trucks were also built to commemorate the company's involvement with the Indianapolis 500-mile Race. These served as "Official Speedway Trucks" during the race.

Vans were the hottest-selling trucks in America in 1978. At the Pontiac, Michigan, factory, GMC ran two assembly shifts, producing an average of 528 vans per day. The Vandura and Rally vans enjoyed a huge 41.30-percent increase in sales together, although Vanduras were still most popular. Model-year production included 32,391 Vanduras and 3,969 Rally vans, compared to 20,560 Vanduras and 6,458 Rally vans in 1978. Both lines continued using the handsome ice-cube-tray grille. The Gypsy and Gaucho packages returned. The Value-Vans were still around, too.

Late in 1978, GMC started work on a limited run of electric-powered 1979 Vandura cargo vans that the American Telephone & Telegraph Co. ordered for use at one of its Southern California Bell System repair shops. The utility ordered 20 vehicles to test under a U.S. Department of Energy grant and said that the test, if successful, could lead to an order of 20,000 more. Thirty-six maintenance-free Delco Freedom batteries powered these vans. They could travel up to 40 miles on a charge at speeds up to 50 mph. They were almost identical to standard Vandura cargo vans in appearance, but weighed 6,600 lbs.

Medium- and heavy-duty truck manufacturing also continued to boom in 1978 and, by the end of the year, GMC's home plant complex had bumped big-truck production up to an all-time high. FMVSS 121, the rule requiring anti-lock brakes on heavy-duty trucks, was quashed by the Supreme Court, which ruled against the National Highway Traffic and Safety Administration on the legality of such a costly measure. It was reported that the equipment required to satisfy the safety standard cost nearly half as much as a small car.

The 7500 Series medium-heavy short conventional models gained the GM 454-cid V-8 gas engine and Caterpillar 3208 DIT diesel V-8 in addition to the Detroit Diesel Allison 6V-53N diesel V-6 that was previously offered.

This 1978 P1500 1/2-ton GMC Value Van has a short seven-foot nominal body length and a 102-inch wheelbase. (KCC)

Left: The Green Machine of Kaltz Lawn Spray Service was a 1978 GMC Series CE6000 97.5-in. conventional cab truck fitted with a special lawn service tanker body. (KCC)

The all-new 1978 Caballero was almost a foot shorter than the Sprint and nearly 600 lbs. lighter, although it offered equal cargo carrying capacity. This one has luxury Diablo trim. (KCC)

Hounds-tooth pattern seats were available to help dress up the interior of the 1979 GMC C2500 3/4-ton Van Dura cargo van. (GDMC)

The highlight of 1978 for GMC heavy-duty trucks was introduction of the Brigadier H/J9500 Series that replaced the old short conventional models. Aimed at the large fleet market, the new Brigadier offered many improvements and refinements resulting in better driver comfort and lower operating costs. Engines available in the Brigadier included Cummins and DDA diesels with outputs from 201 net hp to 334 net hp.

The GMC Astro 95 and General lines were continued with little change. A total of 12 engines were offered in heavy-duty models, including the Caterpiller 3406 DIT diesel and many models were available with several power ratings. The most powerful were the Cummins KT450 at 434 hp and the DDA 8V-92T with 412 net hp. For the year, medium-duty truck sales went up 7.9 percent, while heavy-duty model sales rose 25.8 percent.

1979: 'What We're All About'

"Trucks are what we're all about," General Motors Truck & Coach Division advertised in 1979. The truck-making industry, which had boomed during the two previous years, ran out of gas in 1979. So did the nation, which was shaken by the one-two punch of a sagging economy and politically induced gasoline shortages.

GMC's business looked better than that of the industry as a whole. Its model-year output of light-duty models actually rose 13.45 percent and it built more of every type of truck except 3/4-ton conventionals and Caballeros. Production totals don't tell the whole story however, as model-year sales declined 7.2 percent. Like most manufacturers, GMC had made sales projections based on 1977 and 1978 market conditions and produced accordingly. When the economy "dropped off a cliff," GMC and other vehicle makers were left with excess inventory. Fortunately for GMC, increased sales of both its larger trucks and its RTS buses proved positive factors in what was otherwise a treacherous year.

The American economy technically escaped going into a recession in 1979, but many vehicle makers suffered back-to-back quarterly drops in 1979 sales and the industry wound up laying off some 177,000 workers. By December, following the American hostage situation in Iran and Russia's invasion of Afghanistan, fuel prices shot from 77 cents a gallon to $1.13 a gallon. As had happened in 1973, long lines of vehicles started forming at gas-station pumps.

Overall, light-duty truck sales dropped 17 percent, which made GMC's less than 8 percent decline seem like an outstanding performance. The number of large pickups sold by all U.S. truck makers dropped by 21 percent. It's true that there was actually an increase in Class 1 pickup sales, but this gain went to imported mini-pickups, a genre that had no domestic counterpart yet. GMC's model-year sales of large pickups declined only 9.8 percent. Especially hard hit was the four-wheel-drive market segment, where industry sales fell 10 percent. General interest in recreational vehicles also "took it on the chin" and model-year sales of GMC Suburbans dropped 19.2 percent from 10,664 in 1978 to 8,620.

For the industry as a whole, van sales fell a huge 28 percent, but GMC's van sales fell only 2.1 percent. Nevertheless, by the end of the year, the van business was so dead that GMC was forced to shut down its van plant indefinitely.

In California, 20 electric-powered GMC telephone-company vans went to work for AT&T at one of its Bell System repair facilities in Southern California and 15 others were built for use at other AT&T locations around the country. These trucks looked so much like standard models that when one was displayed at a news conference for electric vehicles, held early in 1979, a member of the organizing group asked utility workers, "Can you please get that phone truck out of there? We have to bring the electric vehicles in." The U.S. Department of Energy provided AT&T with grant money to offset the higher cost of electric power, as well as any maintenance costs above those typical for gasoline-fueled trucks. GMC's new planning director, Richard A. "Dick" Pennell, was probably hoping that the 35 electric vans would lead to an order for 20,000—enough to re-open the van plant again.

The Caballero was one of the few GMC models to suffer a model-year production decline, but only by 19 units. It was, however, the only light-duty model to enjoy a sales increase and its deliveries rose by 343 units to 6,952. It received a new grille for 1979 that had a prominent horizontal emphasis.

Styling refinements for light- and medium-duty conventional-cab trucks included bright trim added to the lower grille portion and a black-colored mesh backdrop for the main grille section. Pickup interiors now had standard vinyl-seat trim. All models, except the Caballero and Value-Van package-delivery trucks, had wider-vent window posts for added theft protection.

Like other "lagging" market indicators, medium- and heavy-duty truck sales did not have an immediate negative reaction to the economic downturn and orders placed before and during the market decline were still being filled. GMC dealers actually posted a 9-percent increase in retail deliveries of Class 6 to Class 8 trucks. Model-year sales of medium-duty trucks rose to 29,406, compared to 27,717 the previous season. Heavy-duty truck sales also increased from 19,952 units in 1978 to 22,394 in 1979.

A new GMC engineering program, designed to increase fuel economy, reduced the weight of many medium- and heavy-duty models to increase fuel economy. Cab styles offered were 93-, 97.5-, and 108-in. bbc conventionals; 54-in. and 86-in. bbc aluminum tilt cabs; a 72-in. bbc steel tilt; a school-bus chassis; and flat-back cowl and a chassis only.

Chevrolet dropped all heavy-duty truck models and got out of that market segment after 1979. The Series 7500 line, which included medium-duty short conventionals, was replaced by the Series 8000 Brigadier.

With its big trucks and buses shoring up business, a year that was bleak for many other truck makers was less so for GMC. Its sales declines were under the industry averages in most categories and the 6.09 percent increase in medium-duty sales and 12.24 percent increase in heavy-duty sales really helped keep the year on track. GMC had total sales of 314,636 trucks. This was enough to push it into third place in industry sales, passing Dodge in the process. While the country and the trucking industry were running out of fuel, GMC Truck & Coach was not ready to join them on the gas line just yet!

This example of the 1979 GMC K1500 1/2-ton Jimmy sport utility features the ZY3 two-tone paint treatment and optional hardtop. (KCC)

This 1979 GMC Astro 95 Special Series tractor included features such as a bright entry system; air conditioning; a Royal Classic interior; a sleeper; a chrome bumper and Perlux lights. (GDMC)

Two-tone Sierra Classic exterior trim added to the looks and luxury of this 1979 GMC C1500 1/2-ton Suburban. (KCC)

Chapter 7

The '80s

1980-1989

1980: No. 3 in American Trucks

The decade of the 1980s started with soaring interest rates, high unemployment, and low-volume car-and-truck sales. The emphasis in the truck-making business was on fuel efficiency, product quality, and safety. New manufacturing techniques were coming on strong, with robotics and electronics the key innovations.

Changes in 1980-model-year GMC trucks were essentially of a cosmetic nature. The Caballero's grille had three rows of short, thin vertical blades. Slightly heavier horizontal moldings separated the rows and there was a vertical center molding. A stand-up hood ornament was used. Trim variations included base, Diablo, and Laredo packages.

Jimmys, conventional-cab trucks, and vans continued with an "ice-cube-tray" grille. The horizontal center strip with GMC letters was painted body color. There was a custom-grille treatment for Sierras and the "GMC Indy Haulers" used as Indianapolis Motor Speedway Official trucks during the Indy 500. Also optional was a Deluxe front end with two vertically stacked headlamps replacing larger single headlamps.

Value-Vans could be had with a variety of bodies built by factory-approved or local independent contractors in either steel or aluminum. An inline six remained standard on the 1/2-ton Value-Van model and the 3/4-ton P2500 and 1-ton P3500 came with V-8s.

Prices started off higher in the new decade. The base Caballero sold for a tad under $6,000. Jimmy prices started a few bucks below $8,000 and the basic 1/2-ton two-wheel-drive C1500 pickup on the shorter 117 1/2-in. wheelbase was $5,005. The base van was $5,748 The Rally STX van listed for $8,680, making it the most expensive

light-duty model in standard-equipment dress. Of course, you got a lot of standard equipment in an STX.

Engine selections grew from eight to 11, but there were no totally new power plants. A different version of the 305-cid V-8 was offered for some models and there were also new versions of the 350-, 400-, and 454-cid V-8s. The 350-cid Oldsmobile-built, diesel V-8, offered since 1978 in GMC trucks, was available again in selected models.

During the 1980 model year, light-duty truck sales declined 39 percent to 160,990 units. For a while, it seemed that the weakening economy and rising concerns about fuel efficiency had all but wiped out the market for personal-use trucks, especially four-wheel-drive and recreational vehicles. Sales of Jimmys and Suburbans were just about sliced in half! Calendar-year production of light-duty trucks dropped off 54 percent.

GMC's medium- and heavy-duty trucks were offered in the same models they came in the prior year. There were several new engine options based on a newly introduced 8.2-liter (500-cid) "Fuel-Pincher" diesel made by General Motors Detroit Diesel Allison Division. It was available in 8.2N (naturally-aspirated) and 8.2T (turbocharged) versions in Class 6 (16,000 to 25,000 GVW) and Class 7 (19,200 to 32,800 GVW) trucks.

Business in the domestic big-truck market bounced around a bit in 1980. Following a slow fourth quarter in 1979, GMC canceled the second shift at its heavy-duty truck assembly plant in Pontiac, only to see orders rise in January and February. A second shift was re-instated, but then the government instituted strict credit and banking controls that sent interest rates rocketing. This quickly resulted in a steep economic decline and the extra shift at the GMC factory was canceled again. Then, Chevrolet and GMC medium-duty truck sales picked up and the GMC plant that produced them added a second shift.

With U.S. sales floundering, General Motors looked toward the international business arena as an alternative and formed a new World Truck and Bus Group in 1980. It consisted of GMC, Chevrolet's truck operations and its partners Isuzu Motors, Ltd., of Japan and Bedford Division in England, plus several parts branches. GMC's role was to coordinate the design, production and parts commonality of Class 6, 7, and 8 trucks and buses built by GM partners and subsidiaries around the globe. Donald J. Atwood was group executive and a GM executive vice president.

Although its calendar-year production fell 4.9 percent in 1980, GMC had only a modest decline in market share and built 11 percent of America's trucks. That was good for third place on the charts, behind only Chevrolet and Ford.

1981: Truckin' Through it All

Double-digit interest rates, truck deregulation, voluntary import trade restraints, tighter credit for vehicle purchasers, and higher vehicle prices combined to make 1981 a horrible year for selling trucks. Through it all, GMC was able to hold its third rank in production for the calendar year and maintain a 10 percent market share. In addition,

The 1980 GMC General road tractor was available with an optional Tri-Tone paint scheme that had lots of eye appeal back then. (KCC)

model-year production was also good for third place. In model-year sales, GMC ran neck and neck with Dodge. The Chrysler division finished only 71 units ahead and that was only because it sold Mitsubishi-built mini-pickups with Dodge Ram-50 badges.

GMC did not yet have a mini-pickup. The Caballero was its smallest model. Its new grille had eight thin, full-width horizontal bars and bright upper and lower moldings. New wheel covers were seen. Inside was a restyled instrument panel with a new pad and glossy appliqué, new seat trim, and international symbols for controls. New options included a 55/45-split bench seat, trip odometer, and resume-speed cruise-control feature. The Diablo came with contrasting lower-body perimeter. The Amarillo package came with the roof and lower-body perimeter painted the same contrasting color. Also new were standard high-pressure tires that decreased rolling resistance and upped fuel economy. Power trains were unchanged, but Computer Command Control came on all engines.

The Jimmy was still available with 4 x 2 or 4 x 4 chassis. New aerodynamic sheet metal that reduced wind drag was used from the cowl forward. The front fenders and hood were restyled with a new front bumper mounted air dam to improve fuel economy. The front fender wells had shields attached to reduce engine compartment splash. A

Tri-Tone paint schemes for the GMC Astro 95 tractor were offered again in 1981. One is seen on this tractor pulling a tanker-trailer. (KCC)

A 1981 GMC Sierra Wideside pickup truck wearing optional white spoked wheels. (KCC)

new grille and bumper were made of high-strength low-alloy steel to reduce weight. A 4.1-liter (250-cid) inline six was standard. There was also a new version of the 305-cid V-8. It had electronic spark control (ESC) and could be ordered outside California.

Conventional-cab trucks had the same attractive new, aerodynamic front sheet metal that was used on the Jimmy. High-strength, low-alloy steel bumpers on wideside models meant reduced weight. The use of other strong, lightweight material reduced the weight of some models by up to 308 lbs. with no reduction in their payload capacities. The front-disc brakes on the 1500s and 2500s and their 4-x-4 counterparts were of a low-drag design. Also introduced were stronger, shot-peened rear springs on 1500 and 2500 series trucks. Most GMC trucks with automatic transmission had re-engineered clutch plates for quieter operation. Interior changes included higher-grade standard interiors with full-foam seat cushions and more attractive vinyl upholstery.

Four-wheel drive was available on all pickups with 6 1/2 and 8-ft. boxes. Dual rear wheels and a 10,000-lb.

GVW rating were available for K3500 1-ton trucks. The 4-x-4 trucks had a new aluminum transfer case and automatic locking hubs that allowed drivers to shift into 4-x-4 mode at speeds up to 20 mph. A new option was a front-quad shocks package for off-roaders. All trim options were available for 4-x-4 models, except that High Sierra trim could not be ordered for Bonus-Cab or Crew-Cab trucks.

New truck options included halogen high-beam head-lamps and quartz clocks. The standard 4.1-liter inline six, three 5.0-liter V-8s and a 5.7-liter V-8 were available in trucks with GVWs below 8,500 lbs. that were governed by one set of emission standards. Above that, a 4.8-liter six and 7.4-liter V-8 were offered. There was a new high-compression (9.2:1) 5.0-liter V-8 with ESC said to give the performance of a 5.7-liter V-8 with better fuel economy. There was a new water-in-fuel warning lamp for diesels and a travel bed option with a 3-passenger bench seat, folding backrest and hinged backrest extension.

Once again this year, GMC was the official truck of the Indianapolis 500. The company provided 50 pickups, Suburbans and vans with "Indy Hauler" graphics for use as general transportation, safety and emergency vehicles during the race.

GMC vans were similar to the 1980 version, with refinements like the ESC V-8 and improved corrosion proofing. On Rally STX vans, the belt line molding was lower on the body sides. This changed the color breaks for two-tone paint schemes. They were now right at the belt line and just above the wheel openings. A 5.0-liter V-8 or ESC V-8 was standard in most models. The new travel bed option came in vans, too. Value-Vans were available again in steel and aluminum, but the 1/2-ton forward-control chassis was dropped.

Like other makers of medium- and heavy-duty trucks, GMC struggled in 1981. With local governments and businesses reducing capital expenditures, sales of GVW Class 6 and 7 city-suburban delivery trucks suffered a sharp decline. At the same time, weakening demand for consumer goods caused a drop in over-the-highway shipping that slashed deeply into the sales of Class 8 tractor-trailer models. As GMC general manager Robert W. Truxell

noted, there were no gains to be had in big truck sales. "The least loss is the best loss," he told the press in 1981. At his division the loss was 25 percent for Class 6 to Class 8 trucks in calendar-year sales. Production of medium- and heavy-duty units was quartered entirely at plants in Pontiac, Michigan, and was a little over half of the 1979 total!

With the market deeply depressed, product changes were minimal. A new Top Kick version of models C6000 and C7000 was added. These versions had a raised cab and extra-large radiator to accommodate the Caterpillar CAT 3208 diesel V-8, which came with output ratings up to 199 net bhp. The SBA (set back axle) version of the 116-in. bbc conventional cab model was dropped. All GMC trucks, including the medium- and heavy-duty models, adopted a new 17-character vehicle-identification number system.

By August 1981, GMC was finally ready to enter the compact pickup field by launching assemblies of the new GM "S" truck in the same factory in Pontiac, Michigan, where GMC motor homes (covered in another chapter) and Chevrolet and GMC G Series vans had been made. The plant was operated by General Motors Truck & Coach Division and was the only factory able to make the new Chevy S-10 and GMC S-15 models in all three configurations: short-bed, long-bed, and chassis-and-cab. These were marketed as 1982 models.

1982: Little Trucks, Big Changes

New-truck sales rebounded more than 13 percent in 1982. Experts suggested that the popularity of trucks could come back to 1978's record levels faster than that of cars for two reasons. First, the '70s had seen a trend toward increased use of pickups; and second, a new generation of smaller vans was in the works to follow quickly on the heels of American-made compact pickups. Mini-pickup sales soared 52.4 percent following introduction of the S-10 and S-15 in the fall of 1981. Both trucks were made by GMC workers.

The new S-15 had been in the works since October 1978. This co-called "compact pickup" was GM's response to imported mini-pickups. Compared to a foreign-built Chevy LUV, the new "S" trucks were 2 inches lower and had a wheelbase just 0.4 in. longer. Styling included single rectangular headlamps and a grille with three big square openings. The standard S-15 came with a 1.9L four-cylinder engine and four-speed manual transmission supplied by Isuzu. The Sierra version had a black bumper, less side trim, and no GMC lettering in the center-grille segment. There was a High Sierra and a Sierra Classic with chrome bumpers, GMC grille lettering, spoke wheel covers, and lower body moldings. Also available was a sporty S-15 Gypsy package. Only wideside boxes were offered, but they came in 6-ft. and 7.5-ft. lengths. Most mechanical components came from the Chevy Monte Carlo and Pontiac Grand Prix.

The 1982 GMC S-15. The 1/2-ton compact pickup was available with Sierra trim and Wideside styling. GM employees also built Chevrolet S-10s. (BLC)

The S-15 hurt sales of the Caballero, which saw model-year production of only 2,738 units. The latest Caballero had new front-end styling with a crosshatched grille and dual rectangular headlights. Five new colors and new two-tones were offered. Technical refinements included dual cowl-mounted fluidic windshield washers and a fender-mounted fixed-mast antenna. Regular equipment included a 3.8-liter V-6. The Diablo added dual sport mirrors, a front-air dam, accent paint color on the lower body, and Rally wheels.

Conventional trucks again had ice-cube-tray grilles. A chrome front bumper was now standard. Under the head-lamps was a new grille extension with three vertical-slot segments. High Sierra, Sierra Classic, and Sierra Grande trim options were offered. An important new option for 1982 was a Chevrolet-built 6.2-liter (379-cid) 90-degree diesel V-8. Previously, a 5.7-liter Oldsmobile diesel had been supplied to GMC in limited quantities. The allocation of engines it received had never been equal to the amount GMC dealers could have sold, but the new Chevrolet diesel was expected to achieve 50,000 sales. It was available in the Jimmy and the Suburban, as well as in all full-size pickups.

Base equipment included a 4.1-liter inline six. A 4.8-liter inline six was standard in C3500, K2500, and K3500 models. A three-speed manual transmission with column shift came with C1500 1/2-ton and 3/4-ton models, while a four-speed transmission with floor shift came in K1500, C2500, K2500, C3500, and K3500 trucks. Diesel-powered trucks featured a standard New Process four-speed over-drive transmission that was introduced during 1981 as a "Special Economy" option. Also available on some GMC models was a new four-speed automatic transmission, called the THM-700R4, which had a lock-up torque

converter that engaged in second, third, and overdrive. Jimmys included the 4.1-liter six, three-speed manual transmission (four-speed manual on K1500), power brakes, vinyl bucket seats, chrome bumpers, and, on 4 x 4s, automatic-locking hubs and power steering.

Industry-wide, medium- and heavy-duty truck sales remained sluggish in 1982. At GMC, sales in the two categories combined dropped 18.2 percent from 1981, although its market share increased from 14.3 to 15.5 percent. This year all of the large Astro 95 cab-over-engine tractors had standard turbocharged, after-cooled engines, and GMC adopted more aerodynamic designs for additional operating efficiency. The Brigadier was available with a sloped hood, as well as the tilt hood and, like all large trucks, offered the Dragfoiler option.

On September 1, 1982, General Motors' new Truck and Bus Manufacturing Division was formed as a branch of the Worldwide Truck & Bus Group that had been announced in July 1981. With former GMC general manager Robert W. Truxell in charge of the new manufacturing division, Donald J. Atwood became group executive in charge of marketing trucks through the existing network of GMC dealers.

John D. Rock was named manager of the GMC Truck and Coach Operation of the Truck and Bus Group and played an important role over the next few years. Rock, a native of Groton, South Dakota, was born January 30, 1936. In 1959, he graduated from the University of Minnesota with a bachelor's degree in psychology and became a salesman in his family's Chevy-Olds dealership in Groton. He began his GM career with Buick in Flint, Michigan, as a district manager trainee in July 1960. Following district manager assignments in Buick's Chicago and Denver zones, he was promoted to fleet-sales manager in the home office in 1963. Four years later, he became director of fleet sales for the division.

Rock joined GM's Detroit marketing staff as the manager of rental, leasing, and commercial sales in 1969 and was promoted to director of fleet and government sales the next year. In 1973, he took over Buick's eastern sales region in New York City and became assistant general sales manager for the Eastern half of the country in 1978. In 1979, he was promoted to executive director of marketing for GM Holden's Ltd. in Australia. His next stop was GMC's new division, where his career flourished.

Rock's new division took over operation of GM truck assembly and manufacturing plants formerly operated by Chevrolet and General Motors Truck & Coach. It immediately became the fourth-largest division of GM with 24,370 employees. GMC Truck & Coach Division was technically no longer in existence. A new entity called GM Truck & Coach Operations became the marketing arm for GMC trucks.

GMC's light-duty models, which now represented 87 percent of all sales, enjoyed their best season since 1979, but sales of Class 4 to Class 9 models fell by 11 percent. This was an irreversible trend that would have a far-reaching effect on the future of GMC.

1983: The A Team

The economy bounced back in 1983 and truck sales followed the bouncing ball. More Americans were working, consumer confidence was high, and many new products helped spark buyer interest. At GMC, calendar-year sales climbed to 265,409 trucks, which was a strong 11.5 percent gain. The major contributors to the upswing were a new S-15 Jimmy and a bounce back in the popularity of full-sized vans and Suburbans, for which sales were up 64.6 percent and 19 percent, respectively.

Added to the S-15 line were 4 x 4 and extended-cab models. Vying for the attention of downsized truck buyers was an all-new S-15 Jimmy. Introduced on September 14, 1982, it was 15.3 in. shorter and 14.8 in narrower than a full-sized Jimmy and had a 100.5-in. wheelbase and two-door wagon body with a tailgate. Sierra interior trim was standard. Sierra Classic and Gypsy options were also offered for only the 4-x-4 model. A Street-Coupe package was available.

The appearance of S-15 pickups was unchanged, but four-wheel drive and an extended cab were new 1983 options. GM's Insta-Trac four-wheel drive was available on all S-15s, except the chassis-and-cab and utility-cab models. In California, the standard engine was the Isuzu-built 1.9-liter 82-hp four. In other states, it was a Chevrolet-built 2.0-liter four with one additional horsepower. A Chevrolet 2.8-liter V-6 with 110 hp was optional in all 50 states.

Caballeros looked virtually the same as last year with a very tight-patterned ice cube-tray grille. The Amarillo trim package was back. With only 1,903 assemblies in the model year (of which about 25 had 5.7-liter V-8 diesel engines), there's little doubt that the Caballero would have been dropped by now, if not for the fact that 22,429 nearly identical models were sold as Chevrolet El Caminos. Russell Lewis, of Chipita Park, Colorado, owns a well-preserved diesel-powered 1983 Caballero that has traveled just under 150,000 miles.

Conventional Class 1 to Class 3 trucks offered a choice of two new grilles. One had a horizontal center bar and two vertical dividers framing six rectangles with parking lamps in the lower, outer rectangles. Twin rectangular headlamps were stacked vertically. A fancier deluxe grille (standard in Sierra Classics) divided each of the rectangles into three smaller squares. Both grilles had GMC letters at the middle of the horizontal center divider. Moving the parking lamps into the grille eliminated the need for a different front bumper on trucks with the deluxe grille. Trucks with Sierra Classic and High Sierra trim had new pewter-toned brushed-aluminum instrument-panel cluster bezels. The same trim was used for the High Sierra's instrument-panel appliqué, horn button, and door-trim panels. A new electronic speed-control system was introduced. Other new developments included the availability of an air cleaner pre-cleaner and an engine block heater for all gasoline engines. Emphasis was placed on improved resistance to corrosion with added use of galvanized steel

in the pickup box front panel, plus a Zincrometal inner hood liner.

Numerous refinements were also part of the 1983 GMC van series. The G2500 and G3500 Vans and Sport Vans were now offered with the 6.2-liter diesel engine, as well as with the four-speed overdrive automatic transmission. The vans had a revised steering wheel angle that was close to that used on pickup models, plus a floor-mounted manual-transmission lever. Also installed on the vans were "wet-arm" windshield washers with wiper-arm-located nozzles, a new rear-door hinge pivot, a new rear latch, and floating-roller mechanism for the sliding door, and an interior-hood release. All vans with manual transmission could be ordered with a tilt-steering wheel. Anti-chip coating was installed along the lower body from the front-wheel wells to the rear doors of all vans. Value-Vans were about the same.

In a popular television series, the "A-Team" drove a modified GMC van into the homes of millions of Americans each week, with "Mr. T" sitting behind the wheel. DailyRadar.com recently included this vehicle in its list of "The 15 Greatest Cars in TV History," noting the television van's "cool ability to drive through virtually any building on earth." While this was a TV-only feature, there's little doubt that the van's national exposure helped to increase the sales of GMC vans this year.

Although light duty-truck sales were on an up-trend, GMC and other truck makers were still struggling in the big-truck market. John D. Rock, the manager of GMC Truck & Coach Operations, estimated that 50 long-haul trucking fleets had gone under since the trucking industry was deregulated in 1979. This and the recession put many almost-new trucks into the second-hand market, thus reducing new-truck sales. Another problem was the specter of new state and federal regulations governing the weights and lengths of truck trailers, which postponed many purchases until firm rules were set.

The 1983 Series 1500 Vandura shown with available Deluxe Front Appearance package. (GDMC)

Few 1983 GMC Caballero pickups were built with 5.7-liter diesel V-8s. This one was purchased from Steve Johnson GMC in Colorado Springs and has traveled over 150,000 miles. (RL)

A new Aero Astro-option package featured a patented, collapsible Dragfoiler air deflector on its roof and large, fiberglass panels closed the gap between the cab and trailer to smooth airflow down the side of the truck. A urethane cab skirt for additional airflow control was also added.

At GMC, sales of Class 4 to 8 medium- and heavy-duty trucks went sliding down another 10 percent. This, combined with stronger competition from International Harvester, reduced GMC's big truck-segment market share to 13.7 percent. However, even despite the 1.8 percent slide, GMC held on to third place in the sales rankings, but the big-truck-manufacturing facilities in Pontiac were operating at only half of their capacity.

1984: XXIII Olympiad Sponsor

"Both the name and the truck carry a lot of weight," said the headline in a 1984 advertisement depicting eight GMC models from an S-15 to a dump truck, a logging truck, a Brigadier, and a giant Astro 95 semi. "GMC: A truck you can work with." It was a fitting message in a year when everything seemed to be working well again. GMC Truck and Coach Operations saw a 22 percent overall gain in retail new-truck sales. Even the sales of medium- and heavy-duty trucks benefited from a strong U.S. economic recovery and hit 42,308 units, compared to 25,738 in 1983. In addition, GMC received a contract to supply the "official" trucks for the 1984 Olympics to be held in Los Angeles, California.

The 1984 light-duty trucks lineup revealed few styling changes, but there were mechanical improvements and refinements in passenger-comfort features. Power windows, power locks, and stereo systems became optional on Bonus-Cab and Crew-Cab versions of the full-sized pickups. Available light-duty truck engines ranged from 1.9-liter fours up to 7.4-liter gas V-8s and 6.2-liter diesels.

Full-sized vans underwent major changes that improved their fit and finish. The use of galvanized steel was extended to the inner and outer hood panels. Standard swing-open side-cargo doors were designed to open at a wider angle.

The S-15 had modest updates for the new model year, but the S Jimmy received an upgraded four-wheel-drive setup with optional Bilstein gas shocks. Improvements were made to the hydraulic clutch on stick shift S-15s and the shift points in the automatic transmission were retuned for better performance.

Based on an increase in orders from big-truck fleets in late 1983, GMC cranked up its medium- and heavy-duty truck-assembly lines for a great year in 1984 and was not disappointed. Sales of medium-duty models went up 53 percent. They were offered in three series: 5000, 6000, and 7000.

The sales gain in the big Class 8-truck category was even more impressive, with Class 8-truck deliveries jumping 92 percent! Also available was the giant-9500 series. Both aluminum tilt-cab models grew a little in dimensions with the former 54-in. bbc model becoming a 55-in. job and the former 86-in. bbc sleeper cab also growing one inch longer. There were 20 engines offered for medium- and heavy-duty models from a 4.8-liter gas V-8 inline six to the 8V-92T Detroit Diesel. New offerings included a 6.1-liter Deutz diesel and a big 10-liter Cummins diesel.

GMC buses did not follow the trucks up the sales charts

Premium turbo diesel power was standard in the 1984 GMC W7 Forward, a medium-duty tilt-cab truck made by Japan's Isuzu Motors. (GDMC)

in 1984 and dropped 58 percent to only 527 units. As a result, the coach plant was shut down from mid-November until February 1985. Patrick J. Coletta, the general manager of the Truck and Bus Manufacturing Division, decided to free some plant capacity for light-duty truck production and combined medium- and heavy-duty production at the GM Truck & Bus Group's Central Manufacturing and Assembly plant, in Pontiac, in February 1985. The vacant 10-year-old East Plant was earmarked to undergo a modernization through which it would be automated and become a "factory-of-the-future" for production of up to 210,000 full-size GMC and Chevrolet pickups per year starting in 1987.

1985: Meet the Family

For some years, trucks had been replacing automobiles as Americans' "family vehicle" of choice. In 1985, GMC Truck and Bus Operations drove this trend home with a marketing thrust that showed families of various types and sizes, with a model from the GMC "family" of trucks that fitted their individual needs. It was a clever way to get across the ever-growing versatility of vehicles that had once been considered purely functional.

The family theme must have worked, at least in the case of light-duty models, which set all-time records. Model-year sales went to 347,920, while calendar-year sales were even higher at 353,075, a 9.2-percent gain over 1984. But, only 41,241 of the model-year sales went to medium- and heavy-duty models. Worse yet, on a calendar-year basis, Class 5- to 8-truck sales declined 4.7 percent and Class 8 sales alone were off 24 percent!

Among the hot-selling light-duty models, the Safari van was the year's hot news. GMC called it a "personal-size, mid-size People Mover" and stressed that it was "garageable." Advertisements said that it was larger than a minivan and smaller than a full-size van, but people still called it a minivan. It had an integral body and frame on a 111-in. wheelbase. The standard power plant was a 2.5-liter inline four. A new 4.3-liter Vortex V-6 was optional. A wide variety of exterior color and trim levels was offered. The Safari had a maximum-load capacity of 145.8 cu. ft.

Ken McCann, the owner of a concrete company in Cheyenne, Wyoming, special ordered this 1984 GMC Caballero with a two-way radio on Sept. 22, 1983. (JWW)

Fire truck maker Emergency 1 built the Dunbar, West Virginia, Fire Department's 1,250-gpm pumper on a 1985 GMC Top Kick chassis. It carries a 1,000-gallon tank. (DFD/GB)

GMC adopted the name Safari—once used for Pontiac station wagons—to identify its new-for-1985 Minivan. This GMC Safari features up-level trim. (© General Motors Corp.)

with the rear seats removed. With them installed, there was room for five passengers and the load capacity was 86.2 cu. ft.

The Caballero had the new 4.3-liter Vortex V-6 as its standard engine and the 5.0-liter V-8 was also available. New stainless-steel full-wheel covers with a brushed-finish center and GMC lettering were standard. The Caballero's standard velour-cloth interior was also new for 1985.

Numerous changes were made in the S-15 line for 1985, starting with a "black-chrome" insert in its three-rectangles grille. There was a Custom two-tone paint option with "Sunshine" striping. All models had restyled fender nameplates and a new paint scheme for the optional-styled wheels. New optional custom-vinyl and custom-cloth seat trim was offered in any of four colors. Standard on all models, except the 4-x-2 short wheelbase regular-cab pickup, was a new 2.5-liter Tech IV inline four-cylinder engine with electronic-fuel injection (EFI). Options included a 2.2-liter four-cylinder diesel engine and a 2.8-liter V-6.

Additional refinements included a partitioned-fuse panel, two side galvanized steel for the hood inner panel and fender skirts, welded-on bumper brackets, adjust-on-release rear-brake adjusters, new valving for the shock absorbers, new controls for the optional intermittent wipers, and a new variable-ratio manual steering gear.

A new front end characterized 1985 full-sized GMC models. It featured stacked-rectangular headlights and a bold three-section black-out-style grille. Wideside models with single-rear wheels were offered with a new custom two-tone option. All models had wet-arm windshield wiper. Interior changes included a new seat-cushion contour and seat-back angle for the bench seat. Both custom-vinyl and custom-cloth fabric options were new. A 4.3-liter Vortex V-6 was base engine for the 1/2-ton C1500 and K1500 models, as well as for 3/4-ton C2500 pickups with light-duty emissions. Other C2500s had a 292-cid inline six as base engine. A 5.7-liter V-8 or 6.2-liter diesel V-8 were available at extra cost.

The Suburban was available with gas or diesel V-8s and two- or four-wheel drive. It had standard three-place seating and 144-cu. ft. of load space. A 5.0-liter V-8 was standard in the C1500. The K1500, C2500, and K2500 came standard with a 5.7-liter V-8. It could haul a 3,903-lb. payload or tow up to 9,500 lbs. The 6.2-liter diesel was optional, as was a Sierra Classic interior.

S-15 Jimmys had a black-chrome tailgate-release handle, full-integral wiper controls, and a new portioned fuse panel. Grille changes and base engines copied those on the pickup. A 2.5-liter in-line four-cylinder gas engine was standard and a 2.8-liter V-6 was optional. New, low-pressure gas shock absorbers were standard. A black-finished rooftop-luggage carrier was available. Options included Sierra-Classic and Gypsy-Sport trims, plus High Country-Sheepskin bucket seats.

GMC's Special Two-Tone paint scheme brightens up this 1986 two-wheel-drive S-15 Jimmy with the 2.8-liter V-6 under its hood. (JAGC)

The full-size Jimmy had new standard and optional grilles matching those of full-size pickups, a new wet-arm wiper system, new optional cast-aluminum wheels, and custom-textured seat trim for the Sierra Classic. The hardtop became available in colors other than black and white. A 5.0-liter V-8 was standard and a 6.2-liter diesel was extra.

Vandura and Rally vans had new front styling. The grille was similar to that of pickups, but had headlight bezels with more rounded outer edges. The high-compression 4.3-liter Vortec V-6 was the base engine. This engine was actually a shortened version of the well-proved Chevrolet 350-cid V-8. It was fuel injected and developed 145-net bhp and 225 lbs.-ft. of torque. The 5.0-, 5.7-, and 6.2-liter (diesel) V-8s were extra. The Vandura offered a choice of a 60-40 swing-out panel door or a standard sliding door that was redesigned for smoother operation. The Rally offered 5-, 8-, or 12-passenger versions.

At the upper end of the medium-duty truck field, GMC had luck selling a new W7 tilt-cab truck built on a chassis that was imported from Isuzu Motors of Japan. It was powered by a 5.8-liter diesel engine. Named the Forward, the new trucks was constructed with a tilt-cab body and designed for city-delivery service. Chevrolet Motor Division also sold it under the name Tiltmaster.

As for domestic models, their production was moved from the East Plant at Pontiac, Michigan, and integrated with the production of heavy-duty models inside the Pontiac Central Facility. The GMC heavy-duty trucks line had a component-standardization program in effect, but few visible product changes. Engine choices were expanded. In the 9500 series, GCW ratings topped out at 130,000 lbs. The 8000 Series was offered in both J8C042 and J8C064 versions. Caterpillar and Cummins engines were increasingly in demand, while customers shunned Detroit Diesel-power plants since GM was in the process of selling its Detroit-Diesel branch to Indy 500 racecar driver and builder Roger Penske.

1986: 'The Classic'

Total U.S. car-and-truck sales had their fourth-consecutive record year in 1986, but bottom-line business wasn't good at GM. The corporation was forced to wage a year-long battle to build up market share, which had dropped to 41 percent of all passenger-car sales by U.S. dealers, a point and a half down from a year earlier. While that may sound small, it translated into a 25-percent drop in net income or a $1.054-billion decline.

Reluctant to see its piece of the pie eaten up by lean-running domestic competitors and growing import sales, GM had its GMAC financial arm send out $25 billion in buyer incentives to preferred customers starting March 2, 1986. GM also laid out $732 million in November to buy out the stock of H. Ross Perot, the founder of its Electronic Data Systems subsidiary, who later made an unsuccessful bid for the U.S. presidency.

Late in the year, GM undertook a massive restructuring to try to get back on track and announced its intentions to close 11 factories and idle 29,000 workers. Analysts pointed out that GM had been overproducing for years and using costly offers to buy market share. It abruptly switched direction in late 1986 to run more efficiently.

Robert C. Stempel assumed the top position at GMC Truck and Coach Operations in 1986. Stempel was a native of Trenton, New Jersey, who graduated from Worcester Polytechnic Institute in 1955, at age 22. Stempel started at Oldsmobile in 1958 as a senior detailer in the chassis-design department. He became senior designer in 1962, transmission-design engineer in 1964, motor engineer in 1969, and assistant-chief engineer in 1972. Stempel was appointed special assistant to GM President Ed Cole in 1973 and in September of the following year, went to Chevrolet as chief engineer for engines and components. A year later, Stempel became Chevy's director of engineering.

Stempel earned a degree in business administration

from Michigan State University and in 1977, Worcester Polytechnic Institute conferred a doctor-of-engineering degree upon him. In November 1978, Stempel was tapped to replace Alex C. Mair as general manager of Pontiac Motor Division. During the summer of 1980, Stempel left Pontiac to become head of GM Overseas Operations and managing director of Adam Opel AG in Germany. By 1982, he was back in the U.S., serving as Chevrolet's general manager.

By 1984, Stempel had been elevated to vice president and group executive in charge of GM's Buick-Cadillac-Oldsmobile group. His 1986 stint with GMC was brief, and he went on to become president and CEO of General Motors in 1988. Stempel was always an automotive enthusiast and an outstanding product-development man. He had a huge ear-to-ear smile and a great knack for remembering peoples' faces and names.

Luckily for GMC's new boss, truck sales held up better than those of cars, although this segment of the market was not without its own import problems. Model-year sales increased 1.67 percent to 353,286 units. This was mainly because trucks now accounted for 29.6 percent of total vehicle sales, compared to 24.2 percent as recently as 1982. The so-called "crossover" buyers who moved out of cars and into trucks were attracted by the new generation of fuel-efficient and dressy-looking pickups, vans, and SUVs that provided cargo space lacking in modern cars. The downside of the trend for American makers like GMC, was that imported models had climbed to 19.1 percent of the light-duty truck mix in 1986 versus 16.4 percent in 1985. In fact, GMC model-year sales numbers included Isuzu W4 Forwards made in Japan and trucks made in Mexico.

GMC's total retail-sales volume for the calendar year wound up at 345,047 units. This was a two-percent decline from a year earlier and the calendar-year totals also reflected slowing sales of 1987 models introduced in the fall of 1986. Light-duty-truck sales also declined in the calendar year, dropping 1.2 percent from 312,274 in 1985

to 305,580 for 1986. While historically good, the lower number was alarming because it directly mirrored the trend toward increased sales of imported light-duty trucks.

Even the Caballero had become a "captive import," with its production quartered in Mexico since 1985. The sedan-pickup offered a four-speed overdrive-automatic transmission with the standard V-6 engine in 1986. Other changes were minor.

New for the S-15 Jimmy was a revamped instrument cluster with warning lights on either side of the combination fuel-and-speedometer gauge. Added to the 1986 option list was a 2.8-liter V-6 with throttle-body fuel injection (TBI). Technical changes included a new higher-capacity Delcotron generator, lighter pistons, 30-degree exhaust-valve seats, low-pressure gas shocks, new paint and trim options, and an optional, hinged rear-mounted spare-tire carrier.

S-15 pickups had the same new instrument-panel treatment as the S Jimmy. It included a package tray and trim plates. The Insta-Trac option provided off-road capability with a shift that could be switched from two-wheel drive to four-wheel drive or back at any speed.

Full-size K1500 Jimmys had new molded front-bucket seats with folding seat backs. The cloth seat-trim option included a reclining-seat back and the passenger seat included the slide-forward, easy-entry feature that was standard on the S-15 Jimmy. Black-and-white tops were available with solid colors, while a new steel-gray top was available to match a similar exterior color. Full-size GMC pickups featured GM's 4.3-liter Vortec V-6 as standard equipment. A 50,000-mile warranty was offered for diesel-engined trucks.

The GMC Suburban had new bucket seats with outboard armrests as a 1986 extra. Of interest to collectors was the method used to promote GMC's 1986 models as the ultimate-upscale trucks. The company contacted the Classic Car Club of America to arrange an advertising photograph that featured an S-15 pickup truck towing an

L-29 Cord to a stately looking mansion. Parked in the mansion's four-car garage were a 1937 Bugatti, 1930s Buick, 1957 Cushman Eagle scooter, and an Indian motorcycle.

The Cord in the photo was borrowed from the well-known collection of the late Barney Pollard. The Bugatti, which had been Ettore Bugatti's personal car, was to be shown at Pebble Beach in 1986. The Buick was a "resto-rod," refurbished with modern appointments. Credit for this "The Classic No Enthusiast Should Be Without" ad theme belonged to McCann-Erickson, GMC's Detroit advertising agency.

A D.U. Limited-Edition Suburban was produced as a joint venture of GMC Truck and Starcraft Automotive. This truck commemorated the 50th anniversary of Ducks Unlimited, a not-for-profit waterfowl-conservation group. It featured a host of special features including a camouflage-style interior, "ducks-in-flight" medallions, and four-wheel drive. Options included a camouflage exterior, Ducks Unlimited emblems, a fiberglass roof storage container with snap-on vinyl cover and boat rack, and a Starcraft 12-ft. Jon boat.

The Safari mini-van, introduced six months earlier, was unchanged for 1986, except for its new Delcotron. Three trim levels: SL, SLX, and SLE, were available. Full-sized GMC vans and other big trucks used a new five-ribbed poly-vee generator-accessory belt. Both the Rally Wagon and Vandura had modest refinements.

A new W4 Forward model, that was technically a light-duty truck, was introduced. The W4 version of the Isuzu-built tilt-cab truck was aimed at commercial users who operated delivery services in which light trucks could be used. GMC dealers reported sales of the first 80 W4s in late 1985.

Big-truck offerings included the medium-duty conventionals, the W7 and W4 Forwards, the Top Kick, and the big Astro, Brigadier, and General models. GMAC financing at 7.4 percent was offered as a sales incentive. Speaking of sales, in December 1986, a merger of GMC's Class-8 heavy-truck operations with Volvo-White was announced. Prompted by lagging sales and the import invasion, the deal, pending approval by the U.S. Justice Department and Federal Trade Commission, gave GMC a 35 percent ownership stake in the new Volvo GM Heavy Truck Corp. based at Volvo White headquarters at Airpark West in Greensboro, North Carolina. The new venture became official on January 1, 1988.

In mid-1986, GMC put its bus operations up for sale. In early 1987, Greyhound Corp. bought this business and formed a new company called Transportation Manufacturing Corp. GMC Truck and Coach then became GMC Truck Division.

The year wound up with calendar-year production of 359,577 vehicles, including buses, for a 10.26 percent share of industry output behind Chevrolet at 32.87 percent and Ford at 39.83 percent. Model-year production of light-duty trucks was 300,730 units.

1987: Not Just A Truck Anymore

To promote the growing appeal of the Safari Wagon, the S-15 Jimmy SUV, and the always unique, station wagon-like GMC Suburban to crossover buyers, a 1987 GMC ad asked, "Do these look like trucks to you?" This particular announcement was aimed at potential GMC dealers and designed to drive home the point that many contemporary buyers saw such models as economical, comfortable, practical alternatives to passenger cars. The "crossovers" were particularly suited to multi-car clans in need of the type of vehicle that could transport more people and cargo than a downsized automobile.

Another interesting thing about the advertisement was that it no longer said "GMC Truck and Coach" at the bottom. Instead, the words "GMC Truck" appeared in bold, red letters. GMC Truck and Coach Operation was re-christened GMC Truck Division of General Motors Truck & Bus Group. It was part of the GM Truck and Bus Group (school

This GMC catalog photo taken at the garage of legendary Detroit-area car collector Barney Pollard shows an S-15 pickup near some of Pollard's classic cars. (JAGC)

"GMC Gem Collector" John Ernst, of Brandon, Florida, purchased this 454-powered red-and-white C3500 pickup shortly after its delivery to Hunt Truck Sales in Tampa. The truck was built on May 12, 1987, in the St. Louis assembly plant, which was closing forever that summer. The truck has never been titled and has gone only 3.7 miles since it was new. (Thomas M. Jevcak photo)

John Ernst decided to buy and preserve a second 1987 GMC C3500 pickup on the last day you could order one. He wanted it to be identical to the first except for color, but was told by a salesman that allocations of 454-cid engines might negate such an order. The blue-and-white truck was ordered with a diesel engine, which has 5.7 miles on it today. This truck was built in Janesville, Wisconsin, on July 15,1987, and has every available option. (Thomas M. Jevcak photo)

buses were still manufactured) under general manager and group executive Charles Katko.

John D. Rock was promoted to general manager of GMC Truck Division. As the year began, he predicted that GM's share of the truck market would rise to 33 percent for Chevy and GMC combined, that the compact van market would grow, and that more Safaris would get aftermarket upgrades by companies such as Starcraft, Inc.

Not many upgrades were needed for the Caballero, which had become GMC's "luxury pickup." The sales booklet said that it looked like a car and worked like a truck, but it didn't say anything about this being the model's last year. Available in standard, Amarillo, and fancy Diablo trim, with a choice of the 4.3-liter Vortec V-6 or 5.0-liter V-8, the sedan-pickup combined three-passenger seating

with 35.5 cu. ft. of cargo space and a 1,250-lb. payload rating. Only 1,907 units were built in a factory in Mexico this year.

Most changes in the S-15 pickup for 1987 were technical. Both the 2.5-liter Tech IV and the 2.8-liter fuel-injected V-6 had a new "serpentine" single-belt accessory drive system. Four-cylinder models had an increased-output 85-amp Delcotron generator and Delco Freedom battery. The four also had an improved throttle-modulation system. A special anti-corrosion coating was used on suspension parts. Regular-cab S-15s offered 108.3- and 117.9-in. wheelbases and the Club Coupe version had a 122.9-in. stance. A 6.1-in. box was used, except with the 117.9-in. wheelbase model which had a 7.4-ft. box. Buyers could add Gypsy or High Sierra trim. Four-wheel-drive versions had GM's shift-on-the-fly system. This featured a vacuum-operated front-axle disconnect and automatically locking front hubs that made it possible to shift into high-range four-wheel drive without stopping, making all-wheel driving much simpler for inexperienced users.

S-15 Jimmys again came in two- or four-wheel-drive models in Sierra, Sierra Classic, or Gypsy Sport trim levels. A super-sporty Timberline decor paint and trim offering was new. It had a Midnight Black top color, with Nevada Gold Metallic on the bottom and a wraparound-center decal that graduated from black to gold, plus gold wheels, gold rocker panels, and black-chrome grille-and-trim parts. Also new were Sunshine striping, the 85-amp generator, serpentine belts, and new batteries. There was a new tailgate appliqué for fancy editions and new colors. The base 2.5-liter four had a throttle-body-injection (TBI) system that increased its horsepower to 92. A strong point of the compact SUV was its shift-on-the-fly four-wheel-drive system.

This 1987 GMC 3/4-ton pickup owned by the Madison (North Carolina) Fire Department carries a 200-gallon water tank, a 9-hp pump, and wildfire supression tools. (MFD/JR)

Refinements for the 1987 Safari included higher-horsepower ratings for the standard fuel-injected Vortec V-6, high-capacity standard and heavy-duty Delco Freedom batteries, and four new solid exterior-paint colors. Safari SL, SLX, and SLE editions were available. The V-6 model gave very lively performance, while the four-cylinder version offered 23-mpg average-fuel economy. *Road & Track* summed the Safari up as a "practical cargo hauler or a luxurious people mover with the strongest engine in the small-van class."

Two types of light-duty conventional-cab trucks were sold this year. The "1987" models had the same basic looks, construction, and creature comforts as the 1986 C/K trucks, with some under-hood refinements. The upgrades included a computer-controlled electronic-fuel-injection system for all gasoline engines, which was a great advance over the carbureted engines used through 1986. Like the smaller light-duty models, C/Ks also had improved generators and batteries. The full-size pickups, Jimmys, chassis-and-cab models, and Suburban all shared these advances. In a tricky use of factory coding, these trucks used a letter R for two-wheel drive or a V for four-wheel drive, as the fifth symbol in their 1987 VIN numbers, although they were essentially the same as the 1986 and earlier trucks coded with a C for two-wheel drive and a K for four-wheel-drive.

In the spring of 1987, an all-new type of full-size pickup made its debut as a 1988 model. GMC called its version the Sierra. It had more aerodynamic styling, more luxurious interior appointments, improved power trains, and anti-lock rear brakes. At the Chicago Auto Show, the powertrain engineer explained that he had been inspired to "style" the V-8 engine's beautiful black, finned valve covers after seeing highly detailed Duesenberg engines at classic-car shows.

These trucks used C (two-wheel drive) and K (four-wheel-drive) as the fifth symbol of their VIN codes. They were produced at a new plant in Ft. Wayne, Indiana, and at the modernized Pontiac East plant and another revamped factory in Oshawa, Ontario, Canada. A unique K-15 Sportside model came out at midyear and was manufactured only in Ft. Wayne. It had fiberglass rear-side panels flanked by functional steps that aided users in loading and unloading cargo. Suburbans and full-sized Jimmys did not change to the new style immediately and continued to be produced as "R" and "V" models, as did crew cab pickups. Things continued this way for several years.

Full-size vans again came as Vandura cargo van and Rally wagons. The Vandura line offered 1/2- and 3/4-ton models on both a 110- and 125-in. wheelbase. The 1-ton and heavy-duty 1-ton versions came only on a longer 125-in. wheelbase. The biggest version had 189.9 cu. ft. of load space and could haul up to 1,700 lbs. of cargo. The 1/2-ton Rally wagon offered Rally versions on both wheelbases, while 3/4- and1-ton versions came only on the 125-in. wheelbase. The Rally Custom and Rally STX options were offered exclusively with the 125-in. wheelbase in the three-tonnage classes.

After divesting itself of most Class-8 heavy-truck business and all transit-coach business in 1987, the renamed GMC Truck Division reorganized its Class-6 and Class-7 truck manufacturing under Thomas S. McDaniel. He became director of medium-duty truck operations and oversaw all aspects of that segment. Part of the plan was to transfer construction of all medium-duty models to GM's assembly plant in Janesville, Wisconsin, in the middle of 1989 and to then close the historic GMC Central Plant in Pontiac, Michigan.

The same line of 12 types of medium- and heavy-duty cabs was offered in 1987, but the number of engine choices grew from 20 to 21. Two new in-line four-cycle Detroit Diesel six-cylinder engines, the DEDEC 60 11.1L and 12.7L, were adopted in Brigadiers and Generals in a range from 250- to 400-gross hp. The other new engine was a medium-duty Deere 5.9L diesel. Carryover options included the 6V-92T and 8V-92T Detroit Diesels and the Caterpillar 3406 and Cummins L-10. GVW ratings were up to 79,000 lbs. A new "Jake-brake" was available.

During 1987, the job of relocating the manufacture of GM-designed heavy-duty trucks to Volvo GM's Greensboro, North Carolina, plant continued. Domestic-make products of the joint venture would be marketed as WhiteGMCs beginning in 1988. In its last year of making Class-8 and Class-9 trucks, GMC sold 7,309 units. Only the Brigadier style was continued beyond 1987.

At the end of 1987, GMC's model-year sales were the lowest in three years at 339,180 units. However, its calendar-year production total rose to 373,859 units because the new Sierra pickups, which were merchandised as 1988 models, were popular, even though hard to get at first. This gave GMC a 10-percent share of industry output.

This catalog photo of the 1988 four-wheel-drive S-15 Jimmy shows one with the Chevrolet-built 2.8-liter V-6 and Special Two-Tone paint scheme. (FHC)

1988: Rugged and Dependable

The new GMC Sierra pickup had to be good. American truck makers were losing market share to the surprisingly high-quality products reaching our shores from Japan. The Sierra was a way for workers in Pontiac, Michigan, Ft. Wayne, Indiana, and Oshawa, Canada, to show the world that North American-built trucks were not ready to take a back seat to any others. The Sierra was modern technology put into action to create a brilliant, smooth, rugged, efficient, and reliable full-size pickup. The Sierra's new aerodynamic styling and technical advances were also exciting enough to bring about its selection as the Official Truck of the 1988 Indianapolis 500 Mile Race.

Though smooth and aerodynamic looking, the Sierra models were anything but small and their capacity was expressed in terms that both suburbanites and tradesmen could understand. The C1500 1/2-ton could hold 26 sheets of 48-lb. plywood. The C2500 could handle 64 sheets and the C3500 could carry 87 sheets in standard configuration or 108 sheets when equipped with dual rear wheels. At press conferences, GM officials showed how the cargo box was designed with depressions that 2-x-4 boards could be snapped into to create cargo partitions. Regular cab models offered 117.5-in. or 131.5-in. wheelbases. Extended-cab models had a 155.5-in. stance.

Base coat/clearcoat finish, a tough new chassis design, rugged cargo box construction, standard anti-lock rear brakes, improved suspensions, better anti-corrosion protection, and easier service access were incorporated into the design of Sierra models. The base engine was a 160-hp Vortec 4.3-liter V-6. Options included 5.0-, 5.7-, and 7.4-liter gasoline V-8s, plus a 6.2-liter diesel.

Styling features included a larger area of glass, flush side windows, and a smoothly curved front bumper. The flush-fitting composite grille ran across the front with a large round-cornered rectangular opening in the center that contained a blacked-out, horizontally ribbed insert and a large, red GMC logo. Smaller rectangles at each corner held the vertical amber-colored parking-light lenses, dual-square halogen-headlamp bulbs, and horizontal-directional lamps.

Sierra styling was also used on chassis cab models, but Suburbans, Jimmys, and Crew Cab pickups did not get the Sierra appearance immediately. Both the two- and four-wheel-drive Suburbans again got either the 5.7-liter EFI V-8 or the 6.2-liter diesel (built in a GM Power Train Division plant in Moraine (Dayton), Ohio) as base engine; the 7.4-liter EFI V-8 was an option. In addition to their "old-fashioned" styling, both 3/4- and 1-ton Crew Cabs—even four-wheel-drive versions—also retained the "old" 4.8-liter (292-cid) inline six with a one-barrel carburetor as base engine. All V-8s except the 5.0-liter job were options. Crew Cabs and Bonus Cabs still featured 155.5-in. and 164.5-in. wheelbases. There was also a version of the 1-ton pickup with a 5.7-liter V-8 that still had the old styling on a 131.5-in. wheelbase.

Its standard solid paint scheme detracts little from the good looks of this 1988 GMC C1500 1/2-ton Sierra Wideside pickup. (© General Motors Corp.)

The compact S-15 pickup's refinements were only cosmetic and included such items as four new colors and an instrument panel with gray trim plate accents. New options included a factory-installed tinted sunroof and the Vortec V-6. The availability of this 4.3-liter 160-hp engine was expected to give the S-15 a big advantage over the four-cylinder-powered compact trucks from Japan. There were also tire-and-brake system improvements. There were four trim levels: Sierra, High Sierra, Sierra Classic, and Gypsy, and three wheelbases: 108.3 in. for short-bed models, 117.9 in. for long-bed models, and 122.9 in. for the extended-cab, which had the shorter-length pickup bed.

Extra muscle under the hood, in the form of a standard 125-hp 2.8-liter V-6, was a new feature of the 1988 GMC S-15 Jimmy. Others included an improved, freer-breathing exhaust system, four new exterior colors, a new Special Custom Cloth seat trim material, new stereo radios, a sun roof, and integral map-reading lights. Taking a page from the book written by Japanese automakers, GMC began bundling specific combinations of options and offering them as part of value-package discounts.

Full-sized vans continued to come in Vandura, Rally Custom, and Rally STX models on 110- or 125-in. wheelbases with the Vortec V-6 as standard equipment and 5.0-, 5.7-, and 7.4-liter gas V-8s optional. A 6.2-liter diesel V-8 was available for the 3/4-ton G-25. The trusty 5.7-liter V-8 was standard in G-35 1-ton models and the 7.4-liter big-block 454 V-8 was the only option there.

With heavy-duty production being phased out at the GMC plant in Pontiac, Michigan, during most of 1988, dealer sales of big Class-8 and Class-9 trucks tumbled. In December, GMC heavy-duty output ceased all together. During the year, the Pontiac factory shipped 16,421 GMCs and 9,278 Chevrolets in the 26,001-33,000-lb. GVW class and 733 GMCs and 277 Chevrolets in the 33,000-lb.-and-up GVW class. Volvo GM shipped 19,837 units, all with GVWs over 33,001 lbs. GMC came in ninth among the top 10 North American Class-8 truck producers and Chevrolet (built by GMC) was 10th. Together they shipped just more than 10,000 Class 8s. Volvo GM was sixth, with shipments of about 20,000 big trucks. In 1988, GMC listed all 12 of the medium- and heavy-duty truck lines and cab types offered in 1987, but in 1989 the offerings were reduced to seven truck lines and cab types.

Although records were set in model-year sales of 33,271 Class-6 trucks in 1988 compared to 32,245 the year earlier, GMC's overall big-truck business also dropped in 1988. Heavy-duty sales were 2,297, compared to 7,507, and sales of W4 Forwards fell from 1,745 to 1,549. Things were expected to get worse in 1989, as the production of medium-duty Class-4 to Class-8 models was transferred from the factory in Pontiac to an assembly plant in Janesville.

There were several big-truck product changes. The 62.2-in. bbc Medium-Tilt Cab of 1987 grew five inches longer from bumper to back of cab and the Deere 5.9-liter and Deutz 6.1-liter 913-model diesel engines were dropped. Added was an Isuzu 6BG1 diesel.

Thanks to the immediate acceptance of the Sierra by

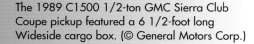

The 1989 C1500 1/2-ton GMC Sierra Club Coupe pickup featured a 6 1/2-foot long Wideside cargo box. (© General Motors Corp.)

the buying public and the residual benefits a hot-selling product produces, 1988 was a record year for GMC light-duty truck sales, which were 352,999. Total model-year sales for 1988 including medium- and heavy-duty trucks, Isuzu Forwards and, for some reason, 325 Caballeros, came to 382,655—a 12.82-percent gain over 1987. There was, however, a worrisome number reflective of the import invasion: GMC's market-share figure fell to 7.3 percent, from eight percent a year earlier.

1989: Business is Good Again

Business was good again in 1989 and full-size pickups were hot sellers. Light-duty truck sales by themselves were 358,202, a 5-percent gain. The new Sierra models sold so well that they made up for a drop in sales of both the compact Safari and the full-size Vandura and Rally models. Large-van sales slowed because many customers were moving to small vans, while Safari sales were driven down by strong competition, including competition from GM's own new GMT200 front-wheel-drive minivans or All Purpose Vehicles (APVs). The APVs included the Chevy Lumina, Pontiac Trans Sport, and Oldsmobile Silhouette.

While GM's truck sales were strong, its passenger-car sales were tapering off slightly. Even more worrisome was a decline in profits, which was industry wide. There were signs that tougher times were ahead due to an economy suffering from high inflation and high unemployment, plus stiff competition from overseas' manufacturers, new government rules and regulations, and the use of high-cost

sales incentives.

There were no major styling changes for 1989 Sierras. All gasoline engines were fitted with throttle body injection (TBI) and the 6.2-liter diesel had a mechanical fuel-injection system with one injector per cylinder delivering fuel to a pre-combustion chamber. Updates included three new exterior colors, changes in option-package contents, a new 4x4 Sports-graphic package, re-routed emergency-brake cables, and semi-metallic brake linings. At the start of the '80s, the standard 1500 wideside pickup had a base price of $5,590. By 1989, the Sierra 1500 short-bed wideside pickup listed for $10,945.

Sierra Club extended-cab pickups featured the short-pickup bed on a 155.5-in. wheelbase and came in 1500, 500, 2500 heavy-duty, and 3500 series. The first two used the Vortec V-6 as base engine, while the heavy-duty 3/4-ton and 1-ton used the 5.7-liter V-8. Four new "Big Dooley" pickups with dual-rear wheels also appeared in 1989 and all used the 7.4-liter big-block V-8 with heavy-duty emissions as their standard engine. There was a 3500HD standard cab long-bed version and, thanks to a new Borg-Warner 1370 transfer case with electronically actuated synchronizers, dual-rear wheels could now be ordered for 1-ton four-wheel-drive pickups, too. GMC offered the K3500 Big Dooley in standard-cab long bed and extended-cab versions.

The Suburban again came in 1/2- and 3/4-ton models with the same sheet metal. However, the grille was restyled to make it look more like the Sierra's grille. The lowest-priced edition of the 129.5-in. wheelbase wagon now had a $15,965 window sticker, compared to $7,923 a decade earlier. The extended cabs were technically dropped from the GMC lineup, but the crew-cab body was available as a chassis model with either two- or four-wheel drive, a 164.5-in. wheelbase, and a new 5.7-liter TBI V-8 engine with heavy-duty emissions.

Also retaining the old look with the new Sierra grille was the full-size Jimmy V1500, which was strictly a four-wheel-drive truck. It rode a 106.5-in. wheelbase, with the 210-hp 5.7-liter V-8 as standard engine and the 130-hp diesel optional. It was base priced at $15,965, compared to $7,975 for its 1980 open-top counterpart.

Compact S-15 pickups had standard rear-wheel anti-lock (RWAL) braking in 1989. There was one new exterior color and a dark-blue interior replaced medium blue. Standard models got a heavy-duty heater. Four-wheel-drive trucks with the base 2.8-liter V-6 used a new transfer case.

S-15 Jimmys also got RWAL brake systems, and all the other upgrades lavished on the S-15 compact pickups. A new option was a wet-arm rear-window washer-wiper system. Sierra-, Sierra-Classic, and Gypsy-trim levels were offered with an additional up-level Timberline package. Both of the compact Jimmys now had the 2.8-liter 125-hp V-6 as standard equipment, instead of the two-wheel-drive version using the 92-hp four.

The Safari vans were upgraded a bit and now came in a cargo model and three passenger versions called SLX, SLE, and SLT. The standard engine in the commercial model was a 2.5-liter 96-hp four, with the 150-hp Vortec V-6—which was standard in passenger models—as the only option.

Full-size Vandura and Rally vans soldiered on as gas-guzzling refugees from the flower-child era and were popular with primarily large families, delivery businesses, and camping enthusiasts.

The commercial-truck lineup was now down to seven truck lines and cab types in Class-4 through Class-7 series: the 76.2-in. and 67.2-in. bbc steel medium-duty tilt cabs; the 97.5-in. bbc medium-duty conventional; two school-bus chassis, one with a flat-back cowl; the forward-control chassis only; and the 97.5-in. bbc models other than chassis and cab. Engine selections were cut from 21 to 14, including only six diesels. In August 1989, GMC started production of a line of all-new conventional heavy-duty trucks that were marketed as GMC Top Kicks and Chevrolet Kodiaks for the 1990 model year.

On July 20, 1989, at the Bonneville Salt Flats in Utah, a GMC S-15 extended-cab pickup created as a special project of GMC Truck Motorsports set new-class records for the flying mile and flying kilometer, besting marks set by a Porsche 928. On August 22, the same truck, with a different engine, set a new record at Bonneville Speed Weeks.

Model-year 1989 sales of all GMC trucks came to 386,968 units, a slight increase from 1988. The Sierra, S-15 pickup and Jimmy, and Suburban registered sales gains. Deliveries of all other models dropped. The figures included 23,620 medium-duty GMC trucks and 1,403 Isuzu-built W4 Forwards. Late in the calendar year, GMC announced that, by 1992, it planned to add about 200 stores to its total of 2,400 existing dealerships.

A new Sierra-like grille was used in an attempt to update the looks of the 1989 GMC Suburban. This example has optional four-wheel drive. (© General Motors Corp.)

GMC TRUCK

Chapter 8

The '90s

1990-1999

Page 116 & 117: For 1999 Yukon buyers, the big news was this four-door luxury version of the full-size sport utility vehicle named after Denali National Park and Preserve in Alaska. (© General Motors Corp.)

A stake rack body from an outside supplier is seen on this 1990 GMC C3500 1-ton Chassis-and-Cab model with optional dual rear wheels. (OCWC)

1990: Racing to the Clouds

GMC Truck Division entered the '90s as a division of GM Truck and Bus Group, which was under the guidance of Clifford J. Vaughan, GM vice president and group executive. John D. Rock continued as general manager of the truck division. Antilock-braking systems were used on 95 percent of all GMC trucks this year and all light-duty models featured engines with electronic-fuel injection.

On February 8, 1990, at the Chicago Auto Show, Rock told the press, "In the past 10 years, light-truck sales in this country have gone from a market of about two-and-a-half-million units to just under five million. In that 10-year span, the light-truck market has basically doubled. But the most important point, from our point of view, is that we more than held our own during that time and, in fact, our share of the light-truck market increased about one percent."

GMC's hottest seller in 1990 was the Sierra, which had modest changes for the year. The headlamps were slightly different. Sierra 1500-series models got a Sports-Handling package with high-performance tires on 15-in. styled wheels, Bilstein shock absorbers, and a 32-mm front-stabilizer bar. The Sierra ST (Sport Truck) offered a sporty-appearance package for 1500-series pickups with a short 6 1/2-ft. cargo box. A heavy-duty version of the 4.3-liter Vortec V-6 was added for 2500-series Sierras with gross-vehicle-weight ratings over 8,600 lbs.

R/V10 and R/V20 Suburbans and R/V3500 Crew Cab chassis-and-cab trucks again had sheet metal that dated to 1987, although an updated grille made them look more modern. Rear-wheel antilock brakes were made standard on '90 Suburbans, as well as an electric speedometer and electronically tuned AM radio with clock. Electric outside

mirrors were offered for the first time.

The S-15 pickup had a standard five-speed manual transmission, with fifth-gear overdrive. The Vortec V-6 was available. There weren't many changes because GMC was working on the aerodynamic Sonoma pickup, which was due to bow in the fall of 1990 as a '91 model.

Full-size Jimmys had rear-antilock brakes that operated in two-wheel-drive mode only, new non-asbestos brake linings, and more use of double-sided galvanized steel. A 5.7-liter V-8 was standard with a four-speed manual transmission. The 6.2-liter diesel was an available option. Jimmys also had an electric speedometer, an electronically tuned AM radio with clock, electric outside rear-view mirrors, and rear-seat shoulder belts for the first time.

The compact S-15 Jimmy now had a standard Vortec V-6, but the hottest news in this truck line was a new four-door model. It debuted at the Chicago Auto Show in February 1990, although it was sold as a 1991 GMC. The four-door had a 6 1/2-in. longer wheelbase, giving it 10 percent more cargo room than the original S-15 Jimmy. Suspension improvements, combined with a longer wheelbase, resulted in a smoother ride than earlier models.

To attract more compact van buyers, GMC offered a new Safari XT model that was 10 in. longer and 18.6 cu. ft. roomier than the regular models, although it shared the same 111-in. wheelbase. It was available as a rear-wheel-drive model, as well as with another new-for-1990 Safari feature—all-wheel drive (AWD). Standard rear-wheel antilock brakes were added to the equipment list and standard four-wheel antilock brakes were featured on AWD models, passenger models, and cargo models used for aftermarket-conversion vans. A high-output 4.3-liter 170-hp V-6 was available in two-wheel-drive Safaris.

Safari vans featured a restyled instrument panel with

larger glove boxes, improved air distribution, and gauge-type instrumentation. Electronic instruments were optional. A high-back driver's seat was made standard in cargo vans. There was a new Safari GT with a blacked-out grille, sport-appearance package, and sport suspension and steering.

Extended versions of the full-size Vandura and Rally vans were offered for all passenger and cargo models in 1990. They had a 146-in. wheelbase and offered a 12.3-ft.-long load area, with 306 cu. ft. of cargo space or 12- and 15-passenger seating options. These models used the 5.7-liter V-8 with heavy-duty emissions equipment. Rear air conditioning was available in the extended-passenger vans. Rear-wheel antilock brakes and an electric speedometer were now standard.

After the Volvo GM Heavy Truck deal, GMC no longer sold Class-8 trucks, so the division started a strong push to create new products, new business, and more sales in the medium-duty market niche. This was partly related to the shift of most medium-duty truck production from the Pontiac, Michigan, home plant to GM's Janesville, Wisconsin, assembly plant. Truck & Bus also announced its intentions to transfer school-bus production to Janesville from the Pontiac central plant, which was scheduled to close by the end of 1990. Production of P-series forward-control trucks was headquartered at the Piquette Rd. plant in Detroit, Michigan.

GMC workers continued building the GMC Top Kick C-5000, C-6000, C-7000, and C-7000 Tandem models introduced late in 1989, as well as their Chevy Kodiak counterparts. These trucks had a 104-in. bbc cabs and were available as trucks or tractors in single- or tandem-axle models. GVWRs ranged between 22,000 and 54,600 lbs. Nine different wheelbases from 132 in. to 261 in. were offered.

The Top-Kick cab featured streamlined aerodynamics with a rounded-corned fiberglass hood and front-fender assembly, an angled windshield, and flush-mounted windows. The hood tilted forward for service and hood-access

panels were optional for trucks with snowplows or other front attachments. Five bumpers were available. Engines included 6.0- and 7.0-liter gas V-8s and a Caterpillar diesel. The gas engines were the most technically advanced GMC engines ever offered. They included electronic-fuel injection, a high-pressure fuel system, electronic-spark control, computerized-spark control, automatic-altitude compensation, and an integrated electronic governor.

A five-speed Fuller transmission was standard and five-, six-, 10-, and 13-speed gearboxes were optional, along with four- and five-speed Allison automatics. Other features included a tapered-leaf-spring front suspension on two-wheel drive models, a new-design chassis for easy body and equipment mountings, and a high-tech electrical system with Metri-Pack harness connectors.

The medium-duty line also continued to offer Isuzu-built low-cab-forward medium-duty trucks marketed as GMC Forward and Chevy Tiltmaster models. These were suited for a variety of jobs, from delivery vans to refuse trucks.

To build excitement in the new product line, GMC showcased a pair of concept trucks in 1990. The Mahalo was a soft-top convertible based on the soon-to-be-released 1991 Sonoma pickup. The GMC Transcend was a full-size pickup with a remote-controlled retractable roof that made it a hardtop convertible. On July 29, 1990, another exciting event took place when GMC Truck Motorsports took a C1500 Sierra with a 403-cid 625-hp V-8 to the Pikes Peak Hill Climb and won "The Race to the Clouds" in its class.

GMC did not do as well in the 1990 sales race, however, as it sold 325,065 domestically built trucks and 1,280 Isuzu medium-duty W4 Forwards, with GMC badges, during calendar 1990. On a model-year basis, GMC held just a 7.1 percent share of the light-duty market. It also sold 22,567 medium-duty models. Those numbers were just slightly off 1989's levels.

An all-new, aerodynamic Sonoma compact pickup replaced the S-15 in 1991. This is the SLE version with regular cab styling and a Wideside cargo box. (JAGC)

1991: Clouds of War

Former GMC general manager Robert C. Stempel replaced Roger Smith as chairman of GM on July 31, 1990. Two days later, Iraq invaded Kuwait in an act of aggression that eventually led the U.S. into a war. For the automotive industry, 1990 had been the worst year since 1983, but the clouds grew darker in mid-January 1991, when the Gulf War began. The conflict exacerbated the economic recession and drove motor-vehicle sales into a deeper hole.

Still, GMC had some exciting new products in 1991. Attention was focused on compact light-duty models, with an all-new, aerodynamic Sonoma pickup replacing the S-15 and siring a high-performance Syclone spin-off. In addition, the four-door S-15 Jimmy, released in mid-1990, was technically a "new" model.

GM's first electronic transmission for GMC light-duty trucks was a 1991 innovation. The Hydra-Matic 4L80-E was available in full-size pickups, the Chevy and GMC Suburbans, vans, chassis-and-cab models, and motor homes. It provided 50 percent greater torque capacity than similar transmissions and upped fuel economy by 20 percent. Alexander H. Rasegan, general director of Hydra-Matic's product and process engineering, said, "This transmission was specifically designed to meet customers' needs for a fuel efficient, yet hearty, transmission capable of hauling heavy loads." It made trailer pulling smoother because its "smart"-control module could sense and adjust for temperature, altitude, and engine variations.

The all-new Sonoma pickup featured a restyled front end that copied the look of the Sierra, except for single-rectangular headlamps. It offered base SL, SLE-comfort, and SLX-sport trim levels. Regular-cab Sonomas came as short-bed trucks on a 108.3-in. wheelbase or as long-beds on a 117.9-in. wheelbase. An extended-cab version with the shorter bed rode on a 122.9-in. wheelbase. A 2.5-liter 105-hp inline Tech IV four-cylinder engine was standard on two-wheel-drive editions. A 2.8-liter 125-hp V-6 was optional. Four-wheel-drive Sonomas used the 160-hp Vortec V-6, which was optional in other models. Prices ranged from $8,916-$25,950.

The extremely wide price bracket is explained by the Syclone, which bowed as a mid-year model in January 1991. The Syclone name had first been used on a concept vehicle at the 1989 Detroit International Auto Show. The production version was a joint venture between PAS, Inc., a Troy, Michigan, engineering firm and GMC. All 632 Syclones made in 1991 were built at GM's Truck-and-Bus-Group assembly plant in Shreveport, Louisiana. The turbocharged and inter-cooled 4.3-liter Vortec V-6 included special new pistons, a unique exhaust system, pintle-style individual-port injectors, and a L98 throttle body. It developed 285 hp at 4400 rpm and 350 lbs.-ft. of torque at 3600 rpm. The only transmission offered in Syclones was a Hydra-Matic 4L60 four-speed unit.

Other Syclone features included full-time four-wheel drive, four-wheel antilock brakes (a pickup truck first), air conditioning, an AM/FM stereo cassette, a tilt wheel, intermittent wipers, analog gauges, cruise control, power windows, and power-door locks, all as standard equipment. Despite such luxury touches, the truck's basic appeal was that it could go from zero to 60 mph in under five seconds and cover the quarter mile in 13.4 seconds.

The Syclone was finished in monochromatic two-tone black, with subtle red accents. The exterior featured a unique and aggressive body-decal package, with exclusive badging. For added corrosion protection and cargo security, the Syclone had a tonneau cover that snapped to an aluminum frame attached to the truck bed. The interior featured sport-bucket seats, a floor-mounted shifter, a center console with a pair of cup holders, and a leather-wrapped steering wheel. High-performance wheels and tires were included. *Popular Hot Rodding* magazine called the Syclone "the performance enthusiast's dream come true."

The full-size Sierra pickup featured a new self-aligning urethane four-spoke steering wheel and new heating, ventilation, and air-conditioning (HVAC) controls. The 4.3-liter V-6 and fully synchronized five-speed manual transmission were standard on 1500- and 2500-series models, with GVWRs below 8,600 lbs. A new option was an under-the-rail GM Duraliner bed liner for wideside Sierras and an analog-instrument cluster with tachometer. In midyear, high-back bucket seats became optional for regular-cab models. The Sierra was also offered in two- and four-wheel-drive chassis-and-cab models, with GVWRs up to 12,000 lbs.

A new Sierra-based commercial cab-and-chassis model, the Heavy Hauler, joined the GMC lineup in October 1990 as a 1991 model. It had a distinctive front-end treatment with single rectangular headlamps and a more truck-like lower grille panel and bumper. Known as the 3500HD or heavy-duty 1-ton, it was actually a Class 4 truck and a direct competitor to the industry's category leader, the Ford F-Super-Duty model. The 3500HD GVWR was 15,000 lbs. The chassis came in 135.5- and 159.5-in. wheelbases and featured 34-in. wide, straight frame rails from the rear of the cab, for easy mounting of commercial and motor-home bodies.

Full-size Jimmy, Suburban, and crew-cab pickup bodies still dated back to pre-Sierra days. New frontal treatments helped cloak this fact until these models could be refreshed in 1992.

The S-15 Jimmy was promoted as "the compact sport utility with full-size features." Buyers could choose from two- or four-wheel-drive models in two- or four-door versions. Features included a standard Vortec V-6, available shift-on-the-fly Insta-Trac four-wheel-drive system, antilock brakes, and a new optional SLS-sport trim package. At the Chicago Auto Show, GMC announced the SLT Touring package for buyers who wanted to dress up their four-door S-15 Jimmy. It included special SLT trim, reclining leather seats, a console, and much more.

For 1991, a standard 4.3-liter Vortec V-6 powered all Safari vans. Changes included an optional sliding tray under the front-passenger seat and a new sport-appearance package for the Safari XT extended-body model.

GMC's large Vandura and Rally vans offered 25 options including a new 7.4-liter EFI V-8 and a Hydra-Matic 4L80-E heavy-duty automatic transmission. To improve ride smoothness and tire wear, G3500 models again had standard steel-belted radial tires.

The GMC Top Kick and Chevrolet Kodiak GMT-530 medium-duty conventional trucks, both built by GMC, offered two new GM EFI gasoline V-8s and a new C-6000 LoPro model with a lowered frame height and nine available wheelbases from 131.6 in. to 260.6 in. A 6.0-liter

210-net bhp gas engine was available for all but Tandem models. A 7.0-liter 235-net bhp gas V-8 was available for all C-7000s. A 6.6-liter Caterpillar 3116 turbo diesel with ratings of 170, 185, 215, or 250 gross hp was also offered. Other changes for the year included: new 11,000- and 14,600-lb. front axles, a new raised roof option to better meet the needs of utility workers and tractor drivers (especially with air-ride seats), and a new midlevel cab-insulation-and-trim package.

The Low Cab Forward (LCF) line had W4, W5, W6, W7, W7HV, and W7T GMC Forwards and Chevy Tiltmasters made by Isuzu. These highly maneuverable trucks had many uses and offered a variety of wheelbases and power trains. They had provisions for body lengths up to 24-ft. The W7T was available as a tractor with a 126-in. wheelbase, a 60,000-lb. GCWR, and an 8.4-liter turbo diesel engine with 225 gross horsepower.

Also falling into the medium-duty category were new P3500 chassis and cab models spun off the P-series package-delivery chassis. These were available as a commercial chassis, with steel or aluminum Value Van delivery truck bodies, or as motor homes. The Value Vans came in four lengths between 10.5-ft. and 18 ft. on 125-, 133-, 157-, and 178-in. wheelbases. Motor home models were available on 137-, 158.5-, 178-, 190-, and 208-in. wheelbases.

GMC also introduced a line of 10 medium-duty trucks with GVWRs from 8,600-10,500 lbs. that were based upon the full-sized vans. These Magnavans, Rally Camper Specials, and Vandura Specials were cutaway-van models combining the front end of the van with a "cube"-type body. They came on 125- and 146-in. wheelbases. Calendar-year sales of GMC trucks fell 7.5 percent. Model-year sales included 289,810 light-duty trucks (seven percent of the total light-duty market) and 19,017 medium-duty units.

A new SLT Touring package was available for the 1991 S-15 Jimmy, as shown here. (JAGC)

1992: 80 Years of Experience

The Gulf War lasted only six weeks. While America's economic problems didn't go away as quickly as the fighting, GMC's 80th-anniversary-year sales went in the right direction. Total calendar-year 1992 deliveries rose to 359,365, with gains in all categories. The small-truck total was almost 7.5 percent of the overall light-duty market and a nice gain from 1990's levels. Medium-duty truck sales were 20,258, up from 18,110 in '90.

GMC Truck Division had many new product developments in its 1992 light-duty lineup. The full-size pickup truck line got an all-new Sierra four-door long-bed Crew Cab model. It was available on the heavy-duty C3500 two-wheel-drive and K3500 four-wheel-drive chassis at prices of $18,174 and $21,174, respectively. The wheelbase was 168.5 in. and overall length was a massive 255.25 in. The 5.7-liter V-8 was standard in both versions. The sportside-style cargo box was now available with extended-cab models.

The 1992 Suburban was also an all-new model that came in 1500 and 2500 series models. A choice of SL or SLE trims was offered. The Suburban's wheelbase was stretched two inches to 131.5 in., but the overall length was slightly less than before. A 5.7-liter V-8 was standard and a 7.4-liter V-8 was optional on 2500 series models. The Suburban's trailering capacity was increased to a maximum of 17,000-lb. GVWR. Prices were in the $19,033 to $22,437 range.

GMC's full-size SUV was also totally redesigned and renamed. Instead of the Jimmy, it was known as the Yukon. The base price was $20,113, up more than 10 percent. The Yukon came only as a 1/2-ton, four-wheel-drive vehicle with a two-door body and a choice of SL or SLE trim packages. A 5.7-liter 210-hp V-8 replaced the Vortec V-6 as base engine. A four-speed automatic transmission and ABS brakes were standard. The Yukon's wheelbase was lengthened five inches, compared to the Jimmy's. Overall length was 188 in., up three inches from the Jimmy's. Yukon prices started at $18,249.

In the compact pickup line, there was a revved-up Sonoma GT for 1992. It was powered by a 195-hp high-performance version of the 4.3-liter Vortec V-6. There were no major changes for the extra-high-performance Syclone, which continued to carry GMC's steepest base price for a light-duty truck, at $25,950.

Compact SUV buyers who wanted to go fast now had an all-new version of the S-15 Jimmy four-wheel-drive model dubbed the Typhoon. It included a 280-hp version of the 4.3-liter V-6 that could take it from 0 to 60 mph in 6.5 sec., as well as ABS brakes. The optional STS Touring Package was again offered on four-door compact Jimmys and a 200-hp high-output 4.3-liter V-6 was optional on both two- and four-door Jimmys.

Safari vans offered the new high-output version of the 4.3-liter V-6 as optional equipment on two-wheel-drive vans. The power increase was achieved through the use of a central-port fuel-injection system. A new rear-door option was added as a running change during the model year. The "Dutch-Door" treatment featured a new one-piece lift-gate, with split-panel doors below and an electronic door-release mechanism. Among the Safari's new interior features were adjustable-bench seats and an optional premium sound system with a compact-disc player.

The Vandura and Rally vans were the only light-duty GMCs that were relatively unchanged in 1992. Light-duty 1500s came on 110- and 125-in. wheelbases, while 2500- and 3500-passenger vans were built on the 125-in. wheelbase. The 3500HD Rally XT had an extended body on a 146-in. wheelbase chassis. A 4.3-liter 150-hp V-6 was standard in all but 3500s, which substituted the 5.7-liter 190-hp V-8. Engine options included the 230-net-bhp 7.4-liter gas V-8 in 3500HD models and the 6.2-liter diesel V-8 in 2500 and 3500HD models. Prices ranged from $14,963 to $17,927.

After spending $300 million to bring the GMC Top Kick and Chevy Kodiak out, GMC general manager Lewis B. Campbell admitted there were "no plans to bring out new products next month or anytime soon." Campbell said that his division's goal was to take 40 percent of the market for Class 6-7 trucks.

Roy S. Roberts became GMC's new general manager in

The 1992 GMC Syclone pickup featured a turbocharged V-6 that produced 283 hp. It could move the limited-production model from 0 to 60 mph in 4.9 seconds. (© General Motors Corp.)

The 1992 GMC Topkick C7H042 extended-cab model was available with gasoline or natural-gas engines. This one carries a cherry-picker crane. (© General Motors Corp.)

October 1992, after Lewis B. Campbell joined Textron Corp. as executive vice president and chief operating officer. Roberts came to GMC Truck at the right time, as 80th-anniversary model-year sales rose 11.3 percent to 322,812 light-duty and 20,957 medium-duty units.

1993: Back on Track

In its 1993 issue, *Ward's Automotive Yearbook* said that GMC was "back on track." The GMC Truck Division was again in charge of marketing both light- and medium-duty trucks, while the former Truck & Bus Division, which took care of medium-duty-truck, motor-home, and school bus manufacturing, was transformed into a new entity named GM North American Truck Platforms (NATP). Both groups were headquartered at 31 E. Judson Street in Pontiac, Michigan, with Roy Roberts as general manager. Group executive Clifford J. Vaughan and group director of operations Guy D. Briggs (both GM vice presidents) were the executives in charge of overall NATP operations.

Due to its strong sales history since 1988, GMC started sourcing the Sierra pickup from a fourth factory in 1992. In addition to continuing production at Pontiac, Michigan, Ft. Wayne, Indiana, and Oshawa, Ontario, additional manufacturing was carried out at the Janesville, Wisconsin, assembly plant. There was a new GT package for 1500-series models and a new 4L60-E electronically controlled Hydra-Matic transmission became standard with 4.3-, 5.0-, and 5.7-liter V-8s. A fully synchronized five-speed manual transmission was standard in all full-size

pickups and chassis-cab models.

This new "smart" transmission monitored every element involved in driving including the fuel-injection rate, the driver's habits, ignition timing, internal transmission temperature, ideal speed, and exhaust gas re-circulation several times each second and then determined the proper shift points and shift smoothness. The "seamless" power train even had a built-in learning feature that allowed the system to adapt to its environment and make clutch pressure adjustments. In the case of a problem, the transmission "defaulted" to operable gear ratios to get the driver safely home. A second safety feature permitted second-gear starts when increased traction was required.

New Sierra features included improved corrosion protection, Solar-Ray window glass, seat recliners, Scotchguard fabric protection, and front cup holders. A 7.4-liter gas V-8 and two diesels became optional in crew cab and extended-cab models with 10,000-lb. GVWs. A 6.2-liter diesel was used in Sierra 2500s and 3500s. A 6.5-liter turbo diesel, built by the GM Power Train Division, went into about 4,000 of the 2500 and 3500 Sierras. A modified version of the 5.7-liter V-8 was available for conversion to compressed natural gas, propane, or dual fuel capability with gasoline. Base prices were $14,418 to $21,910.

Suburbans also got the new four-speed 4L60-E Hydra-Matic as standard equipment on all models. Other improvements for 1993 included an AM/FM radio with more "user-friendly" buttons, a larger radiator, an air

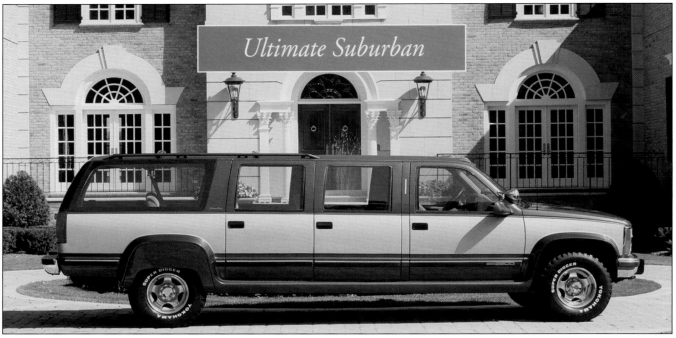

Ultimate Suburban

A vehicle converter named Limousine Werks constructed the "Ultimate Suburban," a stretched version of the 1993 GMC C2500 Suburban with three doors on each side. (GDMC)

cleaner with better sealing, and additional underhood and underbody corrosion protection. The tilt-steering column was redesigned to be more theft-proof. Suburban prices started at $19,170.

The '93 Sonoma had minor power-plant and drive-train improvements, since a total revision of this model was coming in 1994. There was no Syclone high-performance package this year. Base prices started at $9,238 and went as high as $14,665.

A GT sport package was added to the Yukon's options list for 1993 and the new 4L60-E Hydra-Matic became standard equipment. A single-rail shift control was now standard, along with Scotchguard cloth seat protection and Solar-Ray glass. The tilt steering column had a new steel sleeve to help reduce theft. Inside, the passenger side of the split bench seats and the low-back bucket seats reclined for 1993. Under the hood were a new dual-stud air cleaner, more durable oil filter and improved cruise control. Yukons were also built at the Janesville, Wisconsin, assembly plant and they had a base price of $20,838.

In the compact SUV lineup, in addition to the new 4L60-E electronic transmission, there were several new option packages. Two-door Jimmys were available with an SLT touring package and an LS option series was available on the Typhoon. Prices started at $15,497 for the base two-door and ran as high as $29,975 for the Typhoon.

Four-wheel ABS brakes were made standard on 1993 Safari cargo van models. Base prices ranged from $15,308 to $18,258. The full-size Vandura and Rally vans got four-wheel ABS brakes in place of the previous rear-wheel-only system. The new 4L60-E Hydra-Matic was offered with 4.3-, 5.0-, and 5.7-liter engines. Big van prices were in the $15,248 to $22,788 range this year.

The medium-duty product lineup was very similar to 1992, with trucks being sourced from GM factories in the U.S. and Canada and from Isuzu of Japan. There were six

series, W4, W5, W6, W7 tilt cabs and 6000 and 7000 conventional cabs. The 7000 series was available with either single or tandem rear axles.

Line and cab types consisted of the Isuzu-built W4 and W5 steel-tilt cabs, with 68-in. bbc cab measurements; the W6 and W7 Isuzu-built 76.2-in. bbc steel-tilt cabs; the 104-in. bbc Top-Kick conventional cabs; the P-type chassis-only; the S-type chassis-only; and the T-type bus chassis. Three Isuzu diesel engines used in 1992 were dropped: the 3.9-liter 4801, the 5.8-liter 68D1-T and the 8.4-liter 6SA1-T. GM added the 5.7-liter gas V-8. A different version of Isuzu's 3.9-liter four-cylinder diesel was used in the W4. A 6.5-liter six-cylinder diesel engine powered the other W models.

The medium-duty conventional-cab engine line up included 6.0- and 7.0-liter gas V-8s and the Caterpillar 3116 six-cylinder turbocharged diesel. A new hand-pump air-ride suspension was used on 1994 Top Kick LoPro (low-profile) conventional trucks, which also featured new Eaton five- and six-speed transmissions.

GM's truck platform consolidated GMC and Chevrolet medium-duty truck marketing and both brands enjoyed a happy 1993, with market share for the two combined rising from 24 percent in 1992 to 24.4 percent in 1993. It was the GMC brand that turned in the best performance, with its market share rising to 16.2 percent, from 15.6 percent the previous year. GMC led Chevrolet in Class-5 and Class-7 sales, with Chevy taking Class 4, but actually dropping in its overall "piece of the pie."

GMC's calendar-year light-duty truck sales rose 15 percent to 389,881 units and now represented 94.33 percent of all trucks the company manufactured. It also sold 2,045 W7 Forwards and 23,428 medium-duty trucks. Total calendar-year numbers were 413,309 units versus 359,365 the previous year. Model-year sales included 378,501 light- and 22,466 medium-duty trucks.

1994: The Strength of Experience

Light-duty truck sales had taken off in 1993, leading the entire U.S. truck market to higher sales and triggering resurgence in passenger-car sales along the way. Medium-duty trucks were also making impressive gains. Leasing was among the hottest trends in the medium-duty niche and GMC Truck officially expanded their lease offerings to Class-4 through Class-7 trucks because consumer awareness of leasing options had increased to 65 percent, from just 23 percent only two years earlier.

The Sierra, which was introduced in mid-1987, remained one of the most modern full-size pickups on the road, with a handsome shape and a long list of options including nine engines from a 4.3-liter 155-hp V-6 to a 7.4-liter 230-hp "big-block" V-8. There was also a 6.5-liter 155-hp diesel and a 6.5-liter 180-hp turbo-diesel. Sierras came with regular, extended, and four-door cabs, with long and short beds, and in sportside or wideside models. Sierras could be built to handle giant payloads or to haul the family's travel trailer to Florida. Changes for 1994 included a CFC-free air-conditioning system, even better corrosion protection and side-door guard-beam construction. Sierra extended-cab models were now offered with an optional six-way-power driver's seat, with memory control for seat-back adjustments.

GMC Suburbans could haul as many as nine passengers, tow up to 10,000 lbs., slog through a bog (when equipped with four-wheel drive), and then proudly show up at the country club after a quick "bath" at the local car wash. The big news for 1994 was the availability of a 6.5-liter turbo-diesel V-8 that went into only 437 Suburbans. It combined high-torque output with good fuel economy. Like the Sierra, the "super" wagon got side-door guard beams and CFC-free refrigeration. The 5.7-liter 210-hp V-8 was standard equipment.

The Yukon two-door sport-utility vehicle had many of the same upgrades as other full-size GMC models, including the 6.5-liter turbo diesel that developed 180 hp at 3400 rpm and 360 lbs.-ft. of torque at 1700 rpm. The Yukon's top towing capacity was 6,000 lbs.

The Jimmy had minimal change since an all-new truck-and-power train had originally been expected in June 1994. Pilot production of the new model began in May, but there were problems and the launch was delayed until August, making it a 1995 model. The carryover model available earlier had side-door guard beams, increased undercoating, and a center high-mounted stop lamp. Two- and four-door models were available, but the high-performance Typhoon version of the two-door version was dropped. Four-door models got a new 60/40 bench seat. New under the hood was the optional 4.3-liter 195-hp Enhanced V-6. A 165-hp version of the 4.3-liter engine was standard, hooked to a five-speed manual gearbox.

The 1994 GMC Sonoma SLS regular-cab pickup was available with two-wheel drive and Special Two-Tone paint. (© General Motors Corp.)

Completely new from its aerodynamic nosepiece to its smooth backside and notch-style taillights, the 1994 Sonoma had a stronger frame, "slipstream" body styling, interior upgrades, beefier engines, and more features than ever before. Model options included standard SL, sporty SLS, and luxury SLE levels. A new macho-looking Highrider fit between the SLS and SLE. Regular- and extended-cab models were offered on three wheelbase lengths. GMC offered buyers six coordinated levels of suspension systems: standard, Solid Smooth Ride, Heavy-Duty; Sport (two-wheel-drive only), Off-Road, and Highrider (four-wheel-drive only). Base engine was a 2.2-liter inline four that produced 118 hp. An optional 4.3-liter TBI V-6 raised the output to 165 hp. The Enhanced V-6 with central-port fuel injection produced 195 hp. Five-speed manual and four-speed automatic transmissions were available. In January, a strike at GM's Shreveport, Louisiana, plant idled the assembly line and the production of about 3,800 GMC Sonoma and Chevy S-10 pickups was lost.

Safari vans had a new driver-side airbag, revised instrument-panel graphics, Scotchguard fabric protection, Solar-Ray tinted glass, and a roof-mounted stop lamp. Engineers added a balance shaft to the 4.3-liter V-6 to make it smoother.

Up to 15 people or 10,000-lb. loads could be squeezed into some of GMC's Vandura and Rally vans. New features included in these lines started with a driver's airbag on trucks with GVWRs of 8,500 lbs. or less. Side-door guard beams, undercoating, and small improvements to some of the seven available engines were among model-year highlights. The 6.5-liter diesel V-8, with light-duty emissions, was used in 501 Vanduras and 48 Rally vans. The 6.5-liter turbo diesel went into 862 Vanduras and six Rally vans.

General Motors' North American Truck Platforms group had a flat year in 1994 and saw sales of its medium-duty GMC and Chevrolet models drop. GMC-badge truck sales included 3,386 Class-4 units, 372 Class-5 trucks, 4,097 Class-6, and 13,135 Class-7 models. GM was in third place in the overall market, with its two brands pulling down a 21.4 percent market share.

On a model-year basis, GMC sales rose 10 percent. Model-year sales of medium-duty units fell by 1,742 trucks. That included 20,990 medium-duty models compared to 23,428 in 1993. As a footnote to 1994 GMC history, in June, General Motors sold its remaining 13.7 percent equity share in Detroit Diesel Corp., which had built many of the diesels used in GMC trucks when it was operated as the Detroit Diesel Engine Division.

The Madison, North Carolina, Fire Department owns a 1994 GMC C3500 cargo van with a 20-foot body and roll-up rear door. Its equipment includes a 4.5-hp Onan generator; 2,500-watt tri-pod scene lights; 75 gallons of AFFF foam; self-contained breathing apparatus (SCBA), and crew seating. (MFD/JR)

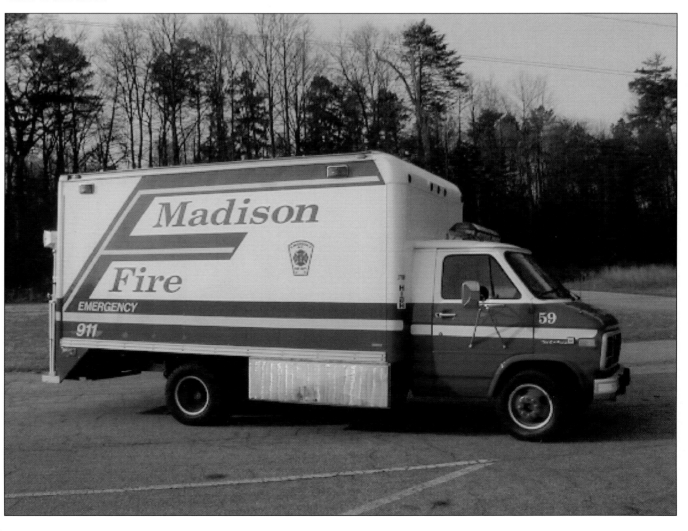

1995: Sweet Trucks

"A tower of classic styling, strengths, capabilities, and refinement, Sierra will definitely elicit strong reactions from your family and friends," said the first page of GMC's 1995 Sierra catalog. "Not only the usual comments, about how convenient it is to know you, but other comments more from the heart. Like two, simple, admiring words: 'Sweet Truck.'" And many truck buyers did consider their GMCs "sweet" indeed, as reflected by record model-year sales of 469,853 units.

It was a historical year for GM, as a 45-year-old former Bausch & Lomb Corp. executive named Ronald L. Zarrella, who joined GM's North American Operations in November 1994 as group vice president of sales, service, and marketing, began making changes. His new brand-management initiative identified 35 customer-needs segments and set up a system under which brand managers, to be appointed later, would be in charge of specific vehicles, with their compensation tied to that vehicle's profitability.

GMC's sweet-selling Sierra, Yukon, and Suburban models were in such demand during 1995 that GM assembly workers had a formidable job keeping up with sales. It was decided to stop making large, rear-wheel-drive Cadillac Fleetwoods, Chevy Caprices, and Buick Roadmasters in Arlington, Texas, and the assembly plant there was converted to build large SUVs by 1997. While the conversion was taking place, regular-Sierra production was maintained in three plants, but crew-cab models only were built in Flint, Michigan. The launch of a new four-door Yukon sport-utility vehicle that perfectly filled the gap between compact Jimmys and cavernous Suburbans, helped to fill the booming demand for "SUVs."

The 1995 Sierra had an all-new interior, driver's air bag, shift-interlock mechanism, electric mirrors, a redone dash, and seating choices that included genuine leather. The base SL-frontal treatment had single-lens corner lamps, single headlights, narrower parking lamps, and a wider grille insert with a more open crosshatch. The SLE/SLT-type up-level grille had split corner lamps, narrower dual headlights, wider parking lights and a

narrower, deeper grille insert, with tighter-spaced bars and a chrome-grille surround. Sound system upgrades—a must in this era—were massive. An important chassis improvement was a three-channel four-wheel antilock-braking system. Among the six engines offered, the base 4.3-liter V-6 had a reinforced block-and-balance shaft. Small-block V-8s were fitted with new exhaust manifolds and a new dipstick. Powdered metal rocker-arm pivots and new valve springs enhanced big-block V-8s. Five-speed manual-transmission advances included shorter shift throws, a new composite shift tower, and closer gear ratios. The 4L80E automatic used with 7.4-liter gas V-8s and 6.5-liter diesels had faster 1-2 shifts for better gas mileage and smoothness.

The Suburban, now built in Janesville with Yukons, had a new interior with energy-absorbing steering column and instrument panel, driver's air bag, and shift interlock set up. It could be configured for 3-, 5-, 6-, 8-, or 9-passenger seating, with cargo volume increasing from 47.5 to 149.5 cu. ft. as auxiliary seats were folded or removed. A 5.7-liter 200-hp V-8 was standard and a 7.4-liter 230-hp gas V-8 was optional. A 6.5-liter 190-hp turbo diesel was also on the list. The diesel produced the same peak net torque as the 7.4-liter gas engine—385 lbs.-ft.

One of GMC's big-news items for 1995 was the Yukon four-door introduced on January 3. It rode on a new computer-designed ladder frame with a 117.5-in. wheelbase. Its body structure from the B-pillar back was all new. No compromises were made in its construction. To maximize cargo-space utility, the spare wheel and tire stowed neatly underneath at the rear, where it contributed to the frame's stiffness. The Yukon's interior width and cargo capacity compared favorably to those of the Ford Explorer and Jeep Grand Cherokee. At the Chicago Auto Show, Jim Kornas, director of full-size truck marketing for GMC, pointed out

that the new four-door Yukon's "specific mission is to offer Grand Cherokee and Explorer owners the opportunity to move up to something better." The base engine was the 5.7-liter 200-hp V-8. The 6.5-liter turbo diesel was extra. The two-door Yukon rode a 111.5-in. wheelbase. It had the same engine options as the four-door, but came in both two- and four-wheel-drive versions.

A Highrider special-equipment package was made available on the Sonoma in 1995. Sonoma extended-cab models and all of the compact pickups were fitted with driver's-side air bags. Other changes for the year included minor power-train improvements, an optional remote keyless-entry system, and the addition of a new on-board-diagnostics (OBDII) engine-control system for trucks built for sale in California with the optional 4.3-liter Vortec V-6. Sonoma's base engine was the 2.2-liter 118-hp four-cylinder with a new one-piece flywheel, powdered-metal connecting rods, low-resistance spark-plug wires, a larger air cleaner, and improvements to the exhaust and emissions system. Sonomas also had new door handles that automatically lighted the interior, bucket seats with new adjustments for lumbar support, and an elastic strap on the driver's sun visor for stowage of loose items.

GMC's compact sport-utility model, which officially changed its name from S-15 Jimmy to just plain Jimmy, had originally been updated for mid-1994, but the launch was delayed until late in the summer and it came in as a 1995 model. The design update featured more interior room and a stiffer frame. Two- and four-door models were available at base prices in the $18,759 to $22,690 range. Both came with two- or four-wheel drive. The base engine was the 195-hp version of the 4.3-liter V-6. Also standard was a driver's side air bag and antilock braking.

The Safari van's front end had been criticized almost since its 1985 introduction, so for its 10th birthday, it got a new look, plus some chassis modifications. The frontal appearance looked more like that of a large van with headlamp, parking lamp, and grille options resembling those of the Sierra models. An air dam was integrated into the front fascia. Color-matched wheel "spats" and body side moldings appeared. Overall length was increased by 2.3 in., as a result of the front-end redesign. The 4.3-liter 190-hp Vortec V-6 was made standard. The compact commercial and passenger models were also enhanced by a new optional FE2 touring suspension package and remote keyless-entry system.

The large Vandura and Rally vans saw modifications to their base 4.3-liter V-6 to reduce noise and vibration. The exhaust manifolds on the 5.0- and 5.7-liter V-8s were redesigned and they also got the new-design dipstick with a T-handle and O-ring seal. The automatic transmission used with the 7.4-liter V-8 was recalibrated for smoother operation and all models got a new electronically controlled solenoid that engaged the torque-converter clutch.

In the medium-duty segment, all models with air brakes got new GM/Bendix antilock units. In the Class-5 category, there was a new W5 GMC Forward. No longer offered in medium-duty models was Isuzu's 6.5-liter 6BG1 diesel. It was replaced by a 7.1-liter 6HE1TC diesel also made by the Japanese company. GMC also beefed up its offerings in the "smaller" medium-duty niche with new 10,000-lb. GVW Sierra 3500 HD model. Total GMC calendar-year sales of domestic-built models included 441,039 light- and 20,990 medium-duty units, giving the division 7.6 percent of the total U.S. market for comparable-size trucks.

After 10 years of success in the marketplace with its original front-end styling, the GMC Safari van got a new frontal treatment for model-year 1995. (© General Motors Corp.)

General Motors' Pontiac and GMC divisions were merged in 1996, with Roy S. Roberts becoming general manager of the new Pontiac-GMC Division. (© General Motors Corp.)

1996: GMC Merges with Pontiac

In 1996, General Motors continued reorganizing the way that it planned, designed, engineered, and sold vehicles. Outside GM Board Director John G. Smale, a champion of brand management, stepped aside to let president and CEO John F. Smith, Jr., become chairman. By October 1995, Smith had appointed Donald E. Hackworth (mid-size and luxury cars), Richard G. "Skip" LeFauve (small cars), and Clifford J. Vaughan (trucks) to supervise 13 Vehicle Line Executives (VLEs) and more than 35 brand managers. The VLEs had the job of bringing a vehicle to the market and the brand managers, many from outside the auto industry, were charged with establishing a marketing image for each vehicle and selling it. *Ward's Automotive Yearbook* reported that the goal was to cut development costs 25 percent.

Like any major corporate reorganization, this one was not without cutbacks, transfers, job moves, and changes in corporate structure. It brought about an historical change on February 20, 1996, when Ronald L. Zarrella, vice president and group executive for North American vehicle sales, service, and marketing, announced that the GMC Truck Division and Pontiac Motor Division were being merged to form Pontiac-GMC Division. A news release explained that the word "truck" was dropped from the name to reflect GMC's "emerging image as GM's premium producer of trucks, vans, and sport-utility vehicles."

GMC General Manager Roy S. Roberts was selected to head the newly joined division as general manager and he announced his executive team members at the same time. Roberts chose Darwin E. Allen as communications director, Michael L. Heisel was finance director, Michael O'Malley was marketing services manager, Elwood M. Schlesinger was general sales and service manager, and Gay G. Tosch was in charge of personnel. The merger was expected to take over a year to accomplish, but was finished by November.

The new Pontiac-GMC division had 12 brand managers, who reported to their respective Pontiac or GMC category director. Frederick E. Cook was appointed GMC category director. Lynn C. Myers, who became Pontiac category director, would later go on to become general manager of the Pontiac-GMC Division.

At this time, GMC was viewed as a leader in delivering "premium" trucks, vans, and innovative service with a personal touch. The division had 2,451 dealers, 275 central-office employees, and 361 zone-office employees. A total of 1,585 or 65 percent of GMC dealers operated GMC-Pontiac dual dealerships. Over the past five years, GMC's calendar-year sales had increased steadily from 303,534 in 1991 to 462,185 in 1995. During those years, its share of the truck market ranged from 6.9 to 7.3 percent, and peaked at 7.3 percent in 1992 and 1993. Pontiac had 2,870 dealers, 194 central-office employees, and 314 zone-office employees. Its sales went up steadily between 1991 and 1994 and fell slightly in 1995, but its market share rose steadily over the period to 6.5 percent in 1995.

Product-wise, the headliner for 1996 was a total redo for the full-size vans. The former Vandura/Rally models became the Savana. With full-frame construction, this series offered 135- and 155-in. wheelbase rear-wheel-drive models in 1500, 2500, 3500, and 3500HD series. A modern, aerodynamic design characterized the large van's new appearance. The Solar glass and door handles were flush mounted and the rear-door hinges were hidden. Savana buyers could choose between a sliding-side door and a 60-40 hinged door. SL or SLE trim packages were offered and there was also a recreational conversion package. Other features included dual air conditioning, ABS braking, and up-to-15-passenger seating.

Revised versions of the 4.3-liter V-6, 5.0-, 5.7-, and 7.4-liter gas V-8s and 6.5-liter turbo diesel were available on specific Savanas. Vans with GVWs under 8,500 lbs. came with standard dual air bags and those with GVWs

The 1996 G3500 Savana full-size van offered an extended-body model. It was available on 135-inch or 155-inch wheelbases. (© General Motors Corp.)

An extensive interior redesign characterized the 1996 Safari van. It included standard dual-air bags and an optional, integrated child-safety seat. An overhead console was optional. The new 190-hp Vortec 4300 V-6 was standard.

For the first year of the merger, the Pontiac-GMC Division remained headquartered at 31 E. Judson Street in Pontiac, Michigan, with the Pontiac employees located at their former offices nearby in Pontiac. The GMC badge continued to identify a line of Class-4 to Class-7 medium-duty trucks.

In the lightest medium-duty-truck category, GMC continued marketing Isuzu-designed W4 Forwards and sold 911 fewer Class-4 trucks than the year before. In Class 5, sales of C -series conventionals and W5 Forward were 103 units less than the previous year. This trend held true in Class 6, where sales of the W6 Forward declined by 13 units. Sales of the Class-6 Top-Kick conventionals and P6 Value Vans also dropped, coming in at 4,427. Similarly, in Class 7, the captive-import W7 lost 228 sales from 1995. Sales of B7 school-bus chassis, C7 four-door Crew Cabs, C7 Top Kicks, and D7 chassis fell to 16,075 from 18,731.

The overall model-year sales of all GMC-badged trucks were recorded as 441,273 light-duty models and 18,429 medium-duty models. The light-duty total included 919 W4 Forwards made in the United States and 2,251 of the same model built overseas. The combined model-year output of 459,702 units was down 2.16 percent from 1995 and GMC's share of the truck market dropped from 7.7 percent in 1995 to 7.1 percent. The dip was only temporary and perhaps understandable, given the many corporate changes taking place.

1997: Comfortably in Command

By 1997, Roy S. Roberts was "comfortably in command" of the Pontiac-GMC Division, which had brand-spanking-new headquarters at 100 Renaissance Center in Detroit. Lynn C. Myers was elevated category director for both the Pontiac and GMC brands.

Corporate reshufflings also continued within General Motors, with Vice President and Group Executive Tom Davis now in charge of all truck operations. GM consolidated commercial-truck production in Flint, Michigan, in order to free up production capacity so more SUVs could be built at the Janesville, Wisconsin, assembly plant. In North Carolina, Volvo Truck Group bought out GM's remaining shares in the former Volvo GM Heavy Truck Group. The Swedish company's U.S. operation was renamed Volvo Truck North America.

GMC promoted its 1997 line of premium trucks, vans, and sport-utility vehicles as one that would put the driver "comfortably in command." Design innovations, powertrain improvements, speed-sensitive power steering, gas-saving transmission upgrades, improved safety and convenience, new colors, and an upscale "Gold Edition" Jimmy were the brand's headline attractions.

Sierra pickups got dual air bags, additional horsepower, and three new colors: Bright Blue, Laguna Blue-Green,

over 10,000 lbs. could get the turbo diesel engine. GMC also offered some Rally G3500 and Rally G3500 15-passenger vans in 1996.

Sierras got a new passenger-side "third door" as an option for extended-cab models. The third door was placed on the passenger side, since passengers were often carried back there and usually entered from the passenger side. A revised Vortec 4300 V-6, with sequential central-port fuel injection and other refinements, was standard. All V-8s also had Vortec technology. Federal law required all 1996 light-duty trucks to have the ability to detect emission-system deterioration. The Sierra did and was therefore "OBDII compliant." Among a host of other new features were 12-volt power outlets with spring-hinged doors, entry lights, and an electrochromic rear-view mirror.

Suburbans, which had previously been built only in Janesville, Wisconsin, were now produced in Silao, Mexico, as well. The base 5.7-liter V-8 and the 7.4-liter V-8 that was optional on 2500 models were both revised with new sequential central-port fuel injection, two-part intake manifolds, and other improvements. The automatic transmission was made smoother shifting. Other upgrades included OBDII compliance, daytime running lamps, long-life engine coolant, and quieter tires with less rolling resistance.

Like other large trucks, the Yukon used the new Vortec 5700 V-8. The two-door model now came with two-wheel drive. An improved automatic transmission was standard. Daytime running lights were also made standard and long-life engine coolant was provided. The Yukon was also OBDII compliant.

Extended-cab Sonomas got a driver's-side third door similar to that used on Sierras. There was also a new sportside box and an available Sport suspension. The five-speed manual transmission used with the base 2.2-liter four was revised to operate more smoothly and quietly. The Vortec V-6 was revised and ABS braking was made standard on 2.2-liter models.

A Highrider sport package with higher-ground clearance, a beefy chassis, and graphics was new to the Jimmy's options list. At midyear, a five-speed manual transmission was offered for the two-door model. Also new was a Vortec 4300-engine upgrade, a brake-transmission interlock system, long-life coolant, an integrated vehicle control module, and standard daytime-running lights.

and Dark Toreador Red. In addition to twin air bags, an air bag-suppression switch was added so that a rear-facing child-safety seat could be used in the front-passenger seat. A new vehicle-control module managed the HVAC functions better to decrease fan noise and coolant temperatures and to increase economy of operation. Engines included a 200-hp Vortec 4300 V-6, a 230-hp Vortec 5000 V-8, a 255-hp Vortec 5700 V-8, a 180-hp 6.5-liter turbo diesel V-8, and a 290-hp Vortec 7400 V-8, all with evaporative-emissions improvements. Commercial versions of the two-wheel-drive Sierra 3500 were prepared for bi-fuel use to run on either gasoline or natural gas.

A passenger-side air bag was also fitted to Suburbans, which offered all the same engines except the V-6 and smallest V-8. All K1500 gas-engined versions had front-suspension revisions that produced a tighter-turn circle for improved handling. An optional electronic transfer-case shift mechanism made it easier to shift modes and eliminated a floor-mounted shift lever on four-wheel-drive models. There were air-conditioning improvements and a convenient door-lock switch was placed in the rear.

The Yukon had many of the same upgrades as Suburbans, such as dual air bags, improved handling, easier four-wheel-drive operation, a rear door-lock switch, better air conditioning, and the same new colors. Engines were basically the same offered for the Suburban, but the turbo diesel was limited to Yukon two doors with four-wheel drive. In January 1997, Pontiac-GMC announced plans to build a new upscale SUV derived from the Yukon. The GMC Yukon Denali was slated for introduction in the spring of 1998.

For the Sonoma, GMC continued to promote the third door, Sport suspension, and sportside box introduced in 1996. The 2.2-liter four-cylinder engine got an improved starter motor. Four-wheel-drive models had a new weight-cutting front half-shaft design, with a fluid drain plug added to the differential case.

Key features of 1997 Jimmys included an available power sunroof, optional leather-seating areas, a CD player, and choices of two-wheel drive, Insta-Trac four-wheel drive, or all-wheel drive, two- or four-door bodies, and lift gates or tailgates. A new endgame design for four-door models featured a large lift gate to provide easier access to the rear-load floor. In addition to getting the same four-wheel-drive system improvements as Sonomas, the Jimmy got a new ABS controller and four-wheel discs for four-door models with all-wheel drive. Another innovation was the use of aluminum calipers on the rear-disc brakes, replacing the former cast-iron drums to save a considerable amount of weight. An optional three-channel transmitter and trip computer package was designed to fit into an overhead console. Key fobs were also redesigned to feature clearer lock-and-unlock buttons and the console and floor shifter were integrated in combination with bucket seats on Jimmys with automatic transmission.

Safari vans got a luxury SLT trim option with gray or neutral leather seating, Euro-style stitching, and a folding armrest. A Gold Package added special aluminum wheels with gold ports and metallic gold decals. New items included an improved starter, new front half-shafts, new key fobs, and a three-channel transmitter that memorized the activation codes for up to three remote-controlled devices.

Savana vans, totally redesigned in 1996, got few updates in 1997. Chrome wheels were a new option. Engine choices were the same as those offered for Sierras.

A new line of medium-duty T55-T-85 forward-control tilt-cab trucks arrived in 1997 called the T-Series. These had 86-in. bbc cabs. The C-Series conventional cab was modified to have a two-and-three-quarter-inch-longer bbc measurement of 106.75 in. A new 5.7-liter center-point-injected gas V-8 was introduced, along with a new 6.5-liter GM diesel. Also available were a GM 6.0-liter 225-hp TBI V-8 and a 7.0-liter TBI V-8, an Isuzu 7.1-liter 6HE1TC diesel, and a Caterpillar 6.6-liter 3116 diesel.

This Fire Red with Quicksilver Metallic 1996 K1500 Sierra SLE Club Coupe pickup was available with a new passenger-side access panel called simply the third door. (© General Motors Corp.)

Three all-new 1997 GMC medium-duty trucks are shown here with C-Series conventional (left and center) and T-Series tilt-cab (right) styling and construction. (© General Motors Corp.)

Innovative service with a personal touch designed to achieve customer enthusiasm was a big initiative at Pontiac-GMC after the merger. To enhance GMC's image as GM's premium brand of trucks, complimentary oil changes at 3,000 miles, 24-7 premium roadside assistance, courtesy shuttles for same-day warranty service, and travel-planning benefits were offered to GMC buyers.

Calendar-year sales of light-duty GMCs, including W4s, came to 447,971 units in 1997. The addition of 19,566 medium-duty trucks brought the total to 467,537, for a 7.1-percent increase from 1996. Model-year sales included 450,613 light-duty trucks and 19,235 medium-duty models. The total of 469,848 was a 2.2-percent gain over the previous year and virtually even with 1995. However, since the truck market was booming, with car companies like Oldsmobile joining in with trucks and SUV models, GMC's share of the total market fell to 6.9 percent.

1998: Premium Lineup

In 1998, GM reorganized to a structure like that of Saturn Corp. This reduced the autonomy and independent-marketing functions of the five divisions. Pontiac-GMC General Manager Roy S. Roberts was promoted to vice president and general manager of field sales for a new VSSM (Vehicles, Sales, Service, and Marketing) staff. In October, International Operations (IO) and North American Operations (NAO) were consolidated to create a new Automotive Operations (AO) arm. G. Richard Wagoner, Jr., became its head, as well as GM's president and chief operating officer. Marketing general managers were in charge of each division. Lynn C. Myers was appointed Pontiac-GMC general manager.

Myers took over at a time that was particularly critical for the GMC brand, since the launch of the first all-new Sierra pickup in 11 years was scheduled for model-year 1999. "There was no mistaking the significance of the Silverado/Sierra to GM's future," said the 1998 *Ward's Automotive Yearbook*. *Ward's* pointed out that GMC was

tripling its advertising budget for the Sierra and had secured a starring role for it in the motion picture, *Lethal Weapon 4*, featuring Mel Gibson.

Myers had also played a "starring" role in launching two midyear-1998 models that were introduced as the 1999 Envoy and 1999 Yukon Denali. While only available for part of the year, these helped to raise model-year sales of all GMC and Pontiac light-duty trucks (including domestic- and foreign-built W4s and Pontiac Trans Sports and Montanas) to 530,132 units, compared to 511,758 in 1997.

Running down the product line, the "1988-style" Sierra was in its final days and had only very minor changes for 1998. The size of the driver's-side air bag was reduced to make deployment safer. Optional for the two-wheel-drive 2500 regular cab was a bi-fuel engine that could run on gasoline and compressed natural gas (CNG). The truck operated on CNG, as long as there was fuel in the cylinder, but if CNG pressure fell below 240 psi, the system switched automatically to gas. Also new were rear-floor heaters for extended-cab models.

As in the last redesign cycle of 1987-1988, the Suburban was to be changed after the new Sierra arrived. However, this time GMC was only going to wait a year before introducing the new version as a 2000 model. Since that was two years down the road, the Suburban introduced in January 1998 was promoted as a 1999 model to get around government rules. It had only a few revisions. GM's OnStar navigational system was a new option. The 6.5-liter diesel V-8 got some minor improvements and the Autotrac push-button shift-transfer case was made standard equipment on four-wheel-drive models.

GMC introduced the new 1999 Yukon early in January 1998. As with the Suburban, this allowed GM to avoid fines for failing to meet 1998 CAFE (Corporate Average Fuel Economy) requirements. The "1999" came only in a four-door model and an Autotrac electronically controlled transfer case was standard on four-wheel-drive versions.

The 4L60-E Hydra-Matic had enhancements that increased power train stiffness to reduce vibration and noise. An electronically controlled clutch increased fuel economy while maintaining drivability. Transmission efficiency was improved by software that compared engine and vehicle operating parameters and set precise transmission line pressure accordingly. The transmission also had a deeper oil pan to improve overall transmission durability and fluid life.

In 1999, Yukon buyers eagerly awaited the luxury version of the full-size sport-utility vehicle, to be named Yukon Denali. It took its name from Denali National Park and Preserve in Alaska, the home of the highest mountain in North America, Mt. McKinley. The word "Denali," means "the high one" in the language of the native Athabascan people and refers to Mt. McKinley's south peak that rises 20,230 feet above sea level.

Then Yukon Brand Manager Denny O'Donnell described the model as one that took premium SUVs "to new heights in luxury, styling, and content." It had a distinctive front end, with a rectangular port grille, and a host of creature comforts, convenience features, and technical enhancements that justified its $44,035 price tag. A Bose Acoustimass sound system and OnStar navigation were standard, along with a 255-hp Vortec 5700 V-8 with 330 lbs.-ft. of torque.

Exterior-styling changes for the redesigned mid-size Jimmy included revised front-and-rear fascias and front bumper. Less-powerful air bags were adopted. The climate-control system was improved and four-wheel antilock brakes now used the all-disc system. Derived from the 1997 show truck, the Envoy was a $34,650 luxury version of the Jimmy. Its standard equipment included high-intensity discharge headlights, a Bose music system, leather seating, electronically controlled four-wheel-drive system, a luxury-ride suspension, and an automatic load-leveling system. It even had a compressed-air port in the cargo area. The Envoy fit the growing need for a GMC entry to the compact sport-utility market.

Sonoma got a rear-step bumper that gave all models a smoother, more integrated new look. A redesigned instrument panel included less forceful "next-generation" air bags, a new gauge cluster, a backlit-headlamp switch, and radio and HVAC controls angled toward the driver. Air conditioning, seating, and braking systems were improved and four-wheel disc brakes became standard on four-wheel-drive models. A 120-hp Vortec 2200 four-cylinder engine was standard with two-wheel drive and the Vortec 175-hp 4300 V-6 was standard in four-wheel-drive models and optional in others.

The least changed 1998 GMC models were the compact and full-size vans. The headline in GMC news releases was that the Safari brand was sponsoring Detroit's Continental indoor soccer league team to connect with "soccer" families. Still, the Hydra-Matic was tweaked to give better gas mileage and the SLT offered a new leather seating option in pewter gray or neutral colors. The button for the Dutch Door option was moved from the instrument panel to the lower edge of the rear hatch.

Savana had the new smaller air bags, with a standard passenger-side bag. Also, a new steering wheel housed the driver's-side air bag. GM's PassLock theft-deterrent system became standard. Use of the proper key triggered a control module to keep sending fuel to the engine. If the code didn't match, fuel delivery would be disabled for ten minutes. Savanas also got new rear seat belts, a new 195-hp version of the 6.5-liter turbo diesel V-8, and a new diesel-fuel gauge.

Model-year sales of GMC medium-duty trucks increased to 21,031 units this year, up from 19,235 in 1997, but still at the same 7.3 percent share of the total market. The distinction between a light-duty truck and a medium-duty model continued to get blurrier. Some of the larger "light-duty" models were now being counted as

The 1998 Sierras—like this K1500 Sportside—were the last in a styling cycle and had very minor changes. A smaller driver's side air bag made deployment safer.
(© General Motors Corp.)

medium-duty or "mid-range" trucks. On the other hand, sales of the Isuzu-designed W4 Forwards, which were built both here and in Japan, were counted with light-duty truck sales.

The W6 and W7 Forwards, which had both been dropped in 1997, came back for 1998. The truck lines and cab types were again the 72-in. bbc Forward medium-duty tilt cab; the 67.9-in. bbc Forward medium-duty tilt cab; the T55-T85 86-in. medium-duty tilt cab; the C series 106.75-in. conventional cab (in C55 or C85 series), the C-series special-equipment crew cab, and the B7 bus and commercial chassis and cowl. GVWRs for medium-duty trucks ranged from 18,000 to 61,000 lbs. Thirteen wheelbases, from 133- to 259-in., were available on "C" models.

For these trucks, there were three new or reissued engines, in addition to all six truck engines offered in 1997. Added were a GM 7.4-liter MFI gas V-8, a 7.2-liter Caterpillar 3126 turbo diesel V-8, and an Isuzu 7.8-liter D-1 turbo diesel V-6. The CAT engine was available with 11 different power and torque ratings, from 175 to 300 gross bhp.

1999: Do One Thing. Do It Well.

During 1999, truck sales reached 48.5 percent of the total U.S. motor-vehicle market. That was a .8-percent gain from 1998 and suggested that at least half of the vehicles sold in 2000 would be trucks. Pontiac-GMC and GM Truck Group wanted to take advantage of this trend by emphasizing their image as a builder of quality, premium trucks. The slogan selected to get the concept across was "Do one thing. Do it well."

The year's banner attraction was an all-new Sierra pickup, the first fruit of the GMT800 revision of full-size, light-duty trucks and SUVs. GM committed between $4 billion and $5 billion to the program, which would eventually create more than 40 models to sell. The trucks featured hydroformed frames made in Magna, Inc.'s, St. Thomas, Ontario, Canada factory. Box-shaped modules replaced full-length frame rails and could be arranged in various ways to make different models. By using four front modules, four midsections, and two rear-frame modules, 14 new trucks were developed for 1999. Later, other modules were added to produce 26 additional models. This technology reduced the time needed to build or update trucks and made different models more distinct.

Sierra Brand Manager Jim Kornas said the new design was the end result of "listening to our customers, then engineering their requirements into the design." The new Sierra was said to have "honest truck styling," which meant that there wasn't a drastic change from the previous look, although the front end was smoother and curvier. A black, trapezoid-shaped grille carried the ruby red GMC logo. New composite headlamps incorporated the parking lamps and turn signals into a broader, single wraparound unit. The step-in height was lowered and 16-in. wheels were used. Wet-arm windshield wiper blades were new.

Both standard and extended-cab models had more interior room. A third door was standard on the passenger side, which also had "best-in-class" rear seat legroom and a wider rear seat-back angle. The cargo-box volume of both the wideside- and sportside-body styles had additional

According to an October 15, 1997, GMC press release the 1998 GMC Envoy was a four-door, $34,650 luxury version of the Jimmy derived from a 1997 concept truck. (© General Motors Corp.)

New styling graced the all-new 1999 GMC Sierra pickups. This is the C2500 3/4-ton version with an extended cab and Wideside box. (© General Motors Corp.)

volume. Built-in slots were provided so lumber could be used to secure cargo in place. Both styles had stake pockets at all four corners, built-in tie-down brackets near all four corners and pocket shelves to provide two-tier loading. Integrated tail lamps were used with wideside boxes. The sportside's contoured rear fenders were made of composite materials.

A new Vortec 4800 V-8 replaced the Vortec 5000, but had 255 hp, 25 more than before. Also new was an optional 270-hp Vortec 5300 V-8. Truck buyers with heavy-duty hauling in mind could opt for a Vortec 6000 V-8 with 300 hp. Another new technical feature was four-wheel antilock brakes. Available automatic transmissions featured a "tow/haul" mode that raised shift point speeds when a button on the end of the range selector lever was pushed.

Full-size Sierras with GVWs more than 8,500 lbs. were called Sierra Classics because they used the old body and ladder-type chassis. These trucks were made in Mexico. Carryover models included the Sierra1500 short-box, extended-cab pickups and all previous 2500 and 3500 models with GVWs above 8,500 lbs.

The Suburban was considered a continuation of the "1999" model, introduced in January 1998. About the only changes were three new colors called Topaz Gold Metallic, Meadow Green Metallic, and Storm Gray Metallic. The Yukon and Denali were also considered "continuation" models with no major changes, except for the same new colors the Suburban offered.

Sonoma compact pickups got next-generation air bags in 1999, larger side mirrors, and a standard AutoTrac transfer case on four-wheel-drive versions. A theft alarm was now included with the optional remote keyless-entry system. Heated-power mirrors were a new option.

Jimmys and Envoys got next-generation air bags, AutoTrac, and a transmission shift-preference selector (for four-door models). The Jimmy offered upgraded premium radios with steering-wheel controls, a re-tuned Euro-ride suspension, and available power passenger seat and power memory driver seat.

A customized look with Silvermist "plastic" body cladding had proved popular with Safari buyers, so GMC offered this cosmetic upgrade in three new colors called Topaz Gold Metallic, Bronzemist, and Medium Dark Teal for 1999. Also available were running boards that integrated with the cladding. SLT-type mirrors were made standard, new aluminum wheels were seen and four-wheel-drive models had a new AutoTrac transfer case.

Savana vans featured automatic transmission modifications for increased durability and two new-for-1999 exterior colors called Fernmist Green and Dark Bronzemist. Inside, Dark Pewter was a new interior color.

There were also very few changes in the medium-duty truck lineup, with GM Truck Group offering the same series, truck lines, and cab types in the GMC-badged model range. Engine offerings dropped from nine to eight. Gone were the GM 6.0-liter and 7.0-liter TBI gasoline V-8, but a second LP4 option based on the GM 7.4-liter MFI gasoline V-8 was added. Medium-duty sales for the model-year rose to 23,627 units, but that did not include 3,794 W4 Forwards that fall into the light-duty category or the large Sierra 3500s considered medium-duties.

Total model-year sales of trucks by the Pontiac-GMC Division, including Pontiac Trans Sport and Montana mini vans was 585,465 units for a steady 7.3 percent share of the total market. It was the third year in a row that GMC trucks broke a half million. Calendar-year totals were 606,050 or a 7.4 percent share.

Chapter 9

The New Millennium

2000-2002

2000: The Right Tool for the Job

GMC entered the new millennium as the official sponsor of the U.S. Olympic team. The division had its sights set on the gold medal for first place in the truck market. Its 2000 GMC Product Guide to Professional Grade Trucks said, "Reputations are not born overnight—they are justly earned as people measure expectations against experience. Over the course of nearly a century, GMC vehicles have earned a reputation as professional grade vehicles that serious truck owners recognize as, quite simply, the right tools for the job."

Last year's new Sierra pickup truck was unaltered, but the Sierra K1500s had a new wheel-flare option. Both rear doors were hinged at the back of the cab, which made it easy to get in and out of the truck. The optional Vortec 4800 V-8 was upped to 270 hp and the Vortec 5300 engine was also boosted to 285 hp and 325 lbs.-ft. of torque. Programmable automatic door locks were added to the list of extras and the new-style Sierra series was expanded to include models with GVWs over 8,500 lbs.

Sierra Classic was again the name applied to the large 2000 pickups with the same styling as 1988-1998 models. This series still offered regular, extended-cab, and crew-cab styles, but no longer came in the SL-, SLT-, and SLE-trim levels. For comparison, the Sierra Classic C2500 two-door extended cab on a 131.5-in. wheelbase was base priced at $21,935. The new Sierra C2500 SL three-door extended cab on a 157.5-in. wheelbase was base-priced at $25,439.

The GMC Suburban got GMT800 styling and a new name. It was now called the Yukon XL to make it distinctive from its Chevrolet counterpart. The body was stiffer and stronger than the previous model to improve its ride and handling characteristics. The front end was designed using extra hydroformed-frame modules and was said to interact better with passenger cars in a collision. The new,

two- or four-wheel-drive model was available in SLE or SLT trim. The Yukon XL could seat up to nine passengers or provide 131.6 cu. ft. of cargo space, with the second seat folded flat and the third seat removed. The base engine was a Vortec 5300 with 285 hp at 2500 rpm and 325 lbs.-ft. of torque at 4000 rpm. The least expensive version was $35,178.

The regular Yukon was also new for 2000. It was wider and roomier than the 1999 edition and came in two- or four-wheel drive, four-door SLE, or SLT models. The upscale Denali stayed on the previous 117.5-in. wheelbase and at 201.2 in. was also 1.4 in. longer than the other 2000 models. Agile handling was provided by a suspension with torsion bars up front, five-link coil springs in the rear, and self-leveling shock absorbers. A 50/50 third seat was now available for nine-passenger seating. Standard side-impact air bags in front, a driver message center, and programmable automatic door locks were other new features. Prices ranged from $32,402 for the 1500 series SLE to $44,210 for the Denali.

New features for 2000 Sonoma compact pickups were mainly under the hood. Four-wheel-drive versions got a hotter 190-hp Vortec 4300 V-6. A handling-and-trailering suspension that cost extra in 1999 was now standard. At midyear, all two-wheel-drive models with the base 2.2-liter four were alternative-fuel compatible. Sonoma prices began at $13,124.

GMC's compact SUV came in two- and four-door Jimmy and four-door Envoy models on 100.5- and 107-in. wheelbases, respectively. Both body styles offered two- or four-wheel drive, but the $34,820 Envoy was strictly a 4-x-4 model. Jimmy prices started at $19,620 and ranged to $32,120 for a 30th-anniversary Diamond Edition with a grille guard, side steps, and interior upgrades.

The passenger version of the midsize Safari van received a standard third-row seat that increased passenger capacity to seven or eight, depending on the overall seating configuration. A 190-hp "enhanced" Vortec 4300 V-6 was the only engine. The automatic transmission was revised and a new composite gas tank increased fuel load to 27 gallons.

Valve trains in the full-sized Savana vans were improved for better quality, reliability, durability and quieter operation. New features included a rear window defogger, top-mounted child seat tether anchors, and increased trailer-towing capacity. A 200-hp Vortec 4300 V-6 was standard, but Vortec 5000, Vortec 5700, and Vortec 7400 V-8s were available at extra cost, as was a 6.5-liter turbo diesel.

In the medium-duty GMC lineup, once again a revised range of engines was the primary change. C-Series engines included the Vortec 7400 MD V-8 gas with either 210 or 270 hp and the CAT 3126B inline 6 diesel with ratings from 175 to 300 hp. The T-Series offered the Duramax 7800 diesel with 200 or 230 hp in addition to the CAT 3126B. The GM-built 6.5-liter turbo diesel V-8 and the Isuzu 7.1-liter 6HE1TC turbo diesel were dropped and not replaced.

The GMC Suburban got GMT8000 styling and a new name. For added distinction from its Chevy brother, it was now called the Yukon XL. This example has four-wheel drive and SLT trim. (© General Motors Corp.)

For the show circuit of 2000, GMC thrilled the public with a high-tech glimpse of the future in a robotic-looking concept truck called the Terradyne which featured GMC's design direction, "industrial precision" and a number of functional "professional grade" features that exceeded expectations.

2001: Professional Grade

2001 was quite simply a watershed year for GMC with an unprecedented introduction of seven all-new trucks—Yukon Denali and XL Denali, Sierra heavy-duty and C³ pickups, Envoy, Sonoma Crew Cab, and Savana SLT. The Sierra C³ was the world's first 1/2-ton extended cab pickup with all-wheel-drive. The "C" stood for "centennial" and the little "3" stood for "third generation."

The $38,305 C³ was designed to cut across GVW and trim levels. In addition to monochromatic paint, a distinctive frontal treatment and a leather-trimmed interior, the C³ also included many features that resulted in segment-leading on-road performance and control. Dubbed Performance Biased Driveline, content included a 325-hp Vortec 6000 V-8, four-speed automatic transmission, and all-wheel drive. Four-wheel disc brakes with twin-piston calipers and an advanced suspension included specially tuned gas-charged shocks and a weight-distributing heavy-duty trailering kit was standard.

Also added to the Sierra lineup was a new GMT800-style heavy-duty pickup series, which set a new standard for heavy-duty truck power, payload, and pulling. The 2500HD and 3500 HD models offered a wide range of two- and four-wheel-drive trucks in regular-, extended-, and crew-cab formats, as well as cab-and-chassis models. These could be ordered with a standard 300-hp Vortec 6000 V-8, a new 340-hp Vortec 8100 V-8, or a new 300-hp Duramax 6600 V-8 turbo diesel sired by a joint venture with Isuzu. Transmission options included a ZF six-speed manual gearbox or an Allison five-speed automatic, with a $2,295 price tag!

A Yukon XL Denali was introduced in 2001. Among the standard features on both the Yukon and Yukon XL Denali models were all-wheel-drive; a 320-hp Vortec 6000 V-8 engine; a new electronically controlled heavy-duty four-speed automatic transmission with GM's exclusive driver-controlled tow/haul mode; computer-controlled Autoride shock damping; 17-in. brushed-aluminum wheels and Michelin cross-terrain touring tires; a Bose Acoustimass 11-speaker music system with an in-dash 6-CD changer; a Driver Information Center; and OnStar system. All 2500 Yukon XL models were available with the Vortec 8100 V-8.

Why change a good thing? The photo of an Indigo Blue over Pewter four-door Jimmy SLT in the 2001 GMC product guide looked the same as the one in the previous year's guide. The reason, as *AMI Auto World* put it in its September 12, 2000 issue, was that "the Jimmy name will be struck from the GM lexicon entirely."

The plan was to drop the two-door Jimmy in December 2000 and bring an end to all Jimmy production in June of 2001, so there was little reason to change the 2001 models.

However, the Envoy—previously based on the 107-in. wheelbase four-door Jimmy—was in for a change...and a big one!

Introduced in the spring of 2001 as a 2002 model, the all-new Envoy was designed as a mid-size SUV that was larger, roomier, and much more comfortable than the Jimmy. It came only as a five-door, five-passenger model with a 113-in. wheelbase and 191.6-in. overall length. It was offered in cloth SLE trim or as an SLT with leather and wood trim. An extended version with a third-row seat was planned.

Envoy brand manager Tony DiSalle said Envoy was created with three "pillars of excellence" in mind. They were: 1) Interior roominess and thoughtful design for greater driver and passenger comfort, 2) A full complement of comfort features and amenities to make it one of the most accommodating SUVs in its class, and 3) an exceptionally smooth, comfortable ride no matter what the road conditions. Under the hood was a new 270-hp Vortec 4200 inline six. Engineers used the latest technology in this all-new engine to make it smooth and quiet at idle or when accelerating.

GMC's 2002 Envoy was an instant it. It won equal raves from customers and automotive critics, such as *BusinessWeek* writer David Welch, who compared Envoy to Ford's Explorer. He wrote, "I like the Envoy better. It handles just as well as the Explorer, but has a better engine and drinks a little less gasoline. Plus, the Envoy looks more contemporary."

New for the 2001 Sonoma was a Crew-Cab model with four full-size, forward-hinged doors. It featured graphite-toned fabric front-bucket seats, a rear-bench seat, center and overhead consoles, and a 190-hp Vortec 4300 V-6 with four-wheel drive or 180 hp with two-wheel drive. The Insta-Trac four-wheel-drive system and a factory-installed liner to protect the 55.2-in.-long cargo bed were standard. A bed extender was available for big-job capacity and a maximum payload of 1,111 lbs. A driver-friendly interior had radio and HVAC controls angled 15 degrees toward the driver for greater accessibility.

Valve trains in the full-sized 2000 Savana were improved for quality, reliability, durability, and quieter operation. Here's a short-wheelbase conversion van version.
(© General Motors Corp.)

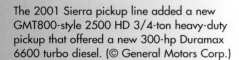
The 2001 Sierra pickup line added a new GMT800-style 2500 HD 3/4-ton heavy-duty pickup that offered a new 300-hp Duramax 6600 turbo diesel. (© General Motors Corp.)

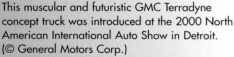
This muscular and futuristic GMC Terradyne concept truck was introduced at the 2000 North American International Auto Show in Detroit. (© General Motors Corp.)

In other Sonoma news, the Vortec 2200 four-cylinder engine offered the option of running on gas or a fuel comprised of gasoline and up to 85 percent ethanol. A third door became standard equipment on all extended cab models. Rich Johnson tested a GMC Sonoma High-Rider extended cab for a week and wrote about it in the November 7, 2000 issue of *AMI Auto World*. He found the V-6-powered pickup "sporty and sexy" and capable of 0 to 60 mph in 9.9 sec. with 16-21-mpg fuel economy. "This is a little truck that can do a big truck's work," he said. "It fits easily in the garage, sips fuel, brings a grin to your face while driving and carries heavy loads without fussing. That's what the world has needed and GMC has delivered."

Savana SLT was GMC's new-for-2001 full-size luxury passenger van. Some of its standard features included seven-passenger walk-through seating, a Bose premium sound system with CD, a Home-Link three-channel universal remote (for opening garage doors, etc.), two flip-down video monitors, rear air conditioning, and heated-exterior mirrors. Other Savanas shared the SLT's full-length box-frame construction and offered a choice of two wheelbases and five different engines. All models came standard with four-wheel antilock brakes. Unfortunately, due to a dramatic drop in demand for full-size conversion vans, production of the Sarana SLT ended in December 2001.

Safari vans had enhancements to their Vortec 4300 V-6 including a new power train-control module located on the intake manifold that saved weight and wiring connections. Also, a more sophisticated detonation sensor was designed to reduce engine knock. GMC repackaged its equipment choices into three preferred equipment groups containing 34 distinct features as standard equipment or options. For 2001, there were two-passenger-van trim levels—SLE and SLT.

GMC's 2001 trucks quite literally offered trucks for many different types of buyers by building in capabilities that exceeded customers' expectations. The product line appealed to a wide range of people from home-improvement expert and Sierra owner Michael Holigan, to show-dog enthusiasts and Yukon owners Joel and Genevera Koonce, to television chef and Yukon XL owner Keith Famie.

Michael Holigan had hauled many loads of lumber while building thousands of homes in the Dallas, Texas, and Nashville, Tennessee, areas. That was before he made an infomercial that eventually led to his GMC-sponsored, nationally syndicated "Your New House" program on the Discovery Channel. In addition to his red Sierra extended-cab pickup, Holigan said he owned a Yukon XL. His wife Debbie traded in her Mercedes-Benz for her own Yukon XL.

The Koonces, of Wayzata, Minnesota, needed to take their award-winning Labrador show dogs to Chicago and

Canada. Joel convinced Genevera to buy a GMC Yukon by pointing out how practical it was for carrying their three 90-lb. dogs Rocky, Reggie, and McCoy. "We have a lot of fun traveling to the different shows," she said. "And thanks to the Yukon, we get there safely."

Keith Famie, a Detroit chef and contestant on "Survivor: The Australian Outback," also had plans to travel a lot. His flame-decorated, bright-orange Yukon XL—which he nicknamed "Max" after a favorite dog of his—carried 800 lbs. of cooking gear and camping equipment for his GMC-sponsored television cooking show "Famie's Adventures in Cooking." Keith's plan was to travel the country and the globe as an international-gourmet chef living up to the slogan painted on his truck: "You really haven't been there until you've eaten the food." Thanks to "Max," Famie could cook anything, anywhere. GMC helped outfit the Yukon XL with Denali trim and 18 special devices including a retractable-cooking center.

2002: Beyond the First 100 Years

Making the rounds of the auto shows in 2001 was a unique vehicle that carried the GMC brand beyond its first 100 years in concepts for the future. The five-passenger GMC Terracross SUV of Tomorrow was promoted as "part sport utility and part truck and all innovation." GMC's brand character chief designer Carl Zipfel described its appearance as continuing the "industrial precision" styling introduced on the Terradyne concept truck, which debuted a year earlier.

The concept truck's features included a glass roof and mid-gate that could be reconfigured to transform the Terracross from an SUV into a full-function pickup or a five-passenger convertible. Inside was an instrument panel that could be customized to the driver's personal tastes. The front-passenger seat swiveled to face the rear passengers for business or social interaction and a laptop computer with cellular modem was provided for the front-seat passenger.

In addition to the OnStar system, the Terracross featured a 3.4-liter transverse-mounted V-6 and four-speed automatic transmission. It rode on 19-in. tires and came with a sure-footed Versatrak all-wheel-drive system. There was also a sound system that could handle cassettes, CDs, or digital-music files from a Sony "Memory Stick" flash-memory device.

"Just as last year's Terradyne concept represents GMC's vision for the ultimate 'professional grade' pickup, Terracross creates an innovative type of SUV, designed to exceed the expectations of the most demanding customers," said Pontiac-GMC General Manager Lynn Myers.

While GMC was making no claims that the Terradyne or Terracross would be coming to dealerships soon, one has to believe that they embody the future vision of a truck builder with a 100-year history of excellence and innovation.

GMC expanded its Professional Grade lineup with a series of uniquely designed and competitively superior trucks for 2002 and beyond. "Our lineup of professional-grade products is growing year by year," said Lynn Myers, Pontiac-GMC general manager. "What began with our light-duty Sierra pickup in 1999 and has continued through to our latest entry, the all-new Envoy, will continue in 2002 and beyond."

The new Sierra Denali debuted in the fall of 2001 as a 2002 model. Sierra Denali featured the amazing control of the full-size truck industry's first-ever four-wheel-steering system, called Quadrasteer. With such a phenomenal feature in place, it was only natural for Sierra C^3 to evolve to Sierra Denali. The Denali name, which was used on the upscale Yukon Denali, became synonymous with the pinnacle of GMC models. The automotive press lauded the Sierra Denali with Quadrasteer as a "game changer" in the pickup-truck market. Jerry Flint of *Forbes* magazine praised it, writing, "I saw a miracle. GM's 4-wheel steering. I did figure eights with a giant travel trailer behind my pickup truck. It was amazing. I mean, figure eights. I did sharp lane changes, no quiver, no nothing. I didn't side swipe anyone."

Another new Sierra model, the Sierra Professional, also came to market as a 2002 model. Sierra Professional provided the ultimate in work capability because it could be turned into a mobile office; and alternative fuel models could be ordered either with bi-fuel capability or as a dedicated compressed natural-gas vehicle. It came in a choice of four models and helped contractors, landscape architects, and other professionals to increase their productivity by allowing them to carry equipment and even convert their vehicles into mobile workstations.

In sport-utility vehicles for 2002, an all-new seven-passenger Envoy XL, with segment-leading performance and comfort, included the industry's first factory-installed DVD rear-seat entertainment system. The third-row seat comfortably accommodated two adults at up to 6'2" and 200 pounds each. It set a new standard for roominess by providing more first- and second-row head, shoulder, and hip room than most competitors.

The GMC Terracross Concept truck debuted at the 2001 North American International Auto Show in Detroit. (© General Motors Corp.)

Chapter 10

Buses and Coaches

Used on a route between Memphis and Kerrville, Tenn., thus Yellow Coach Model X is a type of bus that was sold from 1925 to 1928. (OCWC)

A 1924 Yellow Coach Model Z double-deck bus operated by New York City's Fifth Avenue Coach Co. on Riverside Drive in upper Manhattan. (OCWC)

Right: Four Yellow Coach Type W 17-passenger parlor coaches from a fleet operated by Wisconsin Power & Light Co. headquartered in Madison, Wis. The buses are of 1927-1929 vintages. They sold for about $6,200 and had Cadillac V-8 engines. (WPL/AE)

In the mid-1920s, General Motors decided that it should get into the rapidly growing business of making buses or, as GM preferred to call them, coaches. Automakers such Studebaker, of South Bend, Indiana, and Pierce-Arrow, of Buffalo, New York, had done quite well by expanding into the manufacturing of coaches. A number of market studies indicated that GM could generate profits in this field. By 1924, GMC had the Model X "Bob Tail Coach" on the market. It was styled like a large sedan on a long, long wheelbase with individual doors for each row of passenger seats.

To make its entry into bus building a smoother and more successful one, General Motors Truck Co. engineered a merger with Yellow Motor Coach Manufacturing, a Chicago, Illinois, company. John D. Hertz—later famous for his Hertz rental cars—was president of Yellow Motor Coach. Hertz started with taxicabs, but later became interested in buses. He obtained the Chicago Motor Bus Co. and its manufacturing arm the American Motor Bus Co., as well as New York City's Fifth Avenue Coach Co. Hertz set up a holding company called The Omnibus Corp.

In April 1923, Hertz established Yellow Coach Manufacturing Co., as a new subsidiary of Chicago Yellow Cab. Some experimental work was done at the old American Motor Bus Co. factory and, in August, a new factory on Dickens Avenue, in Chicago, was opened. The first Yellow Coach double-decker transit bus—the Type Z-200—was built there. Production hit 150 in 1923 and more than 700 in 1924. According to the book, *Modern Intercity Coaches*, by Larry Plachno, Yellow Coach started advertising its buses before the end of 1923 and received large orders from Philadelphia and the New Jersey Public Service Co. In 1926, the company made an all-time record 1,700 buses.

Yellow Coach was America's largest-bus builder, with about 33 percent of the market, while GM was its largest automaker with a 30 percent market share. In 1925, General Motors bought control of Yellow Motor Coach from Hertz and his associates for $16 million. Yellow Truck & Coach Manufacturing Co., a holding company, evolved out of Hertz's deal. Yellow acquired the stock of General Motors Truck Co. and General Motors Truck Corp. in exchange for giving GM controlling interest in Yellow Truck & Coach.

Also making history in 1925 was GMC's introduction of the Model Y Yellow Coach, a handsome bus that resembled a railroad parlor car. Wheelbases between 185 in. and 225 in. were offered. It was the earliest of a long line of GMC highway coaches and all but a few featured a sleeve-valve engine (built by the Yellow Sleeve Valve Engine Works division of Yellow Truck & Coach Manufacturing Co.), leather seats, window curtains, rooftop ventilation, and a rooftop-luggage rack. Large shock absorbers near the front bumper helped reduce bouncing and jarring.

From 1925-1936, General Motors Truck Co. was a sales subsidiary of Yellow Truck & Coach. General Motors Truck Corp. was the manufacturing subsidiary. During the late 1920s, a big step in the evolution of Yellow Coaches was the "Safety-Coach" design. Buses of this type featured a low center of gravity, more powerful engines, improved air brakes, and road shock absorbers. Pneumatic tires were adopted to provide a softer, more-cushioned ride.

California led the way in use of long-distance buses called California stages. These stretched "taxicabs" serviced many areas in the state that didn't have rail lines. One of the state's largest operators was the California Transit Co., which became part of Pacific Greyhound Lines. The company made its own buses and that branch became known as Pioneer Stage Manufacturing Co.

By 1927, bus business was booming. Riders could travel to all major cities in the U.S. by bus. During January 1928, GM opened a new truck and bus factory in Pontiac, Michigan. By midyear, all Yellow Coach sales and manufacturing departments were moved from Chicago to Pontiac. Hertz's Yellow Sleeve-Valve Engine Works was closed. Several GM divisions then began supplying engines for the buses. Some of the Yellow-Coach buses had Cadillac V-8 engines and others had six-cylinder Buick engines.

Many utility companies of this era operated bus lines and bought GMC-made Yellow coaches. In 1929, three brand-new Type-W Yellow Coaches were purchased for use on the "Orange Line" route that Wisconsin Power & Light Co. provided in southwestern Wisconsin. These 1929 Yellow Coaches—produced in Pontiac—were top-of-the-line buses designed specifically for over-the-road passenger-coach use. They were actually commercial versions of a Cadillac-passenger car using a Cadillac engine and modified-Cadillac chassis. Each bus was 24-ft. long with seats for 21 passengers. The rear end of one model—the Z-225—was similar to that of a railroad car, with an observation deck, awning, and scallops. Type W coaches had a plain, vertical-rear end.

WP&L workers outfitted the three new rigs at the

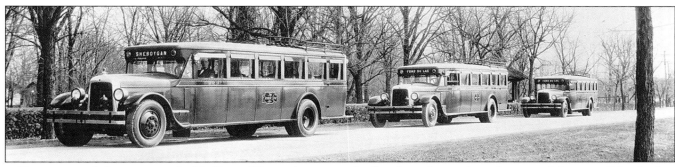

Left: Destined for the Wisconsin cities of Sheboygan and Fond du Lac, these 1928 GMC Type Y parlor coaches had six-cylinder engines and $11,000 price tags. They were operated by The Orange Line, a branch of Wisconsin Power & Light. (WPL/AE)

utility company's bus garage, in Madison, Wisconsin, on the morning of June 21, 1929. A promotion cooked up by the company's Traffic Department was for the buses to participate in an inaugural convoy traveling down Wisconsin Highway 19 while distributing oranges, timetables, and promotional materials. The slogan, "Have an Orange on The Orange Line," evolved from this sales campaign.

Walter Frautschi—of the Democrat Printing Co. in Madison—was invited to ride along on the bus trip as a guest. Frautschi (writing as "Walt Typeslinger") observed that "to float a big bus on a river of orange juice through 114-odd miles of dairy country probably would be worth seeing. And oranges enough there were. Oranges to the right of us, oranges to the left of us, the garage floor was covered and we weren't sure that we could find room enough in the cars for them."

The shiny GMC buses first stopped at Madison East Side High School to pick up the school band. They then set off through Verona, Blue Mounds, Barneveld, Dodgeville, and Mineral Point. Riders chucked oranges at farmers in the fields along the way and gave them away by the crate in small southwestern Wisconsin towns. "Mineral Point seemed to have an unnatural appetite for oranges," Frautschi wrote, "and plenty of rinds were left around as a problem for the street-cleaning department." Nobody along the route was likely to forget those new 1929 Yellow Coaches or the day they had oranges on The Orange Line.

One of the largest intercity-bus lines was operated by Greyhound, which started out as Motor Transit Co. Like other bus companies, Greyhound built some of its own coaches. It even purchased the H.E. Wilcox Motor Co. as a manufacturing arm and changed its name to C.H. Will Motors Corp. In 1929, Motor Transit Co. became associated with California Transit Co. and merged C.H. Will Motors Corp. with Pioneer Stages, though both operated separately.

C.H. Will was located in Minneapolis, Minnesota, near the birthplace of Greyhound Lines in Hibbing, Minnesota. It specialized in building models for Greyhound. After the merger with Pioneer Stages, a model called the "Pioneer-Will" was brought out. After 60 of these were made to order between 1929 and the summer of 1930, the Pioneer Stage plant in Oakland, California, was closed.

The Great Depression was making it hard for bus companies to build their own coaches. In November 1929, Yellow Coach and Greyhound inked a contract that called for Greyhound to underwrite part of the cost of developing new GMC buses made to Greyhound specifications. This deal led to the April 1935 introduction of a new model Z-250 intercity bus, which was based on the Will Stage Coach. Will continued to operate as Greyhound Motors & Supply Co. of Chicago, where Carl Will operated a bus overhauling and rebuilding plant for the company. In 1947, Will played a role in developing prototypes for the first GMC Scenicruiser buses.

Bus historian Larry Plachno—editor and publisher of *National Bus Trader*—describes the 1930s as "the greatest single decade of development for the intercity coach" and Yellow Coach remained the leader in the field in terms of both innovation and sales. New ideas coming out of Pontiac included the invention of angle drive, improved integral construction, and pioneering work with diesel power through GMC's Detroit Diesel Division. The use of rear-mounted engines and below-the-floor luggage compartments were other advances of this era.

The advantages of using a "pusher" engine layout were obvious, but engineers had struggled with how to get the short drive shafts used in rear-engine designs to work reliably. A man named Dwight E. Austin had resolved these problems by using a transverse engine and angle drive to the rear axle in his famous Pickwick Stages (large buses used on rural bus routes in the South). Austin's design also permitted lower floors and greater passenger capacity.

In 1934, Yellow Coach hired Austin. His engineering talents—along with the design genius of James J. St. Croix, who worked in the Yellow Coach Styling Section—were teamed up to create the new Model 719 Super Coach. This 1934 bus, developed jointly with Greyhound Lines, was the first "modern" intercity coach. It had a "flat-front" appearance, integral body-and-chassis construction, a rear engine, and under-the-floor luggage compartments.

There was another change in truck and bus operations in 1936, when Yellow Truck & Coach assumed the manufacturing responsibilities for all GMC trucks, tractors, trailers, taxicabs, and Yellow Coach buses. Sales activities were carried on by General Motors Truck & Coach, which was then considered a division of Yellow Truck & Coach Manufacturing Co., of Pontiac, Michigan.

A new, enclosed double-deck bus—the Model 720—was introduced in 1936. This model was sold to New York City's Fifth Avenue Coach Co. and was dubbed the "Queen Mary." The 1936 Model 736 transit bus was promoted as the first to use a diesel engine.

The use of Pontiac sheet metal on 1932 taxis, the Cadillac sheet metal on this 1933 Yellow Coach S-400 and the relocation of production facilities to Michigan were clear signs that General Motors was calling the shots at the former Chicago company, even though the Yellow Truck & Coach name was retained into the 1940s. (BDKC)

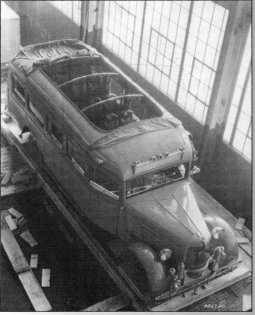

Another photo from the rail-shipping-methods study. Note that the wheels and U.S. Royal tires have been removed from the bus in this case, possibly to make it lower so that it could pass damage-free under bridges and trestles. (BDKC)

Union Bus Company, a part of Blue Bus Lines, operated this 1929 Yellow Coach Type W bus on special routes. "Tampa" appears above the driver's door, but the setting does not look like Florida. It has a body made by Lang. (OCWC)

Judging by their 1929 Wisconsin license plates, these are Yellow Type W models parked outside a Wisconsin Power & Light facility in Madison. The first bus on left ran to Madison, the center bus traveled to Dodgeville and the bus on the right took passengers to Dubuque, Iowa. (WPL/AE)

A restored 1929 GMC Coach formerly used by the Allington Moto Bus Co.

Diesel engine advancements were the big news of 1937. Yellow Coach and Detroit Diesel Division engineers started development of the "71" series of inline diesel engines, with 71 cu. in. in each cylinder. There were two-, three-, four-, and six-cylinder versions identified as the 2-71, 3-71, 4-71, and 6-71. These were two-cycle engines, based on a Winton automobile-engine design. GM preferred this type over the more fuel-efficient four-cycle designs that had lower power-to-weight ratios.

These engines came into use in 1937 buses, such as the new 743 (the basic Greyhound coach and the first with air conditioning), which was a follow up to the 719 Super Coach.

The 1938 Model 729 "hybrid" transit bus had a gasoline-fueled engine. Another 1938 milestone was the use of partial monocoque construction on new 1200 series buses. These were designed for intercity use and became Yellow Coach's top-of-the-line models. However, some 700 series models were built for both inner-city transit service and intercity use through 1941.

With its wide range of models and innovations, Yellow Coach commanded more than 55 percent of the bus market in the U.S. by 1939, but the many model designations became confusing to customers and a new system of descriptive coding was devised. The first letter indicated the type of bus, such as P for parlor coach (on intercity models) or T for transit bus. The second letter was a G for gas engine or a D for diesel engine. Sometimes there was a third letter, G for Greyhound or A for automatic transmission. Then came four numbers. The first two indicated model, series, and seating, and the last two indicated the sequence in the series. For instance, 02 would be the second model issued in the series.

The famous "silversides" bus design was first seen on a prototype displayed at the 1939-1940 New York World's Fair. This handsome model had fluted aluminum siding like many streamlined passenger trains of the era. During 1940 and the early World War II years, more than 500 transit buses per year were built. Some had steel bodies that were designed to conserve aluminum. The 1940 Model TDE-2501 was a diesel-electric model. In 1943, output fell to 100 buses before February, when the bus assembly line was converted to the production of amphibious military vehicles called DUKWs or "Ducks."

On October 1, 1943, the GMC Truck & Coach Division was formed after General Motors purchased the property and assets of Yellow Truck & Coach. On October 1, the Yellow Coach operation officially became a division of GM and buses made from that date on were described as GM or GMC coaches.

Some records show that the first General Motors transit coach was built in February 1944. At that time, motor coach production was controlled by the Office of Defense Transportation (ODT). With ODT and WPB (War Production Board) authorization, the company produced 397 PGA3702 models on an assembly line in the Pontiac Motor Division factory. This was followed by the production of 903 additional PD3302 and PDA3702 models in 1945.

In February 1945, diesel engines became available again. In that same year, single rub-rails replaced the double rails used on 1941-1944 models. The first GM diesel transit-bus model was the TD-4007. By July of 1945, Pontiac Motor Division was ready to start making Pontiac passenger cars again and military vehicle production in the Pontiac factory ended. Plans were made to move GM bus production back to its regular home at GMC's Pontiac, Michigan, plant. Unfortunately, a four-month strike throughout General Motors' divisions kept total production in 1946 down to a trickle. Due to the company-wide strike, only 1,100 TG-4007 and TD-4007 models were made between 1944-1946.

The TG-4007 and TD-4007 models were followed by the TDH-4008 and TDM-4008 models. The new third symbol in the model numbers, indicating "H" for Hydra-Matic or "M" for manual, was added in 1947. The two types of buses had square, lift-up windows and the upper windows for standing passengers to look through (used on most, but not all "4008" series buses) were round-cornered rectangles above the passenger windows. Since GMC was not building a true suburban coach in these years, some of the transit buses made without the upper windows were fitted with all forward-facing seats and overhead parcel racks. These were used as suburban coaches until 1949.

The first 65 examples of the TDH-4008 buses were delivered to the Union Street Railways and Louisville Kentucky Railways in 1946. The first TDM-4008s were delivered to New Jersey Public Service lines in May 1947. The 4008s were powered by a 165-hp version of the famous GM-built 6-71 diesel engine. They had a top speed of 53 mph, with a 2,000-rpm governor. The 4008 had basically the same steel-and-aluminum body as the 4007. It was a sturdy design and many of these buses remained in service more than a quarter of a century!

In 1946-1949, GMC Truck & Coach Division's full-model line up encompassed some 347 different body-and-chassis models in 78 different lines of trucks and buses. The country was starved for all kinds of vehicles and bus makers, like car manufacturers, had no time to develop new models. Prewar designs were put back in production and sold like crazy. GMC literally built a transit bus, parlor coach, or school bus for every purpose. Its favorite customer for big buses, Greyhound, alone ordered 2,000 intercity coaches.

Many GMC buses adopted the use of "Thermomatic" vents above their destination signs in November 1946. These were used on all models except small 27-, 31-, and 35-passenger coaches through 1953, when they became an option. People call buses without the option "baldies." In 1947, transit coaches got new recessed headlights that remained a GMC tradition until the release of the "New Look" series in 1959. Wider bumpers replaced the narrow spring-bar type in 1949 and a new suburban-coach model, with paired-passenger windows with sliding sashes, also arrived that year. These included the 3209, 3612, and 4509 models.

The production of coaches, other than school buses, rose to 2,251 units in 1950, but GM probably made a lot more money because there was a postwar trend toward sales of larger models than before. Some of the smaller intercity models that had been popular in the early '40s were totally discontinued. To replace them came a new PD4102, which was characterized by its rounded front-end design and offered an optional restroom. A similar bus called the PD4103 of 1951-1953 was the last GM intercity coach to use conventional springs.

In the coach-building field in 1953, GMC developed a radical new GMC PD4501 Scenicruiser. The evolution of this revolutionary new bus traces back to the late 1940s, when Greyhound commissioned industrial designer Raymond Loewy to create a prototype called the Highway Traveler or GX-1 (Greyhound Experimental 1) bus. The result was a double-deck interior, a suspension that employed an air bellows in place of leaf springs and other advances.

While too far out for practical use, the 1947 GX-1 led to the GX-2 of 1949, a 40-ft. long deck-and-a-half coach with tandem rear axles, air conditioning, and air suspension that became a prototype for the Scenicruiser. The bus was also used as a public relations tool to lobby for new laws permitting longer buses. On July 14, 1954, coach general sales manager E.P. Crenshaw got a new product to sell when the first GMC Scenicruiser bus rolled off the assembly line. A total of 1,000 were made exclusively for Greyhound Lines between 1954 and 1956.

The extensive development work that went into the Scenicruiser also led to the creation of two other new products. The first was the PD4104, a modern new large-windows coach with the Air Ride suspension system and options including power steering and a restroom. The PD4104 had a 6-71 diesel engine, with a smaller engine

used to power the air conditioning system. This became the most popular intercity bus in GMC's history and 5,065 were manufactured.

On May 17, 1954, GMC also expanded the availability of Hydra-Matic Drive to all lines, which represented an industry first. It then introduced its third new intercity bus—the PD4901 "Golden Chariot" 47-passenger model—on September 15. Brochures for this tandem-axle bus suggested it was a 40-ft. model that operators other than Greyhound could get, but only one prototype was made.

On April 6, 1956, coach general-sales manager E.P. Crenshaw announced that GMC's coach-making branch had developed a safer and simpler-to-operate 72-passenger school bus with forward control. The division's total coach production climbed to 2,912 units in calendar year 1956, a gain of 29 buses. That added up to industry domination with 84 percent of the U.S. market and led to U.S. Justice Department antitrust charges that were never proven.

In *Modern Intercity Coaches*, Larry Plachno states that the charges made against GMC, Greyhound, and three other bus lines may have been misguided and points out that, "Regardless of other situations, operators were buying GMC coaches because they were the most attractive, durable, and reliable on the market. For the most part, the competitors simply could not match what GM offered." A consent decree ultimately settled the case years later. It required GMC to share its technology with other companies and to provide financing to buyers of other brands.

E.P. Crenshaw's final year as coach general-sales manager was 1957, which proved to be a banner year with calendar-year production of 3,108 units. C.S. Dick took over the sales position in 1958, when 2,405 GMC coaches were produced. Some of the decline may have been based on the fact that the Justice Department's action inspired GM to make its diesel engines available to other bus manufacturers through the Detroit Diesel Division.

Replacing the PD4104 in 1960 was the 35-ft.-long PD4106 coach with a new 8V-71 diesel. Larry Plachno, of *National Bus Trader*, says, "There is some justification to the claim that the PD4106 was one of the finest 35-ft. coaches ever built. It got 10 miles to the gallon, was very

Ms. Rosa Parks refused to give up her seat on December 1, 1955, while riding this bus. The Henry Ford Museum & Greenfield Village recently purchased it at auction for some $492,000. (The item shown was sold in a recent MastroNet, Inc. auction. Photo property of MastroNet, Inc.)

Chicago Motor Coach Company's No. 146 bus was another 1936 Yellow Coach 72-passenger double-deck transit coach. "See Chicago – the beautiful city," said the lettering. "Go the motor coach way." (OCWC)

The advantages of a "pusher" bus engine were obvious, but getting short drive shafts to work reliably was a problem. Dwight E. Austin solved it by using a transverse engine and angle drive system, such as found in this 1935 Yellow Coach Model 718 41-passenger coach. (OCWC)

Los Angeles Motor Coach Co. used this 1940 Yellow Coach TD-4502 on a "Wilshire Local" route. This same basic type of bus was offered in many sizes and models from 1940 to 1952. (OCWC)

Yellow Coach commanded over 55 percent of the bus market in the U.S. by 1939. The first letter of the company's model numbers was a P for parlor coach (on intercity model) or a T for transit bus. Seen here is a 1940 Yellow Coach transit bus. (OCWC)

City buses of this type were produced by GMC from 1959 until 1975. Shown is a 1959 TDH-5301 model that the CTS bus line used on its Route No. 3 to the public square. (© General Motors Corp.)

easy to drive and maintain, and had no apparent faults other than a penchant for bulkhead cracks in its old age." In addition to squarer styling motifs, the new model featured a revised driver's panel inspired by contemporary transit buses.

In 1963, GMC's coach-building department introduced a line of advanced "New Look" buses and put both 45- and 53-passenger models into production. They featured styling refinements over the 1960 version and had a new V-hydraulic transmission that shifted under full power. A $16.3-million order for 605 of these buses was the coach division's largest in seven years. Production started in May at the rate of 60 buses per week.

In terms of both production and sales, 1963 was a banner year for GMC. Counting both trucks and coaches, the division hit an eight-year peak and increased its overall production by 13.2 percent. More than 90 percent of production—including all manufacturing of coaches—was done at Pontiac, Michigan.

The popular PD4106 was replaced by the 35-ft. PD4107 "Buffalo Bus" in 1966. This model's nickname came from its humpback roof styling. History was made because this was the last model produced under the Yellow Coach and Greyhound agreement that dated back to 1929. That deal made Greyhound the biggest buyer of Yellow Coach and GMC buses between 1929 and 1966.

In 1968, a new PD4903 intercity bus with greater passenger capacity and storage room was introduced. It had a retractable auxiliary axle. This third axle could be raised or lowered according to state road weight restrictions. It was 40 ft. long, held 49 passengers and provided 400 cu. ft. of luggage capacity. Its introduction marked the first time, since 1952, that GMC had more than one intercity bus model available, since the PD4107 was continued.

A GMC first for 1969 was an experimental Rapid Transit Experimental turbine-powered bus designed for use in congested cities. It featured triple headlights, gas-discharge turn signals, carpeting, lounge-type seating, and a lift-ramp for handicap access. A new "kneeling" suspension lowered it to the ground for easier entry and egress. The RTX, as it was called, was put together with structural adhesives, rather than rivets.

In 1970, GMC expanded and modernized its coach-building facility. PD4108 and PD4903 intercity buses, with

very minor changes, were introduced. GMC wound up having the best year in its history in 1972, but bus production was not a record. For the calendar year, it came to 1,795 units—all built in Pontiac. Gasoline-engine transit buses were discontinued, meaning that all models now relied on diesel power. Since it was no longer necessary to code the type of engine, the second symbol in model numbers was changed to a "6" or an "8" to show the number of cylinders. Another letter was added to indicate transmission type, "A" for automatic and "M" for manual.

Following the end of the long-standing relationship with Greyhound Bus Lines, GMC began to switch its emphasis from the intercity-bus market to the transit-bus market. Reportedly, sales of large over-the-highway coaches averaged about 230 a year from then on. However, a 1973 announcement revealed that the division was about to spend $32 million, in 1974, for the equipment and tooling needed to build a new coach. This RTS model evolved from an prototype bus called the Rapid Transit Experimental (RTX) that was developed in 1968. It incorporated modular construction and was made in the modern new 500,000-sq.-ft. coach-building facility in Pontiac.

The all-new RTS transit coach hit the market in 1976. However, late in the year, bus production slowed to a snail's pace because AM General Corp. (a branch of American Motors) filed a suit against the Urban Mass Transit Administration over a contract awarded to GMC, even though AM General placed the lower bid. UMTA said that the higher bid was justified by special features of the RTS model, but no immediate decision about the suit was reached.

In 1977, GMC bus sales continued to be artificially suppressed by legal issues surrounding the RTS Transit Coach model. AM General's lawsuit over Urban Mass Transit Administration design standards had been resolved in a manner favorable to GMC, which allowed production to resume. However, several subsequent UMTA rulings, related to what cost offsets would be acceptable for special material requirements, threatened to halt RTS production by mid-1978. As a result, GMC built only 507 of the buses in 1977.

In 1978, production of the RTS bus finally got going at full speed. However, GMC was still unsure of its future in bus making and discontinued the 35-ft.-long P8M4108A intercity coach. The division's transit-bus business wasn't in much better shape. The RTS was proving expensive to build and public utility firms that operated bus lines were not inclined to offer cost-offset allowances when bidding. Fortunately, GMC was able to put in low bids on several new UMTA contracts and get enough orders to up production to 1,339 units.

Sales of the RTS Advanced Design Bus increased in 1979. After the federal government relaxed rules requiring special equipment for handicapped passengers, new orders came piling in and GMC built 1,719 units. While the increase was nice, few intercity coaches were being purchased, and in June 1979, it was decided to build only transit buses and school buses in the future.

With its U.S. sales floundering, GM looked toward the international market as an alternative and formed the new World Truck and Bus Group in 1980. It consisted of GMC, Chevrolet's truck operations, and partners Isuzu Motors, Ltd., of Japan, and Bedford of England, plus several parts branches. GMC's role was to coordinate the design, production, and parts commonality of large trucks and buses built by GM partners and subsidiaries around the globe. GM Executive Vice President Donald J. Atwood was named group executive.

In bus production, GMC became the number-one maker in both the U.S. and Canada in 1980. Calendar-year production here was up 45.1 percent to 2,495 units. In Canada, production jumped 40.7 percent to 850 units, from 604 the previous year. GMC was building as many as 12 buses a day early in the year. It then cut back to as few as eight per day, by October 13, after government funds for community bus purchases were cut back.

Despite growing competition for dwindling government funding for public transportation systems, GMC remained the country's number one maker of buses in 1981, although its production total of 1,957 units was down 21.6 percent from calendar year 1980. A single shift of workers at the Pontiac plant built eight Advanced Design Buses per day. These were modern, rounded-looking coaches with sealed windows and wheelchair lifts. North of the border, GM of Canada produced 1,000 "New Look" coaches with styling that dated back to the 1950s.

Business in the bus market in 1982 was lagging and GMC's model-year output dropped 42 percent, leading to cutbacks in the bus-building operation and layoffs at the Pontiac bus plant. "We've built all we've had orders for," Don Atwood told the press. He noted that increasing competition from smaller domestic firms and overseas manufacturers led to loss of a market that, he said, "Once belonged to GMC and maybe one or two others." On September 1, a new Truck and Bus Manufacturing Division was formed as a branch of the Worldwide Truck & Bus Group that had been announced in July 1981. Robert W. Truxell, former GMC general manager, was put in charge of the new manufacturing division.

GMC remained the giant among bus makers in 1983 and production rose 10.6 percent to 1,264 units. Unfortunately, this was 40 percent below the 1980 total and, worse yet, no substantial growth was anticipated for 1984. The problem was that federal funds to help cities buy buses were still being tightly held onto. GMC had the capacity to make 5,000 coaches a year, but the demand needed to sell them wasn't there.

Up north, GM of Canada, Ltd., introduced a new Classic bus at midyear in 1983. It was still based on the 1959 New Look model, but had improvements designed to ease serviceability. These included the use of new easy-access electrical components. The Canadian branch in Oshawa, Ontario, built 506 buses.

GMC bus production dropped to only 527 units in calendar-year 1984. As a result, the coach plant was shut down from mid-November in 1984 until February 1985.

Patrick J. Coletta, general manager of the Truck and Bus Manufacturing Division, decided to free some plant capacity for light-duty truck production. In February 1985, he combined medium- and heavy-duty production at the GM Truck & Bus Group's Central Manufacturing and Assembly plant in Pontiac. The vacant 10-year old East Plant was earmarked to undergo a modernization to become a "factory-of-the-future" for pickup-truck production.

Coach sales "fared" a bit better in 1985, despite a four-month shutdown of the assembly lines early in the year. In March, New York City placed the largest single order for 419 RTS models. It was worth more than $70 million. The Massachusetts Bay Transit Authority ordered 200 more. The assembly lines started rolling again and a milestone was hit when the 10,000th RTS Advanced Design bus rolled out of the factory in June.

By mid-1986, GMC decided to sell its bus operations. Despite an influx of orders from East-Coast transit systems, the bus-building branch had too many ups and downs to operate efficiently on a large-scale basis. A buyer wasn't found until early 1987. Then, a long-term association between a manufacturer and customer that dated back to 1929, paid off in Greyhound Corp.'s purchase of GMC's bus business. The new bus-making company became Transportation Manufacturing. Corp. The remaining GMC entity became GMC Truck Division.

Ex-GM executive John Nasi became the head of Transportation Manufacturing Corp., Greyhound's new transit-bus manufacturing arm. The unit was expected to begin operations in January 1988, after bus-making equipment was moved from the GMC factory in Pontiac to its new facility in Roswell, New Mexico. Also moved to Roswell were some partly finished coaches which were completed by Nasi's group, but included in 1987 GMC's calendar-year production of 435 coaches.

After 1988, GMC's only remaining link to bus manufacturing was the production of the 7000-Series school bus and commercial chassis. These were made on a modified truck chassis and had very little in common with either the transit buses or intercity coaches.

East Broadway Transit Co. operated the GMC transit coach shown in this 1975 press photo issued when the company's new RTS transit bus came out. The bus in the photo is believed to be a 1959 model, but this same design was used for 16 years. (© General Motors Corp.)

Starr Transit Co. used this GMC coach on a run to Princeton University in New Jersey. It is a 1968 PD-4903 with modifications produced under another model number. (© General Motors Corp.)

The sleek 47-seat RTS transit bus is seen in this photo issued in 1975. It features standard baseline color trim with one 14-in. wide color accent stripe above the side belt panels and a six-inch wide stripe at the front and rear. A striking "Wrap-Around" option was available at slight extra cost. (© General Motors Corp.)

GMC

GMC Goes to War

World War I

World War I began in 1914 as a struggle between the great European powers, which were grouped into two hostile camps: the Central Powers (Germany, Austria-Hungary, Bulgaria, and Turkey) and the Allied Powers (Britain and the British Empire, France, Belgium, Russia, Italy, and the United States).

The spark that lit the flame of war was the assassination of Austrian Archduke Franz Ferdinand while visiting Sarajevo, the capital of present-day Bosnia (then part of the Austro-Hungarian Empire). Bosnian separatists shot Franz Ferdinand to symbolize their struggle for freedom from the empire in order to unite with Serbia. Urged on by Germany, Austria invaded Serbia in retaliation. Serbia asked Russia (which was jealous of Austria's ambitions) for help. Soon, other countries involved in tangled alliances were drawn into the conflict.

Germany, wanting to expand its empire, declared war on Russia and France, then invaded Belgium and Luxembourg. Both Russia and France mobilized to protect their national integrity. Britain declared war on Germany for its violation of Belgium's neutrality. Initially, the warring nations felt the fighting would end in a few months and that peace would return in 1915.

When the fighting in Europe started in 1914, America had no overseas' alliances. On August 19 of that year, U.S. President Woodrow Wilson declared a policy of strict neutrality. However, supplying war goods to the European combatants helped the U.S. economically and America's exportation of goods to Allied countries increased from $825 million in 1914 to $3.2 billion in 1916.

This level of support made it possible for Britain and France to keep fighting against Germany, so Germany reacted with a policy of "unrestricted submarine warfare." When German subs sank the Lusitania, President Wilson announced that he was increasing the size of U.S. armed forces. On January 31, 1917, Germany stepped up its submarine offensive and Wilson responded by breaking off diplomatic relations. Then the Zimmerman Telegraph was published, revealing that Germany was trying to help Mexico regain territory in Texas and Arizona. This intensified popular opinion in the U.S. against the Central Powers.

On April 2, 1917, President Wilson asked Congress for permission to go to war. This was approved in the Senate on April 4 and in the House of Representatives on April 6. War was then declared against the German government on April 8, 1917. War against Austria-Hungary was declared on December 7, 1917.

World War I led the U.S. to intervene in European affairs for the first time. Like other participants in the world's first "total war," the U.S. was forced to mobilize all of its resources—military, industrial, and human—on a scale once thought impossible. GMC trucks played a major role in the effort.

Once the U.S. was embroiled in the war in Europe, nearly all of the nation's car and truck makers became involved in the production of fighting vehicles. At the General Motors Truck Co., in Pontiac, Michigan, 90 percent of the output of trucks was earmarked for the war.

The U.S. Army grew interested in the idea of standardizing military vehicles after using a rag-tag assortment of cars and trucks to chase down Pancho Villa in Mexico in 1916. The U.S. Army used some GMC Model 15 3/4-ton trucks during this Mexican campaign.

Prior to the U.S. entering WW I, the Army had hoped to avoid sending a fleet of civilian vehicles that had little in common with each other to Europe. It tried to start a standardization program with different companies building the same designs, but this was accepted very slowly. Most manufacturers were already extremely busy filling orders for Great Britain and France. This made them reluctant to convert over to building someone else's vehicles for the military. As a result, the Army wound up using no less than 213 different makes and models, including GMCs, in WW I.

Supplying parts and service to such a diverse range of vehicles proved problematic to many small truck makers, but GMC's ability to provide large numbers of military trucks, and especially ambulances with common features, became very important. Two standardized military models—the M-23A troop carrier and light aviation truck—were among 8,500 purpose-built GMC military vehicles sent to Europe. The company built 2,401 examples of the M-23A.

The casualty rate in WW I was enormous and the quick removal of the injured and dead from the battlefields was found to be of utmost importance in terms of both health and morale. GMC did a great job of building a truck-based military ambulance, called the Model 15, at the rate of 50 units a day in 1917. The Army's original plan was to eventually replace the Model-15 ambulance with a Standard AA truck that Willys, Federal, Reo, and Maxwell were designing for military-only use, but each firm built only one pilot model of the standard design.

When the Army decided not to produce its own standard AA truck, GMC came to the rescue with its 3/4- to 1-ton Model 16AA, which was established as the Army's standard AA 3/4-ton truck during 1918. Like the Model 15, it was used largely as a battlefield ambulance. This model's output in 1918-1919, combined with that of the 1917 Model-15 ambulance, reached 5,000 units. The Model 16 was also used as a cargo truck and in several other applications.

During 1918-1919, GMC also supplied Model-41 two-ton express-truck chassis to the Army. Many of these carried all-steel bodies with built-in tool compartments made by the Budd Co. and a portion pulled utility trailers also made by Budd. With its 282-cid four-cylinder engine, the Model 41 could hit up to 14 mph on a good road. GMC offered the Model K-101 five-ton truck chassis in 1918 and some of these may have seen wartime use as well, although the Army's primary large truck was the 3- to 5-ton Standard B "Liberty" truck. The Liberty truck was built by at least 15 truck makers, but not by GMC.

Between the Wars

Many trucks that had been ordered by the government were still uncompleted when WW I came to an end. A large number of these were diverted to use by government agencies or sold to private companies. In addition, a postwar move toward disarmament pressured the Army to sell even those trucks it needed for peacetime operations. The flood of war-surplus vehicles coming on the market forced many smaller manufacturers out of the truck-building business and also caused a shortage of peacetime-military trucks.

By the 1930s, the Army began to change things and moved toward building a standardized fleet of contemporary "high-tech" vehicles capable of higher speeds than ever before and off-road use. According to military-vehicle historian Fred W. Crismon, GMC provided a wide variety of commercial models to the Army and Navy between 1930-1941. Most were in the 1 1/2- to 3-ton range.

Crismon's book, *U.S. Military Wheeled Vehicles*, shows pictures of a 1931 T-26 Navy tanker, 1932 T-45 vans, cargos, and dumps, a rare 1936 T-14 roadster pickup-artillery truck, a 1938 F-18 cab-over-engine Army-searchlight truck, a pair of 1940 cargo trucks (including a Budd-bodied ACX-353 and a Heil-bodied AC-305), a 1940 AFX-312 U.S. Army recruiting van with a Proctor-Keefe body, and a 1940 AF-361 Signal Corps radio truck with a Luce van body. GMC also produced all-wheel-drive cargo trucks and heavy prime movers in this era.

In addition to supplying U.S. military vehicles, by 1939-1940, GMC was receiving orders for trucks from friendly nations such as Argentina and France, some of which were already involved in World War II. A batch of 2 1/2-ton ACKWX-353 six-wheel-drive models with tandem-rear axles was being built for shipment to France in 1940, but wound up being delivered to England after June 1940. This model was the predecessor to the famous CCKW deuce-and-a-half cargo truck or "Jimmy" that became the most commonly used World War II-tactical truck.

In the years just before and during World War II, General Motors produced an incredible $12 billion of military goods. This 1938 GMC 4 x 2 2 1/2-ton cargo truck was part of an order produced for the U.S. Army. (OCWC)

Another restored World War II GMC 2 1/2-ton CCKW, towing a 40-mm Bofors anti-aircraft gun made by Pontiac Motor Division and is equipped with a winch, a ring mount and a steel cargo box. (CLKC)

GM Prepares for World War II

In the years just before and during WW II, General Motors produced an incredible $12 billion of military goods—probably more than it would have made in peace time. That was a miracle in itself, but amazingly, $8 billion worth of that business came from products totally new to GM. In addition, this amazing transformation was accomplished even though more than 113,000 veteran employees left the company to go into the armed forces!

In his book, *My Years With General Motors*, Alfred P. Sloan, Jr. writes about the corporation's mobilization for WW II. "Our assignment was to transform the world's largest automobile company into the world's largest manufacturer of materials for war," he said. " We not only had to alter the character of our product, but had to increase our total output substantially."

The government prepared for war by forming the Office of Price Administration and the War Production Board to protect against wild inflation, profiteering, and drastic cost-of-living fluctuations if America became embroiled in WW II, and to regulate American industry if the country entered the war. GM's William S. Knudsen served as director of the WPB. Former GM executive Al Glancy became the U.S. Army's Deputy Chief of Ordnance for Automotive.

GM also got its war machine in gear quickly. Organizational changes were required for a rapid shift to all-out war production. On January 5, 1942, a War Emergency Committee composed of six top executives, mostly from the GM Policy Committee, was set up to meet at least once a week and run GM until April 1942. In May 1942, as GM settled into military production, a War Administration Committee consisting of all the general executives and group vice presidents was set up to run the corporation for the next three years.

The Jimmy

For the 1941 model year, the GMC four-wheel-drive ACK-353 truck was replaced by the four-wheel-drive CCK-353 and 100 of these new trucks, fitted with drilling equipment, were built for the U.S. Army Signal Corps. Other CCK-353s with cargo bodies were sent to England. In

The U.S. Navy was another GMC customer. It purchased this 1940 GMC AC-355 2 1/2-ton chassis-and-cab conventional with a Perfection stake body. (OCWC)

January 1941, Yellow Truck and Coach started making the first of 13,187 CCKWX-353 six-wheel-drive trucks with military-style cabs. The "X" indicated "extended" wheelbase. Over the next five years, Yellow Truck and Coach Division (1941-1943)/GMC Truck & Coach Division (1943-1945) would make 527,104 copies of this same basic 2 1/2-ton 6-x-6 truck with dozens of different bodies and several chassis lengths and configurations.

Once mass production began, the Jimmys were built as short-wheelbase CCKW-352s and long-wheelbase CCKW-353s. Models included cargo trucks; dumps; water and gas tankers; utility trucks with a LeRoi air compressor, jack-hammer, and tools; the Wrecker Set No. 7; van, and mobile-shop models; platform hoists; bomb transporters; tractors; fire trucks; oil field equipment and drill rigs; rail engines (used to move railcars, due to a shortage of steam locomotives); oil and fuel service trucks; and chemical-decontamination units.

The CCKW-352s had a 145-in. wheelbase and the 353s had a 164-in. wheelbase. Overall lengths were 231 and 256 in., respectively. Power was supplied by the GMC 270-cid inline six, which produced 91.5 hp at 2750 rpm. A five-speed constant-mesh manual transmission with overdrive was used. These freedom fighters had a top speed of 45 mph and a cruising range of 300 miles with their 45-gal. fuel tanks filled. Standard accessories included a canvas cab top; side curtains and cargo compartment canvas; hand, vehicle, and pioneer tools; spare parts; and a fire extinguisher. The GMCs were fitted with sheet metal cabs through July 1943 and tarpaulin cabs thereafter. Three different types of gun mount rings for 12.7-mm Browning machine guns were used and rifle carriers were an accessory for open-cab models.

Many CCKWs were employed in the liberation of France during World War II and the book, *The GMC 6 x 6 and DUKW: A Universal Truck*, written by Jean-Michel Boniface and Jean-Gabriel Jeudy, is a tribute to this military milestone. It was first written in 1978 and reprinted by Haynes Publishing Group in 1990. It is illustrated with hundreds of fascinating photos showing Jimmys in action in battlefield locales ranging from the beaches of Normandy in 1944 to the sands of the Golan Heights region in 1973.

The 'Red Ball Express'

One of the better-known efforts of World War II, in which GMC trucks had a major role, was that of the Red Ball Express. This operation was organized to get supplies to the American troops, who invaded Normandy and then drove the Germans back to their homeland.

Immediately after the Normandy invasion, Allied troops ran into stubborn resistance and had trouble breaking out of their beachhead. Late in July, they pushed through the enemy's front lines and pursued the German army toward the River Seine. The sudden and speedy German retreat had not been expected. Logistics were quickly changed and General George Patton ordered his Third Army eastward, toward Paris. If the Americans were able to outrun the Germans, the 12th Army Group could trap the Germans between Normandy and the Seine. A speedy supply operation was needed to make this plan work, since the American fighting forces needed about 20,000 tons of supplies a day.

Allied bombers had taken out France's rail lines to keep the enemy nailed down and the Germans still controlled the seaports. As a result, supplies had to be transported by truck—mostly by GMC deuce-and-a-half cargo trucks made in Pontiac, Michigan. If the trucks couldn't get through in time, Patton's tanks—which burned up 800,000 gallons of fuel per day—would simply run out of gas.

The Red Ball Express was conceived on August 25, 1944. The operation lasted barely three months, but that was enough to make the CCKW the war's most-famous truck. More than 6,000 trucks carrying Yellow Truck & Coach or GMC identification plates (and often towing trailers) transported more than 400,000 tons of supplies to the advancing American forces, all the way to the German border.

After encountering traffic snarls early in the operation, the Army set up northern and southern priority routes from Normandy to the city of Chartres. The northern route was for one-way traffic to Chartres and the southern route was used for returning. Civilian traffic, as well as other military traffic, could not use either route. The Red Ball drivers often drove their GMCs down the middle of the road to avoid land mines. They were under orders not to stop for anything, even cars that wandered onto the highways, and accidents sometimes did occur.

Some of the men who drove for the Red Ball Express had never operated a truck before. By the time their three-month stint was over, they probably racked up nearly a year's worth of experience, since the trucks rolled both daytime and nighttime, using blackout lights after dark.

Army mechanics "swept" the roads in both directions for trucks with problems. They had a slogan that said,

"Red Ball trucks broke, even though they never braked." It took huge Diamond T 969 six-wheel-drive military wreckers, with W45 Holmes twin-boom wreckers, to haul broken Jimmys back to repair depots. While some of the Red Ball-Express trucks suffered wear and tear due to the strenuous work, most of the battled-scarred GMCs were still going strong when the operation came to an end on November 16. Some were even used in the less-famous Green Diamond, Lions Express, and White Ball Express operations between September and December 1944, as well as in postwar applications.

The Red Ball Express was only possible because major American companies, such as General Motors, were able to rapidly mobilize and support the war effort. More than 800,000 deuce-and-a-half trucks—including some 540,000 GMCs—were sent off to the battlefields of Europe. No other nation involved in the war had the means to produce the kind of trucks—or the number of them—that were needed to make the Red Ball Express a wartime legend.

"The spectacular nature of the advance was due in as great a measure to the men who drove the Red Ball trucks, as to those who drove the tanks," Col. John S.D. Eisenhower once said after the war. "Without it (the Red Ball Express), the advance across France could not have been made."

You Win Some ...You Lose Some

The CCKW was not the only GMC truck produced for the military during WW II. A second model, based on the CCKW, but using a forward-control cab with the engine mounted below it, was the AFKWX. It was a long-wheelbase (164 in.) medium-duty cargo vehicle used primarily to haul bulky freight. Early models had civilian-style hard cabs with military modifications and 15-ft. wood or metal-cargo bodies. Later versions had open cabs with a removable canvas top and folding windshield. These also featured a longer 17-ft.-long cargo body.

The U.S. Army specified a 15-ft. body with stake rails for this 1943 GMC 6 x 6 Model AFKWX-352 2 1/2-ton cab-over-engine truck. It is powered by GMC's reliable 270-cid inline six. (CLKC)

A World War II advertisement describes the special abilities of the amphibious "Ducks" and encourages Americans to buy war bonds. (OCWC)

A 1943 GMC "Duck." Officially known as the DUKW-353, this 2 1/2-ton-rated amphibious fighting vehicle was based on the CCKW-353. (ST/MV)

This GMC model was designed by the U.S. Army Quartermaster Corp. in 1939 and was built by Yellow Truck & Coach in 1942 and by GMC Truck & Coach Division in 1943. A total of 7,325 were made. It shared its running gear and other parts with the CCKW. The major difference was the cab, which proved problematic. Maintenance was extremely difficult because the cab did not tilt forward and it often had to be completely removed for major engine work.

Yellow Truck & Coach employees also helped to design a heavy-duty military tractor that ultimately went into production in 1941, as the Autocar U7144 four-ton tractor. GMC had first dibs at supplying this truck to the Army and Mack had the second crack at the same job, but Autocar's version won the contract. White assembled some of these as 444T models and Federal built a similar model, called the 94x43A, which had only minor sheet-metal differences.

Duck Tales

One wartime General Motors' ad depicted an imaginary man named "Big Ed Gormley" polishing his prewar GMC pickup, while talking to a boy named "Johnny." Ed tells the lad, "This baby'll do everything but swim," and the ad notes, "Johnny, thinking of the power in that big engine and the strength of the sturdy frame, wouldn't put even that past Big Ed's husky GMC truck."

The copy accompanying the illustration explained how Ed's truck became the basis for GMC's "Duck" or DUKW-353 WW II amphibious vehicle. "When I grow up, I'm going to drive a truck like that," Johnny promises. (This ad must have run in *The Saturday Evening Post* late in 1943 or afterward, as it was from the GMC Truck & Coach

Division of GM, rather than Yellow Truck & Coach Co.)

In addition to changing its corporate identity in 1943, GMC began making Ducks. The original design work started in 1940, when a young Buffalo, New York, engineer, Roger Hofheins, advised the U.S. Ordnance Department of research he was carrying out, privately, to design an amphibious truck. This happened at about the same time that the military became interested in an amphibious Jeep design.

Hofheins' project was considered too complex and expensive to fit into the military services' peacetime budget and he did not get research funding, but he continued his testing and development work. In 1941, the government freed up the money to create an amphibious Jeep and opened an unlimited credit account for P. C. Putman, of the National Defense Research Committee, to use in developing such a vehicle. Putman contacted naval architect Roderic Stephens, Jr. of New York City's Sparkman & Stephens, about designing a hull for an amphibious vehicle. He also asked C. L. Kramer and F. G. Kerby, of Ford, to work out ways to use mass-production methods to build an amphibious Jeep.

Hofeins' Amphibious Car Corp. had constructed prototypes of a medium-duty amphibious truck called the AC-2 Aqua-Cheetah that was based on a 3/4-ton Dodge with four-wheel drive, but the Defense Department still wanted a Jeep-based amphibian. This changed, early in 1942, when Hofeins' already-proven design seemed to provide a ready solution to beachhead supply problems that U.S. troops were facing in Europe. On April 15, 1942, the authorization to order a prototype of the DUKW was given to the U.S. Army Equipment Service.

The Office of Scientific Research and Development,

which had superseded the National Defense Research Committee, was given the job of designing and developing the production version of the DUKW in conjunction with Sparkman & Stephens and GM. Contracts were signed April 30 and the prototype appeared 43 days later. It was built on a GMC AFKWX-353 forward-control truck chassis and tested out so well that 2,000 copies were ordered. Production versions were based on the CCKW-353. In October 1942, the U.S. Ordnance Department classified the DUKW as a standard-military truck.

Basically, the DUKW-353 was an amphibious six-wheel-drive truck with a boat-type hull built on a modified GMC truck frame using a 270-cid inline six for motivation. It could carry a payload of 5,000 lbs. or 25 men. Military specifications called for it to perform equally well on land and in water. The thousands who have ridden in these vehicles at several tourist attractions in Wisconsin Dells, Wisconsin, Washington, D.C., and Branson, Missouri, can readily attest to their outstanding capabilities in "dry" or "wet" modes.

The hull and body was made of lightweight sheet metal attached to a metal framework. Towing shackles and a folding-surf shield were mounted at the lower and upper front end of the vehicle, respectively. Directly behind the surf shields were two deck lids, one for radiator-air intake, bow stowage, air-compressor access, and service, and the other for engine access and service.

Early versions of the Ducks had vertical windshields, while later models used a folding windshield. There was seating for a driver and assistant in the cab. An M36 ring mount for a 12.7-mm. machine gun could be fitted to brackets above the passenger seat.

On land, the DUKW was operated and steered like a conventional truck. It moved through the water by means of a "pusher" propeller located at the rear and driven by a shaft mounted at the output end of the gearbox. In water, a cable-operated rear-rudder mechanism was used to navigate, but the front wheels could be used to help steer. The operating controls were in the cab.

Three bilge pumps were fitted. Two were driven directly by the motor and the third was manually operated. In order to help the DUKWs climb slopes and sand dunes, they could be equipped with a device that raised and lowered tire pressures while on the fly. A Garwood winch was mounted at the rear.

The DUKW's cargo compartment held top bows for a canvas top, a removable plywood floor, stowage areas, the bilge pumps, and access compartments for service. An anchor, two Jerry cans and a spare tire were mounted on the rear deck lid. The DUKW used combat-style wheels, such as seen on armored vehicles, but they were 18-in. in diameter, rather than 20 in., and had a unique offset. The rudder, propeller, and shaft were located under the rear deck and cargo compartment. Rubber boots were used to seal the hollow tubes that housed the drive shafts.

The DUKW used the 164-in. GMC long-wheelbase chassis and had an overall length of 372 in., making it pretty impressive in size. It was 99 in. wide and 106 in.

high and had a 63 7/8-in. tread, which made it look a little "pigeon-toed." The 14,880-lb. vehicle had tandem-rear wheels. Its GVW was 20,055 lbs. Top speed on land was 50 mph, which made for a fairly exciting ride through the woods. It could do six mph in the water. With its 40-gal. fuel tank, it could go about 240 miles on land or 50 miles in the water on a full tank of gas.

According to GMC historian R. A. Christ, the calendar-year production volumes for GMC's 6-x-6 amphibious trucks were 263 units in 1942, 4,720 units in 1943, 11,386 units in 1944, and 4,778 units in 1945. While "Big Ed Gormley's" GMC pickup truck couldn't swim, it had some things in common with the Duck like its GMC engine and its GMC heritage—the same heritage that helped the Allies triumph in World War II.

The 'Boarhound'

One World War II military vehicle built by Yellow Truck & Coach that hasn't received a lot of recognition is the 26.8-ton T-18E2 eight-wheel armored car manufactured for the British Royal Army in 1942. These were designated for use in desert warfare, but were never used for that purpose because the desert fighting died down by the time they were built. British soldiers nicknamed this 8-wheeled, tank-like vehicle the "Boarhound." The turret, which swung a full 360 degrees, carried a Mark III 57-mm. gun and a .30-caliber machine gun. Power came from two rear-mounted GMC engines developing 150 hp each.

Although the Boarhound was 20 feet long and had a hull with 3/8-in. to two-inch thick armor plate, it was capable of 50 mph. Both front axles could be steered and it could ford 48-in.-deep water. Drive was through a selective-speed transmission with a torque converter and the suspension incorporated an articulated spring and torque-tube system. It rolled on eight large 14.00-x-20 all-terrain tires. Only 30 of these fighting vehicles were ever built.

This CCKW-353 is pulling an M17 trailer with a "Quad .50" anti-aircraft gun and gun mount. In January 1941, Yellow Truck & Coach Manufacturing began making the first of 13,187 CCKW-353 six-wheel-drive trucks with military-style cabs that it would produce for World War II. During the war the company changed its name to GMC Truck & Coach Division. (CLKC)

A CCKW 353 2 1/2-ton 6 x 6 military cargo truck goes together on the GMC factory assembly line sometime in 1943. (© General Motors Corp.)

More Military Might

GMC's contributions to America's military might didn't come to a close with the end of WW II. Things slowed down immediately after the war, but revived by the early 1950s, with saber-rattling going on in China and Korea.

The GMC M-211 deuce-and-a-half six-wheel-drive cargo truck—essentially an improved CCKW—was produced in Pontiac, Michigan, from 1950-1955, along with six derivative models. The M-211 featured a larger cab than its WW II counterpart, plus a sealed waterproof-ignition system, an artic-weather heater kit, hinged doors, and roll-up windows. It used a larger 302-cid inline six that produced 130 hp at 3400 rpm and was linked to a four-speed Hydra-Matic transmission with a torque converter and two-speed transfer case gear-reduction unit attached to give it eight forward and two reverse speeds. It came on 144- and 156-in. wheelbases and had a top speed of 55 mph. Heavier sheet metal was used throughout the truck. The M-211 had dual 9.00-x-20 rear tires.

The GMC M-135 was basically the M-211 with single wheels and 11.00-x-20 tires. The tires were larger in size, so the cargo box had wheel wells added to provide jounce space. The M-215 was a 2 1/2-yard dump version of the M-211 with a shorter wheelbase. Garwood supplied the dump body and hydraulic mechanism. The M-221 was a semi-tractor version of the M-211. The M-220 was a van body truck with the same basic chassis as the M-211. Two tanker models were also offered, the M-222 two-compartment for hauling water and the M-217 three-compartment for hauling gasoline. Some of these trucks saw service in the Korean War. The National Guard used M211s as late as the 1960s.

GMC's round-nosed postwar forward-control truck, often called the "cannonball" by truck drivers and enthusiasts, became the basis for a number of early 1950s military applications. The U.S. Navy ordered some short-wheelbase HFX-652 deuce-and-a-half versions in

the summer of 1950 in cab-and-chassis form. They had a 318-cid inline six under their hoods.

An unusual 5-ton cannonball-style forward-control GMC was converted into a specialized 16-liter ambulance in 1952. Its body was mounted on a scissors hoist that could raise it 13 ft. to load wounded soldiers on aircraft. It was a 6-x-4 model, with a 302-cid 145-hp inline six.

By the mid-1950s, trucks that were basically civilian-type GMCs were being used in military applications, such as a 1953 Series-400 wrecker employed at the Aberdeen Proving Ground in Maryland and a 1954 U.S. Army stake truck. In 1955, GMC began offering entry-level "Fleet-Option" trucks with a plain wire mesh grille and no frills. The U.S. Army saved a little money by switching to these for its Model 424-V stake bed. In the same year, the U.S. Air Force had a 414-8V GMC tanker with the standard painted grille. It was used to fuel aircraft and had a new 155-hp V-8. Throughout the '50s and '60s, GMC models, ranging from a 1954 HC854 10-ton 4-x-2 dump truck to a 1955 W635-50A semi tractor, were pressed into service by the armed forces, although they had few real military features other than navy gray or olive drab paint jobs.

Military models of a specialized nature were also produced from time to time for use in peacetime operations and on the battlefields. In 1955, after the Ordnance Department issued technical specifications for a new series of medium-duty trucks, GMC designed the XM434E1 air-transportable amphibian with six-wheel drive. This 19-ft.-long truck rode on a 132-in. wheelbase. The engine was GM's 318-cid 190-hp 6V-53 diesel V-6. The XM434E1 was evaluated at Aberdeen Proving Ground.

In 1953, an experimental XM-147 "Superduck" was tested. It was similar to the famous WW II amphibian, but used an M211 engine and Allison CTP-4 automatic transmission. The XM-147 out-performed the DUKW-353, but sank while being tested at Monterey, California. It was salvaged and underwent additional evaluation at

Wartime production lines at GM. During World War II, General Motors transformed the world's largest automobile company into the world's largest manufacturer of war materials, building all-new products with reduced labor while increasing output substantially. (© General Motors Corp.)

This type of GMC CCKW-353 oil servicing truck with six-wheel-drive was used by the U. S. Army Air Force in World War II. It carries a 660-gal. tank body and equipment produced by the Heil Co. (CLKC)

GMC developed a 42-ft.-long, 8-ton, 8 x 8 vehicle called the XM-157 Drake in 1956. It had a 221-in. wheelbase, a 120-in. width and a 130-in. height, twin 302-55 engines, two Allison Powermatic transmissions and a pair of two-speed transfer cases. The Drake went 45 mph on land and 8.7 mph in the water, but never went past the experimental stage. (© General Motors Corp.)

Aberdeen, but the military never ordered any production versions. In 1955, the U.S. Army did some extensive modifications to an old DUKW to turn it into a "Flying Duck" that flew through the water on hydrofoils. It was powered by a 880-hp Lycoming gas turbine engine and did 50 mph over the water.

Since GMC was still considered the expert in the field of amphibious vehicles, it was tapped to develop an 42-ft.-long, 8-ton, 8-x-8 Duck-like vehicle called the XM-157 Drake in 1956. This huge machine had a 221-in. wheelbase and was 120 in. wide and 130 in. high. A pair of GMC Model 302-55 engines were linked to two Allison Powermatic transmissions and two two-speed transfer cases. The Drake could go 45 mph on land and 8.7 mph in the water. It never went beyond the experimental stage. The last CCKW's were retired from U.S. Army service in 1956.

In 1960, GMC Truck & Coach began manufacturing transporter-erector units for America's guided missile program. The contract called for production of a highway tractor and two carriages to haul Minuteman intercontinental ballistic missiles. These tractors had a very-low-profile cab that sat ahead of two steering axles and rear-driving axles. Power came from a 702-cid GMC V-12 engine. A second military contract issued in 1960 was for a series of tactical trucks.

During 1965, GMC Truck & Coach continued manufacturing transporter-erector units for Minuteman guided missiles. S. G. Little was appointed to the new post of director of defense products, which made sense with U.S. military advisors being sent to Vietnam.

By 1967, the Vietnam War was in progress, and GMC displayed a new deuce-and-a-half AGL-6 six-wheel-drive truck with a wide "telephone booth" cab that was detachable from the low, cargo-style body (actually a trailer). It used a DH-478 diesel V-6 linked to a six-speed Allison TX-200-9X transmission with a torque converter. The 8,600-lb. truck could carry a 5,400 lb. payload, including its crew,

and had articulated steering. GMC also built thousands of special rear-engine ambulances, aircraft fuel trucks, and missile carriers for Vietnam duty.

After the War

Following the end of the Vietnam conflict, GMC continued to sell products to America's armed forces, although the bulk of the trucks and buses it delivered for such purposes seem to be primarily modified civilian models. In 1972, a GMC Model 6500 GMC chassis was used to build a forward-control fire truck used at Aberdeen Proving Ground. It was fitted with a 427-cid Chevy V-8. In 1974, the U.S. Army took delivery of a PD-4107 "Buffalo Coach"-style bus that it used at the U.S. Military Academy in West Point, New York. In Europe, the French army was still operating 8,950 World War II-vintage GMC trucks in 1975.

In 1976, GMC supplied some 2 1/2-ton 6000 Series two-wheel-drive conventional trucks to the military for use in such applications as a short-wheelbase dumps fitted with snowplow equipment.

During 1991, 450 light-military trucks manufactured by GMC were sold to the Joint Forces of the Kingdom of Saudi Arabia. These were the first military vehicles based on the new GMT400 truck design. The sale included 150 GMC K2500 pickups and 300 GMC K3500 ambulances. Later, in 1993, a total of 2,000 troop/cargo carriers based on the GMC K2500 pickup were made for the Saudis, along with 6,000 ambulances based on the GMC K3500 model.

In both the '80s and '90s—as well as the new Millennium—GMC continued its tradition of building both military versions of civilian models and specialized equipment for the U.S. armed forces to employ in the protection of our nation and in the continuing struggle for the seemingly elusive goal of world peace. Whether the guns of war are silent or blasting, the GMC badge is there to offer a shield of safety to Americans around the globe.

The Office of Price Administration and War Production Board regulated American industry during World War II. GM's William S. Knudsen served as director of the WPB. Former GM executive Al Glancy became the U.S. Army's Deputy Chief of Ordnance for Automotive. GM also issued posters like this one urging its employees to purchase U.S. War Bonds. (© General Motors Corp.)

GMC

C h a p t e r   1 2

Taxis, Trailers, and Motor Homes

Page 160 and 161: GM initially produced all MotorHomes, but later produced only the fiberglass body shells and supplied them out to outfitters like Midas, Avaion and Coachmen Industries, which then finished the vehicles. In November 1977, GMC dropped out of the motor home business, but Coachmen continued to offer Royale and Birchhaven "motor homes." (GDMC)

The first Yellow Cab was the Model H, produced in 1915. It had a four-cylinder Continental engine and a Racine body. (MVMA)

The 1938 General Motors Cab had a Chevrolet-like look. This Model O-18, operated by Netherland Cab Co., which was part of Terminal System, Inc., represents the last General Motors Cab. (OCWC)

Taxis

Today when we think of a taxicab, we often think of the color yellow. The idea of painting taxicabs yellow came from John Hertz, a man most famous for the rental-car business he founded. Hertz's background was also intertwined with that of GMC through his connections with Yellow Truck & Coach Co.

In 1905, Hertz was a salesman for the Walden W. Shaw Livery Co., of Chicago, Illinois. Within three years, he became a partner in the company. His early success was based upon purchasing used cars and turning them into taxis. By 1910, the firm was flush enough to buy nine Thomas automobiles—huge cars made in Buffalo, New York—which Hertz had painted yellow to attract more attention.

Shaw started building its own taxi chassis and formed The Yellow Cab Co., of Chicago, Illinois, in 1915. It assembled cabs in the Walden shops, sold them on credit to taxi firms, and provided the cab operators with a manual on how to run a successful livery business. A total of 150 Yellow Cabs were made in 1915, but not all of them were painted yellow. The color choice was up to the buyer.

On June 29, 1920, the Walden W. Shaw Livery Co., changed its name to the Yellow Cab Manufacturing Co. The company then built taxis at a larger plant at Menard and Dickens avenues in Chicago. For 1921, Yellow Cab Manufacturing Co. offered the four-cylinder Model-O chassis with taxi body. It had a 3 3/4- x 5-in. bore-and-stroke, four-cylinder, vertical, side-valve engine, with its cylinders cast en bloc and a non-removable cylinder head. The engine produced 22.5 NACC (National Automobile Chamber of Commerce rated) horsepower. The shipping weight for this vehicle was 3,830 lbs. The following year,

This neatly uniformed taxi driver looks very proud of the 1930 General Motors Cab Model O-10 that he drove for the Palace Cab Co. Livery rates posted on the vehicle are 15-cents for the first quarter mile and five-cents per additional quarter mile. (OCWC)

this cab became the Model O-2, which had no changes to speak of. The Model O-3 of 1922-1923 had the same engine, but came as a Limousine Taxi and weighed 3,980 lbs. A smaller Model A-2 four-passenger Brougham Taxi also arrived in 1923. It had an 18.23-hp four-cylinder engine and weighed only 3,335 lbs.

The Yellow Cab Model O-4 Brougham Taxicab of 1924-1925 sold for $2,340 and weighed 3,775 lbs. The four-door body had an open-front design and was sedan-like in the rear, with the roof extending over the open driving compartment. Standard equipment included a hand horn, cowl lights, electric "Vacant" sign, a "For Hire" sign, a wheel puller, a spare-tire carrier, and a tool set with a jack and wrenches. The Model O-4 continued using the 22.5-hp four. The transmission was of selective-sliding design with three forward and one reverse speed. It had spiral-bevel drive and a semi-floating rear axle. The 32 x 4 1/2-in. pneumatic cord, non-skid tires were mounted on steel-disc wheels.

The year 1924 was a big one for Hertz's company. An order for 120 Yellow Cabs came in from W & G du Cros of Acton, England. They were shipped to London for final assembly there. The company also made a 1-ton Yellow Cab truck called the Model T-2 "Yellow Knight" that had a 124-in. wheelbase and 5,490-lb. gross-vehicle-weight (GVW) rating. It used an 18.99 NACC-hp four-cylinder Knight engine. History was made when John Hertz started a "self-drive" operation, renting out his own Ambassador sedans. This became Hertz Rent-A-Car.

In 1925, Yellow Cab Co. merged with General Motors Truck Co. to form Yellow Truck & Coach Manufacturing Co. For a while, John Hertz remained president and manufacturing operations remained in Chicago. The Yellow-Cab line was expanded and added a Knight Sleeve-Valve engine with 18.99-NACC hp. This was a four-cylinder, vertical, cast-en-bloc motor with a 3 7/16 x 5-in. bore and stroke and force-feed lubrication. The Yellow-Knight model was offered, along with a Continental-engine model. A few Lycoming and GM Northway engines were also used in taxis and Ambassador sedans.

The Model O-5 Yellow Taxicab of 1926 was a larger car with a fully enclosed six-window sedan body, high-crowned

fenders, and much more modern styling than the Model O-4. It was called a Limousine Taxicab and initially priced at $2,340. Later this rose to $2,600. The Model O-5 had a 4,175-lb. shipping weight. It rode on a 114-in. wheelbase and had 30- x 5-in. pneumatic cord, non-skid tires mounted on steel-disc wheels. The engine was of Knight Sleeve-Valve design and the transmission was of selective-sliding design, with three forward and one reverse speed. It had spiral-bevel drive and a semi-floating rear axle. Standard equipment included tools and a jack, an ammeter, an electric horn, a spare-tire carrier and wheel, a spotlight, a sun visor, a cowl ventilator, a headlight dimmer switch, a heater, and a dome light.

The Knight-engined Model O-5 was continued into 1927 with a lower price of $2,450, but by this time, signs of GM's ownership of the company were starting to be seen. A second taxicab with a powerful, overhead valve Buick six-cylinder engine and front-wheel brakes was added to the model line up. The 3 1/8- x 4 1/2-in. bore-and-stroke 207-cid engine came from Buick's smallest Model 115 Standard-Six model and generated 23.4-NACC hp or 63 brake horsepower at 2800 rpm. It had a Marvel carburetor and Delco-Remy ignition. This Model O-6 Limousine Taxicab was priced at just $2,150. Production of the Model T-2 Yellow-Knight truck was also discontinued at the end of the 1927.

In 1928-1929, Yellow operations moved into one of the GMC Truck plants in Pontiac. A new Model D6 Yellow Cab used an updated overhead-valve engine from the 1929 Model-116 Buick Standard Six. It had a 3 5/16- x 4 5/8-in. bore and stroke and 239.1 cubic inches and produced 74 hp at 2800 rpm (26.33 NACC hp). By 1929, all Yellow-Cab models used the Buick Standard-Six engine.

By 1930, the Yellow-Cab name was discontinued and replaced by General Motors Cab. The first General Motors Cabs were called Type O-10s and offered in six-passenger sedan and Town Car-body style. The sedan sold for $2,095 and weighed 4,908 lbs. The Town Car was $200 more expensive at 104 lbs. heavier. Both utilized Buick's Series-40 motor, a valve-in-head six with a 3 7/16 x 4 5/8-in. bore and stroke, 257.5 cid and 80.5 hp at 2800 rpm. Apparently, due to the Depression, sedan prices were lowered at some point during the year and both body styles were then offered in two models. The Sedan Taxicab came as a Model 385 or 386, but both were priced at $1,800 and weighed 4,890 lbs. The Limousine Taxicab came as a Model 388 or

389 and both were priced at $2,295 and weighed 4,960 lbs. There could not have been much difference.

In 1931, the Type O-10 was continued in both body styles. Prices remained at $1,800 for the sedan and $2,295 for the Town Car, but the weight of each model increased by 80 lbs. After 1931, *Branham Automobile Reference Book* indicated "no further data available because of manufacturer's failure to furnish same," so historical details are sketchy. Other books say that later models of the General Motors Cab used a GMC-built six-cylinder engine until 1934.

The 1932 General Motors Cab was called the Type O-12 and the 1933 model was called the Type O-13. Both of these versions were six-passenger Sedan Taxicabs. In 1934, there were two models, the Type O-14 and Type O-15. The 1933 and 1934 taxicabs both had the general appearance of a 1932 Pontiac or Oakland. There was no General Motors-Cab production during 1935.

A new Type O-16 bowed in 1936. It had a "stretched" Chevrolet Master-Deluxe body on an extended chassis with a 124 1/2-in. wheelbase. That compared to the Chevrolet's stock 113-in. stance. The rear axle was from a Chevy truck. Under the hood was a 206.8-cid 79-hp Chevrolet overhead valve six-cylinder engine with a Carter carburetor and Delco-Remy ignition.

The O-17 of 1937 grew to a 127-in. wheelbase, even though the year's Chevrolet Master Deluxe had a one-inch shorter stance than it did in 1936. A new 216.5-cid 79-hp overhead valve six-cylinder engine with a Carter carburetor and Delco-Remy ignition was used. In 1938, the same basic model was carried over as the O-18. Both of these taxicabs had standard rear jump seats. A single front seat and a division window between the front and rear were options. The 1938 model was the last appearance of the General Motors Cab.

Left: The General Motors Cabs took on a new Pontiac-like appearance in 1933, when the Model O-13 was offered. It even wore a Pontiac Indian hood mascot. (OCWC)

Terminal Cab Co. purchased this 1931 General Motors Cab Model O-12. The six-passenger taxicab was powered by a six-cylinder engine. (OCWC)

The 1928 Model O-6 Limousine Taxicab was the next-to-last to carry the Yellow name. (© General Motors Corp)

Trailers

GMC was interested in selling its products to trucking companies and truckers were constantly looking for ways to carry more goods while spending less time, effort, and money. To many truckers, a large trailer pulled by a truck seemed like a good way to expand the truck's utility value and carrying capacity without adding greatly to operating expenses. While it's true that a truck-and-trailer combination would have a higher initial cost, slightly higher tax burden, and higher fuel consumption (due to its heavier weight), truckers realized that trailers had great advantages. They could ship nearly twice as much without investing in a second drive train or a second driver.

As early as 1923, General Motors Truck Co. was building truck tractors. In that year, the Wayne Truck Co. of Detroit—a truck-body-mounting company—bought a hard-rubber-tire Model K-14T truck, with a fifth wheel and a flat-bed semi trailer that was set up to carry three dump bodies. The market for trailers naturally grew, as the trucks pulling them became more powerful and faster.

By the 1930s, interstate-trucking operations were really catching on and the demand for long-distance trailers was growing by leaps and bounds. In 1931, GMC entered the market for heavy-duty trailers with a line up of 21 models including single- and tandem-axle semi trailers and four- and six-wheel full trailers. Over the next nine years, the company would build a total of 8,283 trailers. Except in the case of a model called the Trailabout, GMC provided only the fifth wheel and the trailer chassis. Other firms built the trailer bodies.

The famous Southern California Freight Lines transcontinental run of 1931 involved a GMC T-95-C double unit truck and trailer owned by the Los Angeles, California, trucking firm. The eight-foot-wide truck and trailer were 52 ft. long overall and 10 1/2 ft. high. The truck had a 130-hp engine. Twenty-two 9.00 x 20-in. tires (10 on the truck) carried the load. Both the truck and trailer were equipped with Bendix-Westinghouse air brakes said to be able to stop the fully loaded unit, from 30 mph, within a distance equal to its own length. Both units carried GM Frigidaire Division refrigeration units and refrigerated bodies made by Hammond Lumber Co., of Los Angeles.

The truck and trailer left Los Angeles on September 8, carrying a load of perishable fruits, vegetables, and eggs. A man named Colonel Davis, who was in charge of the Transcontinental Test Run, maintained close records of every aspect of the trip. The GMC and its trailer covered 3,200 miles and ran for 117 1/2 hours at an average speed of 27.39 mph, consuming 1,137 gal. of Texaco fuel (for an average of 2.79 mpg). When the doors on the trailer were opened in New York City on September 16, the average temperature of the produce inside was 35 degrees. The trip was considered a "scientific experiment" to prove the practicality of long-distance transportation of perishable goods.

Among the prettiest tractor-trailer rigs that GMC ever

made has to be a pair of T-46-Ds built for the Washington State Liquor Control Board in November 1934. They featured a very low-slung tractor on an extremely long wheelbase with a goes-on-forever louvered hood.

During the later 1930s, the Yellow Truck & Coach Manufacturing Co. manufactured a wide variety of GMC semi trailers in Pontiac. The 1937-1938 lineup included six models offered in a variety of lengths between 16 ft. and 24 ft. The least expensive was the TT-25 Trailabout, a light-utility trailer that was available with four different light-truck bodies based on pickup beds. It included a hitch for a two-inch ball. The TT-218 semi trailer had a single 10,000-lb. axle with one wheel on each end. It was available in 16-, 18-, and 20-ft. lengths priced at $575, $585, and $595 respectively. The trailer, without bodywork, had an average weight of about 2,255 lbs. A different version of the TT-218 was offered in the same lengths with a 12,000-lb. axle, which added about $210 and 330 lbs. There was also a heavy-duty TT-218H version in the same lengths, with prices from $850 to $870 and weights from 2,820 to 2,900 lbs.

A "W" (for "wide") was used to code trailers with wide-frame construction. These "4-wheel semi" trailers came as TT-218Ws, with a choice of a 10,000- or 12,000-lb. axles in 20-, 22-, and 24-ft. lengths. Prices for the former ran from $1,325 to $1,345 and the 12,000-lb. axle models were $250 additional and weighed more than 4,000 lbs.

Rounding out the 1937-1938 GMC trailer offerings was the TT-252 semi trailer, which came in 16-, 18-, and 20-ft. lengths. These were priced at $1,075 to $1,115 and weighed 3,320 to 3,440 lbs. In 1939, the line was the same and prices on all TT-218 and TT-218H models dropped $50, while all the other models had unchanged pricing.

A fascinating photo in Gini Rice's 1971 book *Relics of the Road No. 1: GM Gems 1900-1950* shows the rear view of a streamlined travel trailer that was used by General Petroleum Co.'s lubrication department. The trailer, which has Venetian blinds and fender skirts, appears to be a rolling office. Even more interesting is the vehicle pulling it, which resembles a mid-1930s GMC pickup with its cargo bed replaced by a custom-built extended-rear deck that makes it look like a coupe-style passenger car. It has unique, fully skirted rear fenders. Unfortunately, there is no caption on this photo, but the implication is that the customized truck-and-trailer combination was built entirely by GMC. GMC historian Donald E. Meyers says this is doubtful.

GMC continued building trailers until the outbreak of World War II. While sales of these units averaged less than 1,000 per year, the extra business did help during the Depression. In addition to giving work to those employed on the assembly lines, the trailers put the company's ever-growing production facilities to good use. However, with the increase of military contracts by 1940, GMC management decided to end trailer building and commit all factory capacity to the manufacture of war goods.

A 1934 GMC Model TT-251 single axle trailer chassis. (© General Motors Corp.)

A 1933 GMC T-51 Tractor with a GMC Model TT-551 trailer chassis. (© General Motors Corp.)

The Crestmont and Birchaven models were based on the 23-ft. GMC MotorHome and described in a February 1976 brochure. The interiors were actually installed by two Indiana firms. Midas International of Elkhart trimed Crestmont models and Coachmen Industries of Middlebury did the Birchaven. (GDMC)

A 1972 GMC motor home built on a Model PE3500 forward-control truck chassis. (© General Motors Corp.)

The GMC MotorHome

During 1971, sales of self-contained motor homes represented the fastest-growing segment of the booming recreational-vehicle movement. Sales of motor homes were at about 60,000 units per year, but only about half of those were the large, expensive units built on a truck chassis. The rest were van conversions. Motor homes had a 10.9 percent share of the total RV market and that had grown from just 4.4 percent in 1969. In addition, a 14-percent share was forecast for 1972, meaning that sales would be up more than 300 percent in four years!

In 1971, the RV industry had sold 57,000 motor homes for an estimated $650,000,000 to $750,000,000. That's one reason that GMC picked late 1971 to announce its intention to build a large, modernistic, self-contained motor home. "With the advent of General Motors entering the motor-home picture, it is conceivable that the motor-home portion of the recreational vehicle market will account for more than half of the revenue brought into the industry from all types of RecVees in 1972," suggested *Ward's 1972 Automotive Yearbook*.

Motor Trend ran an item in its January 1972 "International Report" saying GMC Truck and Coach Division "may start building motor homes next year." It said that prototypes of 23- and 25-ft. models had been built and that the steel-bodied vehicles would be manufactured at the GMC plant in Pontiac. According to *Motor Trend*, GMC denied that it had any plans to enter the market with complete vehicles, but said it would continue to provide chassis to motor-home makers. It added that word of GMC's plans "sent a shiver through the market."

Motor Trend didn't get all its facts just right until April 1972, when a second item near the front of the magazine announced that the GMC motor home was "going to be introduced by the General Motors Truck and Coach

Division early next year." This report clarified that it would come in 23- and 26-ft. sizes, be in the 10,500-lb. weight class and feature a fiberglass-and-aluminum body with front-wheel drive. "The body will be built at the division's Pontiac plant and the interior will be finished by Gemini Corp., a subsidiary of PRF Industries, Inc., the firm that makes the Dodge motor home." A price of $12,000-$14,000 was originally envisioned. One-stop warranty service through General Motors franchised car-and-truck dealers was a part of the plan.

The GMC motor home—initially advertised as the MotorHome—was designed from the ground up to be one of the most comfortable, efficiently haped and totally integrated motor homes ever seen. It was promoted as a joint venture between GMC Truck & Coach Division of Pontiac, and PRF Industries of Mt. Clemens, Michigan. "PRF" stood for "Pre Formed Fiberglass."

The GMC MotorHome brought many innovations to the RV field. It had a 6.7-liter GMC V-8 and a front-wheel-drive system derived from the Olds Tornado-Cadillac Eldorado design. The 26-ft.-long vehicle rode on a special chassis that was equipped with rear air suspension. Large, tinted windows provided excellent all-around visibility. The windshield alone measured 32 sq. ft.

Four interior-floor plans were offered, with options sleeping up to six people. With extensive storage space, a complete kitchen, and a fully featured bathroom, the GMC MotorHome was a home on wheels. Exterior and road noises were reduced through use of a special polyurethane foam barrier that covered the entire floor, interior walls, and ceiling.

At the time it announced the MotorHome, GMC was in the middle of the biggest expansion and modernization program it had ever carried out at its Pontiac facilities. A new 1.6-million sq.-ft. truck-assembly plant was about to

A Camel colored 1973 GMC MotorHome with optional roof-mounted air conditioner. (AJMJ)

An artist concept of the innovative 1973 front-wheel-drive GMC MotorHome. Early models like this one utilized a 455-cid Oldsmobile V-8 and Turbo-Hydra-Matic drive. (AJMJ)

GMC set out to build a motor home that was as close to perfect as possible and started by designng its 1973 MotorHome around a front-wheel-drive unit. (© General Motors Corp.)

Right: A new super-luxurious version of the MotorHome called the "Eleganza II" was introduced early in December 1974. It offered a plush environment to relax, sleep or dine in. It had contrasting stripes running around the body. (GDMC)

go into operation. This opened up space in the former GMC full-size van factory in Lansing, Michigan, for assemblies of the new GMC MotorHome. The factory underwent an extensive re-tooling to allow production of this so-called "multi-purpose vehicle" to start in January 1973.

Innovative Job-Enriching Team Construction methods were used in producing the motor homes. This system allowed GMC Truck & Coach workers to use the vehicles on weekends to make quality checks. Strong attention was also focused on occupant safety features, since the U.S. Government had started considering safety regulations for recreational vehicles during 1972.

Certain GM car-and-truck dealers handled sales of

GMC MotorHomes at key locations nationwide. Warranty service for the entire vehicle was provided at these same retail dealerships, which was a selling advantage. With most other motor homes, chassis service was provided by the automaker, but the RV body and accessories had to be serviced by the companies that built them.

With recreational-vehicles sales increasing 2.1 percent to an all-time record in 1973, GM's timing for the launch of the GMC MotorHome at first seemed just about perfectly planned to take advantage of a boom in RV sales. Even initial production of 3,045 units in calendar year 1973 was encouraging. However, as things turned out, the company could not have picked a worse year to introduce a new motor home.

Beginning in the summer of 1973, negative indicators suggested that trouble was brewing. Government safety regulations and pressure from environmentalists were increasing the costs and decreasing the popularity of RV use. When the Arab oil embargo of October and resulting gas crisis in November led to long lines at the gas pumps, it was a death blow. By the time the National Recreational Vehicle Show was held in Louisville, Kentucky, in November, 30 percent of America's RV makers were on the verge of bankruptcy or already there. Other industry-trade shows were being canceled due to low attendance.

GM struggled with its motor-home business in 1974 when calendar-year production of the GMC MotorHome dropped 64.5 percent, to 1,080 units. The early months of the year were so slow that the motor-home-production line in Pontiac was shut down in March. To keep things going, models outfitted as emergency-medical vehicles, mobile offices, rolling classrooms, bookmobiles, and other job-specific applications were built and sold during the worst months.

Demand for all kinds of recreational vehicles picked up again toward the end of 1974 and GMC-assembly operations started up again in the fall. A new super-luxurious version of the MotorHome called the "Eleganza II" was introduced early in December. Another change at this point was that the motor-home interiors were now installed in Pontiac inside a completely renovated older plant that had once been used to build Yellow Cabs.

GMC's motor-home business was focused on the high end of the market in 1975. The 26-ft. Eleganza II, Glenbrook and Palm Beach luxury models were introduced early in the year and demand climbed 90.3 percent. However, calendar-year production of 2,055 units was still significantly below 1973's level. Even worse, retail sales for the model were only 1,315.

GMC was a member of the Recreational Vehicle Industry Association. Advertising flyers for the motor homes noted that the RVIA seal indicated compliance with federal-construction standards to assure "a safe, dependable travel home." GMC used the RVIA's annual show in Louisville to introduce several new editions late in 1975. The Crestmont and Birchaven were 23-ft. models. The Edgemonte was a 26-ft. twin-bed beauty, with a $25,525 price tag.

GMC MotorHome business continued to pick up in 1976, when calendar-year production rose to 3,497 units and model-year sales nearly doubled to 2,492 units. This year GMC's marketing department said that 25 percent of motor-home sales were expected to go to commercial users. Prices rose to $30,000 this year.

In November 1977, GMC Truck & Coach Division dropped out of the business of making large motor homes. In making the announcement, GMC said that it could make better use of its production facilities to build trucks, which had a better long-term sales outlook.

Coupled with that decision was the fact that the Oldsmobile Toronado, which supplied the engines and front-wheel-drive system for the motor home, was due to

be downsized for the 1979 model year, a move that would take away the motor home's power plant and transmission.

Ward's 1978 Automotive Yearbook noted, "There was more than a touch of irony in GMC's quitting the motor-home field" because industry observers had been worried that the business would be gobbled up by large corporations. As it turned out, GMC sold 9,262 motor homes in three years, plus 2,483 stripped shells of a sister vehicle called the Transmode. In doing so, it had captured nearly 25 percent of the top end of the RV market, but then dropped out because it wasn't making enough profit on the motor-home operations. During 1977, sales rose a modest 6.05 percent to 2,643 units and model-year production was 2,040 units.

GMC MotorHome output for the year 1978 fell to 1,217 units and sales came in at 2,250. Production of GMC MotorHome models was terminated in July. The division then began talks with various outside interests for sale of the motor home-production facilities.

The Glenbrook model of the MotorHome was advertised in a March 1976 dated brochure. It featured a gold-and-brown plaid upholstery, yellow curtains and brown carpeting. (GDMC)

Some GMC workers were allowed to use the MotorHomes on weekends to make quality and safety checks. (© General Motors Corp.)

Presidential limousine builder Hess & Eisenhardt, of Cincinnati, Ohio, described its Para Medic GMC as "the most revolutionary concept in ambulance design." It could accommodate two Ferno ambulance cots and two stretchers suspended from the interior roof. (GDMC)

GMC

Chapter 13

Famous GMC Concept Vehicles

Page 168 and 169: The 1988 GMC Centaur concept truck. (© General Motors Corp.)

A 1936 Cadillac convertible sedan leads a row of eight "Parade of Progress" vans parked in front of a Michigan factory. (MB)

1936: Streamliners

Charles F. "Boss" Kettering was an engineer from Dayton, Ohio. General Motors' famed chairman of the board, Alfred P. Sloan, Jr., once described Kettering as "a world-famous inventor, a social philosopher, and a super salesman." He invented the automotive self-starter and sold Cadillac on the idea of using it on the 1912 Cadillac.

In 1909, Kettering and his partner E. A. Deeds had independently organized Dayton Engineering Laboratories, Co. The first letters of the company name formed the Delco trade name. In 1916, Delco became part of United Motors Corp. General Motors purchased Delco in 1919 and within a year it became the General Motors Research Corp., with headquarters in Moraine, Ohio. In 1925, all of GM's research arms were consolidated in Detroit under Kettering. He remained in charge of corporate research until retiring in 1947.

When Kettering visited the Chicago World's Fair in 1933, he saw that GM's "Parade of Progress" was one of the most popular exhibits. It showcased visions of what tomorrow might bring in the field of highway transport. Kettering decided that it would be worthwhile for GM to take its show on the road. The first of three Parade-of-Progress tours opened on February 11, 1936, in Lakeland, Florida.

Kettering felt that the trucks transporting the exhibit from city to city should seem as advanced as the Parade of Progress. Engineers from the Yellow Truck & Coach Division were given the assignment to create eight special vans with a futuristic look. The red-and-white vehicles were constructed on a 223-inch wheelbase GMC-truck chassis powered by a GMC-truck engine. The ultra-modern bodies for these "Streamliners" were made in Fisher Body Division's Fleetwood plant. In front they resembled giant football helmets perched on an early Oscar-Meyer Wienermobile platform. The overall look was that of a modern-style moving van. They had triple-bar front bumpers and four car-style bucket headlamps, two mounted in the fender catwalks and two on the sides of the huge grille.

The trucks must have gotten lots of attention as they crisscrossed the country over the next four years. When they arrived at one of the cities on the Parade-of-Progress tour route, six of the buses were joined together with canvas awnings to form walk-through exhibition galleries.

When traveling, 29 other vehicles accompanied the Streamliners. They included nine GM tractor-trailers, a Chevrolet car that served as a rolling office, and exhibit vehicles from each of the five GM divisions. Every 2,000 miles these non-Streamliner exhibit vehicles were traded in at local dealers for new ones.

The Parade of Progress made more than 100 stops between 1936 and 1939. It visited mainly small American towns, but did make it as far as Mexico, where it helped to open the Pan American Highway between Laredo, Texas, and Mexico City in January 1938.

The traveling show was free to the public and focused on education, rather than sales. Exhibits ranged from high-tech displays of a stereophonic ping-pong game and a microwave oven to demonstration of a Curved Dash Olds known as "Old Scout" that had crossed the country in 1905. However, the biggest attraction of the tour was the streamlined "trucks-of-tomorrow" built by GMC.

A security guard inspects one of the streamlined "Parade of Progress" vans built by GMC in 1936. (MB)

A woman demonstates how to enter the bus-like 1937 "Previews of Progress" vehicle. (© General Motors Corp.)

In between making the 1936 and 1941 "Parade of Progress" vehicles, GMC workers designed and built this streamlined "Previews of Progress" van. (© General Motors Corp.)

1939: 'Futurliners'

In 1939, General Motors began planning for its participation in the 1939-1940 World's Fair in Flushing Meadows, New York, and the Golden Gate Exposition on Treasure Island, near San Francisco. Industrial designer Norman Bel Geddes was commissioned to design a "GM Futurama" exhibit for the New York event. Like the earlier Chicago World's Fair exhibit, the Futurama's underlying concept was to illustrate how science could change the future of the nation. Included in the show was a "Highways & Horizons" exhibit that predicted how America's personal-transportation system would look and work in 1960.

As he had done earlier, Charles Kettering converted the World's Fair exhibit into a road show so that Americans living in the center of the country could also "see into the future." His plan called for the design and construction of 12 new futuristic transporters, to be built at a cost of $100,000 each, to carry the new Parade-of-Progress tour. The General Motors Styling Studio designed these 16-ton "Futurliners." They were similar to GMC "Silverside" Greyhound buses enhanced with some styling motifs taken from streamline locomotives.

The Futurliner chassis were built at the Truck & Coach plant in Pontiac, starting in 1939. The bodies were again assembled at Fisher Body Division's Fleetwood factory in Detroit. Like the earlier Streamliners, the Futurliners were painted red and while. They were decorated with gold-and-silver trim and fluted aluminum panels on the sides. The original Furturliner driver's compartment was a Plexiglas bubble mounted high on the top of the front end. Large "GM" letters decorated the nose and "General Motors" was written on the sides at just below cockpit level. Below this, in script, were the words "Parade of Progress."

Each Futurliner was 33 ft. long, eight feet wide, and 11 ft. high. The driver sat in the center, perched nearly eight feet above the ground. In addition to a driver's seat, two jump seats were included at the rear of the cabin. Power steering and an autronic-eye automatic-headlamp dimming system were included. The buses had aerodynamic outside rear-view mirrors on each side, an upright exhaust stack on the right side, and huge whitewall tires. The engine was a 145-hp GMC inline six linked to an early Hydra-Matic Drive system. With such a small engine, the 33,000-lb. rigs were not very fast, but they sure looked great.

Each Futurliner was custom-designed for a specific exhibition purpose and the bodies contained different compartments with clamshell doors that opened to showcase exhibits or to provide such necessities as lighting and electrical power. A section of the roof was designed to be elevated above the vehicle and contained florescent-lighting fixtures to illuminate the display area at night. A new tent with fluted aluminum siding and aluminum arches backdropped the Futurliners.

The Futurliners made their first public appearance in Miami, Florida, in February 1941. The original schedule called for them to travel more than one million miles to 251 towns in the U.S., Canada, Mexico, and Cuba. They actually made it to 30 cities in 10 states before the day the Japanese bombed Pearl Harbor. The declaration of World War II brought a premature close to the second Parade of

One of the 1941 "Parade of Progress" buses is seen, in its original "bubbletop" form, at General Motors' Milford Proving Ground. (© General Motors Corp.)

This 3/4 view of the "Parade of Progress" bus at GM's Milford Proving Ground shows off its streamlined body forms. (MB)

From the rear, the 1941 "Parade of Progress" vans could probably pass for a transit bus. (MB)

This 1953 photo shows how the sides of one bus could be dropped to reveal scaffolding for seats. Note the "Parade of Progress" semi-truck in the background with matching trim. (RG/MB)

Thousands of Americans came to experience the General Motors "Parade of Progress" in 1953. Although the buses were over 10 years old, they still looked very modern. (RG/MB)

Progress, although GM was not yet ready to abandon the Futurliners.

Immediately after WW II, a severe shortage of cars and trucks in America prompted the auto industry to rush into production with prewar or slightly updated models. It took three to four years for Detroit to catch up with demand. There was little time or motivation for experimentation during that period, but after all-new postwar-car designs led to record sales in 1950, America's car-and-truck makers realized that a focus on new products and new technology had to be revived.

General Motors launched its Motorama show in New York City and made plans to reactivate the Parade of Progress in 1953. As part of those plans, the Futurliners were taken out of mothballs. A new steel roof was added to each bus, because the original bubble-top design made it unbearably hot inside the cabin for the operator. A Harrison air-conditioning system was installed. New 302-cid GMC engines and improved postwar Hydra-Matic transmissions were fitted and half of the buses had large generators added at the rear to help power the show.

After the Futurliners' roofs were modified, the front ends resembled "Scenicruiser" railcars with panoramic, curved-glass windshields. The futuristic buses toured the country again between 1953 and 1956, but by then the crowds of the prewar era were missing. One of the new technologies that the Parade of Progress showcased, television, made the traveling road show obsolete. Americans preferred seeing the future in the comfort of their homes.

Two Futurliners were donated to the state of Michigan and one was used as a State Police Safetyliner for a few years starting around 1959. By the early 1960s, this pair was sold to a salvage yard and all of the other buses were taken out of service. They were scattered to new owners in different parts of the country. Eventually, America dream-car collector Joe Bortz, of Chicago, Illinois, started buying up the surviving Futurliners. He wanted to restore them to carry some of his dream cars to shows. However, Bortz later decided to sell them.

Bob Valdez of California partly restored one Futurliner as a motor coach. Richard and Mario Petit, of Quebec,

Canada, spent a great deal of money restoring a second one. They then leased it to a cell-phone company that turned it into a promotional vehicle called the "FIDO Phoneliner."

Two other Futurliners were purchased by the owner of Peter Pan Bus Lines of Springfield, Massachusetts. Peter Pan is the second-largest bus line in the country and operates a modern-bus facility, where one of these buses is being restored from parts of both of them. It will be used for publicity campaigns.

Six other Futurliners survive and all have been changed from their original condition. Bortz eventually donated one of the survivors, bus No. 10, to the National Automotive and Truck Museum of the United States (NATMUS) in Auburn, Indiana. It is now being restored to its GM-modified 1953 condition through a restoration program spearheaded by Don Mayton, a Zeeland, Michigan, man who graduated from the General Motors Institute and worked for GM for 40 years.

Mayton saw his first Futurliner several years ago, while he and his wife were having breakfast at an open-air café in Palm Springs, California. Mayton, who had collected and restored half a dozen vintage Buicks, was mesmerized by the sight of the bus. When he returned to

The left side of the streamliners looked like this in 1953. (© General Motors Corp.)

Michigan, he began doing research at the GM Media Archives and Kettering University in Flint. He also learned about the bus that Bortz had donated to NATMUS.

After meeting museum director Ty Bennett, Mayton became involved in the effort to get the Futurliner restored. New tires were purchased and the vehicle was moved to Mayton's shop. More than 50 people from all over the country are now involved in the project and about a half dozen volunteers meet at Don's home every Tuesday to work on the bus. NATMUS is sponsoring the project by raising funds to help with the parts needed for the restoration. More than $10,000 has already been spent to buy spare parts reproduced by the Canadian brothers who refurbished the FIDO Phoneliner.

Mayton's devotion to this project shows that the dreams of one man can be passed on to another six decades later. The vision behind the Futurliners did not die when "Boss Ket" passed away, but patiently waited for people like Joe Bortz, Bob Valdez, Richard and Mario Petit, Ty Bennett, and Don Mayton to come along and showcase it to a new generation. These classic GMC "dream buses" are sure to inspire additional innovation from the people who see them today.

Here we see one of the buses, in 1953, with the side open to show the "A Car is Born" display inside. (RG/MB)

1955: L'Universelle

Along with the Parade of Progress Streamliners and Futurliners, the L'Universelle is one of the better-known GMC concept trucks. In addition to being featured in many contemporary car magazines, this front-wheel-drive, forward-control van created for the 1955 GM Motorama was also replicated as a small toy made by the Midgetoy company. It came in two versions, one with side windows and one without side windows.

A detailed article titled "L'Universelle: Front Wheel Drive in '55," written by Dave Newell and Robert L. Hauser, was published in the August 1982 issue of *Special Interest Autos* and provides a fascinating look inside the GMC Truck and Coach Studio in the 1954-1955 era. William F. Lange was the head of this studio, which was housed in Fisher Body's old Plant 8 in Detroit, while the GM Tech Center was under construction. Located nearby was Luther W. Stier's Chevrolet Truck Styling Studio. A smaller Experimental Styling Group worked in an area that was partitioned off between the two studios.

Well-known GM designer Chuck Jordan was put in charge of the Experimental Styling Group in April of 1954. According to the SIA story, Jordan was seen driving around in a Chevrolet Suburban Carry-All and a VW Kombi bus. As he absorbed the features of each of these vehicles, Jordan began to think of a truck that would merge or blend the best points of each. At this point, Jordan had already finished designing a new, slab-sided "Suburban Pickup" that was due for introduction by both Chevrolet and GMC in early 1955.

Truck design was getting a lot of attention inside GM at that time and Newell and Hauser pointed up several reasons. First was the fact that the 1953 Motorama did a lot to promote interest in new cars and it seemed wise to extend this to trucks. Second, GMC's 40-year-old general manager, Phillip J. Monaghan, had the feeling that truck design had been stagnant for too long, even as passenger cars went through dramatic modernizations. This made sense, since GMC relied on trucks only for its business. In addition to these points, Jordan's Suburban Pickup (which is now better known as the Cameo Carrier) must have shown the GM brass that trucks really could look stylish.

Monaghan shared his idea with styling vice president Harley Earl and it was decided to put Jordan to work on a new type of experimental truck, code named the XP-39, for the 1955 Motorama. Earl had sketched van-like cars in his earlier years at GM and he pushed some of his concepts on the younger designers. "He always had a heavy influence," Jordan was quoted as saying in *SIA*. "We were just young punks. Earl had his own ideas and wanted to make sure we used them."

The thinking behind the L'Universelle has a familiar ring to it and resembles Brooks Steven's earlier concepts for the Willys Jeepster. For example, the van was to be convertible into different configurations such as a station wagon, a taxicab, and a sportsman's version.

Another 1953 photo of a white-topped "Parade of Progress" bus which was used as a mobile office and to entertain VIPs while the show traveled. (RG/MB)

This "Parade of Progress" bus carried a display highlighting the latest developments from GM's Electromotive Division. (RG/MB)

The 1955 GMC L'Universelle van was displayed on the portable circular platform. (© General Motors Corp.)

GM engineers experimented with various preliminary engineering layouts. The VW buses' rear-engine mounting was not adopted for the dream truck. Instead, it was originally decided to use a 287-cid 180-hp Pontiac V-8 placed lengthwise behind the driver (for better weight distribution) and to link it to a forward automatic transaxle. A dropped rear axle was used to make the frame sit low to the ground. After the initial mechanical layout was locked in, stylists began working on clay models to develop the truck's outward appearance. Two early clay models were identified by the names "Livraison" and "Expedier."

Following standard practice, as the styling began to "gel," GM engineers working under vehicle-development head Maurice A. Thorne went back to their chassis and drive-train designs. GMC chief engineer Carl Bock and head of experimental engineering Gil Roddewig went to see Harley Earl and were told that GMC would get the job of building a chassis for the show truck. Even though Roddewig had no budget for this, Bock told him to do it.

According to Newell and Hauser, GMC engineers were worried about how a front-wheel-drive truck would handle, so he found a Jeep, locked out the rear axle, and let them drive it before he told them what he had done. This demonstration made the engineers realize that there was nothing to worry about.

A second chassis with a 110-inch wheelbase was developed under Roddewig and shop superintendent Tony Bego in a few months to replace the original 107-inch wheelbase chassis. It also had reworked steering and the radiator mounting was changed for improved cooling.

Robert L. Hauser, who worked in GMC's engine design group in 1954, recalled that the engine would not fit into the prototype chassis because of insufficient clearance between the distributor, the engine cover and the driver's seat. He said this was solved by drilling a hole in the water pump housing and putting the distributor there. The chassis was non-functional and apparently no one who saw the show truck later noticed that the distributor couldn't work.

Chuck Jordan was transferred off the project in the fall of 1954 and it moved to Bill Lange's studio where Bob Phillips and Stan Trybus did final drawings, finished the clay model (with GMC changes), and called in plasterers to make molds for pouring the fiberglass body.

In November, the chassis was sent to the styling department's metal shop and the body was built on it. The finished prototype was 188 inches long, 78 inches wide, and 71 inches high. It had a 173 cu.-ft. cargo area, a 1/2-ton rating, and a maximum GVW of 4,561 lbs. Coach engineer Bill Strong coordinated the final work between the styling and engineering sections. The L'Universelle was painted in a pearlescent copper color and was displayed at the GM Motoramas in New York, Miami, Los Angeles, San Francisco, and Boston.

For awhile, there were plans to produce the L'Universelle and Harley Earl was so serious about it that he filed a patent covering the entire vehicle a few days before the New York Motorama opened. In its 1955 annual report, General Motors stated that the truck would be going into production in 1956.

When the Motoramas ended, the L'Universelle came back to GM Truck & Coach for further development as an engineering-design project. Engineer Hans Schjolin created a separate frame and running gear unit with a transversely mounted V-8 attached to a Hydra-Matic transmission using a GMC bus angle-drive unit. He did not like the 8.40-x-13 tires that the engineering staff had suggested as replacements for the show truck's 8.00-x-13 tires or the front-wheel-drive layout, but the design work continued and preliminary specifications for a production version were issued on January 3, 1956.

Plans for the production version included a semi-monocoque steel body with separate under frames for the power train and front suspension. Work on a Model-90 station-wagon version and Model-91 panel-delivery version started. A test version was created. The designers used pop-rivets to attach a fiberglass L'Universelle front end to a modified Buick body mounted on a styling buck. A transverse engine was mounted in the resulting vehicle.

Richard Balmer, who was head of the engine-design section, told Newell and Hauser that GMC engineers preferred the use of a Buick V-8, but the final choice was to use a 316-cid Pontiac V-8. This engine was used in the two test beds (T-1443 and T-1478) that used the modified Buick body. These were driven at the GM Proving Grounds and despite the weird appearance, they tested out fine, particularly in winter-driving conditions.

Dave Newell and Robert L. Hauser talked to ex-GMC employee Tom Van Degrift, who told them that the project went as far as ordering a new press, in 1956, to stamp out L'Universelle roof panels. Eventually, the truck proved to be too innovative to build at anywhere near a reasonable cost, but as the two authors noted, "GMC's one and only dream truck (author's note, up to this time)...was so new that it took the cooperation of three GM divisions to build it." They also noted that the "L'Universelle put the 'van' idea in motion at General Motors."

Five views of the Palomino Pickup as it looks today. (JRR)

1957: The Palomino

Both the production-type GMC Suburban pickup and the GMC-built L'Universelle dream van were reflective of the image changes that trucks were going through in the mid-1950s. The same could be said about the one-of-a-kind Western-style 1957 Palomino pickup that was created by GMC designers to display at various auto-and-truck shows as a concept vehicle.

The concept behind the Palomino was pure luxury. It was based on a stock 1957 Suburban pickup, but featured customized treatments on the exterior and interior designed to catch the attention of show goers.

On the outside, the Palomino was painted in a special two-tone combination of gold and cream. Custom-fabricated ribbed-aluminum trim decorated the sides of the cargo box just behind the doors. Accessories galore were added to the stunning-looking truck, including a sun visor, wheel-trim rings, combination spotlights and mirrors, and bright metal-vent shades over the side windows.

The seats inside the truck were done in special two-tone leather trim that was color-coordinated with the body colors. The arm rests and door panels were trimmed to match the interior and gold-colored mats protected the floor. The steering wheel had a special leather covering.

The Palomino had a Pontiac V-8, which was an extra-cost option in regular GMC models. It had a Hydra-Matic transmission, power steering, and power brakes. U.S. Royal tires with unusual-for-the-era narrow-band whitewall tires were mounted on the Palomino.

After its stint on the show circuit, the Palomino was sold to a loyal customer of Seibright Cadillac/GMC in Wheeling, West Virginia. Mr. C. L. Hanna had bought a new Cadillac at the dealership each year that they were available between 1908 and 1957. Based on that record, the dealer was able to get him the retired show truck he had fallen in love with because he thought of it as the "Cadillac of pickup trucks."

When Hanna passed away, the Palomino pickup was bought by collector Clyde W. Horst, of New Holland, Pennsylvania. Horst bought the Palomino in 1979. Although it was 22 years old at the time, the truck's odometer showed only 9,000 miles. Horst had the gold paint re-sprayed to bring the truck back to mint condition. He then resold the truck, about 10 years ago, to car collector Jack R. Robinson, who owns it today. Robinson reported that the truck had only 9,300 original miles on its odometer in July 2000.

1964: Bison

In 1964, GMC caught the imagination of many visitors to the New York World's Fair in Flushing Meadows, New York, with an experimental cargo vehicle called the Bison. This dream truck of the future used two turbines enclosed in a pod behind the operator of the vehicle. The driver sat ahead of the front wheels, in an aerodynamic, forward-tilting canopy. Inside were red, green, and amber lights to warn the driver whenever the truck needed repairs.

1965: Turbo-Cruiser No. 2

Although it had been a decade since GMC developed the "Turbo-Cruiser No. 1" bus in 1955, the concept was not forgotten and resurfaced in 1965 when the turbine-powered "Turbo-Cruiser 2" appeared late in the fall of 1964. The new turbo-cruiser was introduced at an urban-rapid-transit seminar. It featured a power-transfer system designed by General Motors Research Laboratories and the Allison Division of GM that gave it an impressive margin of extra performance over the first GMC turbine-powered bus. It used a variable-speed-ratio clutch to transfer a scheduled amount of power from the engine's gasifier turbine to the output shaft. GMC General Manager Calvin J. Werner told the press that the Turbo-Cruiser No. 2 represented, "A dramatic example of the potential of the motorbus for efficient rapid-transit operations in the community of today and tomorrow."

1989: Centaur

GMC's marketing program for 1988 employed the catchy slogan, "It's not just a truck anymore," and it's probably no coincidence that a 1989 GMC concept truck had both a name and an appearance that underlined that sales pitch. The Centaur was named after Greek mythology's half-man half-horse creature and blended the appearance of a mini-van with the utility of a pickup truck.

The Centaur had some of the characteristics of the early '60s forward-control pickup trucks marketed by Volkswagen, Dodge, and Ford, but it was a much smoother interpretation of the always-popular body style. The front half of the vehicle resembled one of GM's new-at-the-time All-Purpose Vehicles, such as the Pontiac Trans Sport. The rear had a cargo bed like a pickup truck.

A bright-red metallic and silver two-tone finish treatment was done using translucent paint for a high-tech look. Most of the vehicle was painted red, but forward-tapering panels finished in silver decorated the rear quarters and lower doors. Each panel had slanting vertical louvers just ahead of the rear-wheel openings. The high-tech wheel covers carried the Centaur name.

The aerodynamics of the Centaur's sleek front end were enhanced through the use of flush-fitting glass. The roomy interior could accommodate either four or five people (two in front and the others in a rear seat). Inside the vehicle, the instruments and gauges were housed in a free-standing vertical console that wrapped around on the left side of the steering wheel. The center-mounted steering wheel featured redundant push-button controls. The Centaur also boasted self-leveling air springs, electric four-wheel steering, and an anti-lock braking system.

Right: A rear view of the 1988 GMC Centaur concept truck. (© General Motors Corp.)

Right: The 1988 GMC Centaur concept truck looks modern even now. (© General Motors Corp.)

1991: Big and Small Dreams

For many years throughout its history, GMC did not create any concept vehicles, but in 1991 it outdid itself by showcasing two dream machines at events across the country. Both were convertible versions of regular pickups. The GMC Transcend was a customized full-size Sierra and the Mahalo was a restyled Sonoma compact pickup featuring a Hawaiian theme.

Finished in two-tone raspberry and dark-magenta colors, the Transcend had a rakish "hot rod" look with its chopped roof, lowered suspension, and ground effects. The cab and cargo bed were integrated to give a smooth, flush look. When the operator pushed a button, the truck's roof retracted into the sail panels to "park" behind the seats. Then you had a convertible with a "targa" top. The roof also retracted by using a remote transmitter that operated the keyless ignition and remote-entry systems as well.

As with many modern show vehicles, a lot of custom work went into the Transcend's interior, which was trimmed in raspberry-and-black cloth-and-leather upholstery. It featured aircraft-style high-back bucket seats and a console with a CD player, accessory power modules, and all accessory controls, as well as cup holders and storage compartments. The seats had six-way power controls and a memory function that brought them to pre-set adjustments when the cab was entered.

According to GMC, the word Mahalo meant "hello and goodbye" in Hawaiian, but the customized Sonoma pickup using that name was a tightly designed package with soft-top convertible styling, a lowered ride height, and new low-profile rubber rolling on 16-inch wheels. It featured

The 1991 GMC Transcend. (JAG)

full-ground effects, custom outside rear-view mirrors, and an integrated front bumper and air dam.

The small dream truck's paint job was a unique tri-color combination, with the lower body done in coral. This was accented by diagonal "sea-spray" graphics in Seafoam Green with white edging. The interior was leather trimmed to match the exterior finish and had a custom, full-length center console and floor-mounted shifter.

GMC stressed that it had no plans to produce either the Transcend or the Mahalo, but said that many of their advanced systems and components were in the research stage for possible use on future GMC-production models.

The 1991 GMC Transcend. (JAG)

Above and Left: The 1991 GMC Mahalo pickup. (JAG)

The 1994 GMC Santa Fe concept truck.
(© General Motors Corp.)

1994: Sante Fe Pickup

In a way, GMC's full-size Sante Fe concept truck of 1994 was a modern interpretation of the 1957 Palomino pickup's Western theme. Like its predecessor, the Sante Fe had Western motifs inside and outside. It was based on GMC's 1/2-ton Sportside Extended-Cab model and stressed a blend of high-tech engineering with luxurious appointments. It was loaded with extras like cruise control, power windows, power locks, air conditioning, and tinted glass.

Up front was an integrated brush-bar grille that had a GMC character. A bold and aggressive front fascia treatment incorporated "projector" road lamps, tow hooks and a tunneled-in winch. Exclusive side mirrors, created by K. W. Muth, Co., incorporated visible-to-the-rear turn signals on the mirror glass as a safety feature. The wraparound rear bumper had a built-in step pad.

The Sante Fe pickup's rear fascia housed a high-density rear fog lamp and back-up lamp. Its unique tail lamps blended neatly into the pickup box. A neon-lamp high-mounted stoplight was featured and a first-ever rear-window pickup-truck lift glass allowed easy access to the rear-cab compartment.

The Santa Fe exterior was done in a distinctive monochromatic Terra-Cotta color with the all-leather interior trimmed in two-tone saddle shades. Power came from a 210-hp 5.7-liter V-8 that put out 300 lbs.-ft. of torque. A 4L60E Hydra-Matic transmission was used with a 3.73:1 limited-slip rear axle.

The Sante Fe-concept vehicle was equipped with GMC's popular Z71 off-road and heavy-duty trailering packages. Setting off the show truck's custom appearance were specific 20- x 10-inch painted aluminum wheels shod with P295/50R20 Extended-Mobility Tires. Developed specifically for GMC Truck Division by Goodyear, the Extended-Mobility Tires were designed to provide extended operation in the event of a loss of air pressure. They allowed the driver to continue to a service location and eliminated the spare tire and jack.

Continuing the Western motifs inside, the show truck featured reclining high-back leather-bucket seats, with French-sewn seams in contrasting thread, and a center console and armrest. The console contained a compact-disc changer and cellular telephone, with hands-free operation, and automatic-radio muting functions. Custom-leather saddlebag pockets dressed up the door panels and seat backs. The folding rear-bench seat was trimmed in matching leather. The leather-trimmed instrument panel contained a full analog-gauge cluster with a tachometer, speedometer, voltmeter and oil pressure, and temperature gauges. A "heads-up" display function projected gauge readings and turn signals on the windshield. A four-spoke leather-wrapped steering wheel was also included.

1997: Envoy

At the 1997 Chicago Automobile Show, Roy Roberts unveiled a Jimmy-based show truck called the Envoy, saying there were plans to introduce a production version within the next calendar year. The Envoy featured smooth, flowing body lines, HID (high-intensity-discharge) headlights, GM's OnStar mobile-communications system, a Bose sound system, leather-and-wood interior trim, a built-in air compressor, and a "panic-button" alarm system. "Like the diplomatic envoy, the GMC Envoy is refined, sophisticated, and evokes a sense of comfort and security," said Jeff Cohen, brand manager for GMC compact SUVs. "The Envoy emphasizes a luxury approach to the sport-utility market."

1998: The Deuce

At the 1998 Chicago Auto Show, GMC introduced a Sierra "Deuce" concept truck that emphasized the sporty character of GMC's full-size pickup. The Electric Red Sportside regular-cab model was customized inside and out and rode on custom-designed 285/60R18 Michelin tires mounted on 18-in. chrome-plated cast aluminum six-spoke wheels. Power was supplied by a Vortec 5300 V-8 that generated 265 hp at 5000 rpm and 320 lbs.-ft. of torque at 2800 rpm. According to brand manager Jim Kornas, the acronym "Deuce" (a term familiar to American hot rodders) meant Design-Unique Coupe Expression.

Above and Left: The 1997 GMC Envoy didn't take long to reach production. (© General Motors Corp.)

Below and Left: The 1998 GMC Sierra Deuce show truck was a big hit at car shows that year. (© General Motors Corp.)

PLEASE DEPOSIT CIGARETTES
ETC.INTO RECEPTACLES PROVIDED
FOR THIS PURPOSE
HELP KEEP FLOOR CLEAN

GMC

Chapter 14

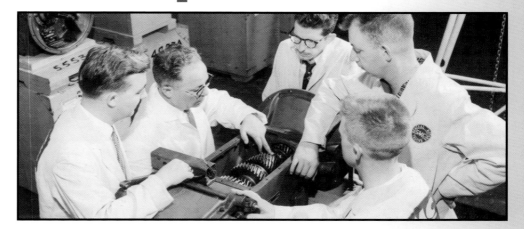

GMC Personnel

The General Motor Truck Company
Early Management Teams

Position	Name	Tenure	Comments
General Manager	William L. Day	1912-1925	Departed when GMC merged with Yellow
Assist. General Manager	K. Kurst	1919-1923	
Assist. General Manager	H.L. Hurst	1924	Was Comptroller of GM in 1914
Works Manager	E.E. Chrysler	1919-unknown	
Works Manager	Jack A. Murray	unknown–1925	
Sales Manager	W.K. Chilcott	1912-1917	
Sales Manager	Otto E. Stoll	1917-1919	
Sales Manager	V.H. Day	1919-unknown	Son of W.L. Day, General Manager
Advertising Manager	J.H. Newmark	1911-unknown	
Advertising Manager	Jim Beard	1914	
Comptroller	W.F. Mayberry	unknown	Per organizational chart of April 1924
Chief Engineer	F.A. Whitten	unknown	Per organizational chart of April 1924
Purchasing Agent	H.J. Crichton	unknown	Per organizational chart of April 1924
Service Manager	S.V. Norton	unknown	Per organizational chart of April 1924
General Manager	Otto E. Stoll	1925-unknown	Also VP of Yellow Truck & Coach Mfg.
Assist. General Manager	A.J. Banta	1925	
Assist. General Manager	H.J. Warner	1925-unknown	
Factory Manager	Jack A. Murray	1925–1932	

Notes: Information compiled from R.A. Christ's *GMC Truck History: 1900-1950*, courtesy D.E. Meyer.
See "Yellow Truck & Coach Manufacturing Company" for events after merger in 1925

Harry G. Hamilton, general manager of the Rapid Motor Vehicle Co., was born in Rochester, New York, in 1861. He developed an aptitude for business after settling in Saginaw, Michigan and later moved to Pontiac and became associated with A.G. North's Pontiac Spring & Wagon Works. He was instrumental in the establishment of Rapid Motor Vehicle Co.

Donald J. Atwood was executive vice president of Truck & Bus Power Products and Defense and Component Operations in 1983. He spent 24 years at GM and joined the board of directors on January 1, 1984.

Selected Organization Charts Related to GMC Truck

Yellow Truck & Coach Mfg. Co.—1928

President . . . . .Paul W. Seiler
Vice President, Engineering . . . . .George A. Green
Vice President, Manufacturing . . . . .Frank V. Hadas
Vice president, Finance . . . . .Irving A. Babcock
Vice President, Truck Sales . . . . .Oscar L. Arnold
Vice President, Taxicab Sales . . . . .Paul A. Geyser
Vice President, Coach Sales . . . . .H.E. Listman
Comptroller . . . . .Ernest R. Breech
Director, Service Department . . . . .O.M. Brede
Director, Purchasing Department . . . . . .B. Livingston
Director, Personnel Department . . . . . . .William F. Rasche
Notes: Information compiled from R.A. Christ's *GMC Truck History: 1900-1950*, courtesy D.E. Meyer.

Yellow Truck & Coach Mfg. Co., Organization—1932

President . . . . .Paul W. Seiler
Executive Vice President & Treasurer . . .Irving A. Babcock

Vice President .George A. Green
Vice President .J.A. Little
Secretary . . . . .T.S. Merrill
Comptroller . . . . .D.L. Tate
Notes: Information compiled from R.A. Christ's *GMC Truck History: 1900-1950*, courtesy D.E. Meyer.

Yellow Truck & Coach Mfg. Co., Officers—1938

President and General Manager . . . . . . .Irving A. Babcock
Vice President, Engineering . . . . .George A. Green
Vice President .H.C. Grossman
Vice President .H.E. Listman
Vice President .J.P. Little
Treasurer . . . . .D.L. Tate
Secretary . . . . .H.C. Grossman
Comptroller . . . . .W.F. Maybury
General Cousel . . . . .John T. Smith
Notes: Information compiled from R.A. Christ's *GMC Truck History: 1900-1950*, courtesy D.E. Meyer.

GMC Truck & Coach Div., Top Management Changes—1945-1953

Date	Position	Name	Action
Jan. 31, 1945	GM VP & General Manager	Irving A. Babcock	Resigned
Feb. 1, 1945	GM VP & General Manager	Morgan D. Douglas	Appointed
Oct. 1, 1949	Assistant General Manager	Roger M. Kyes	Appointed
April 1, 1950	GM VP & General Manager	Morgan D. Douglas	Retired
April 1, 1950	GM VP & General Manager	Roger M. Kyes	Appointed
Nov. 1952	GM VP & General Manager	Roger M. Kyes	Resigned
Jan. 1953	GM VP & General Manager	Philip J. Monaghan	Appointed

Notes: Information compiled from R.A. Christ's *GMC Truck History: 1900-1950*, courtesy D. E. Meyer.

1942

General Motors Truck & Coach Div. of Yellow Truck & Coach Mfg. Co.

President . . . . .I.B. Babcock
Coach Sales Executive . . . . .H.E. Listman
Truck Sales Executive . . . . .J.P. Little
Chief Engineer . . . . .C.O. Ball
Purchasing Agent . . . . .H.J. Crichton

1949

GMC Truck & Coach Div. of General Motors Corp.

Plant Manager . . . . .M.D. Douglas

1950

GMC Truck & Coach Div. of General Motors Corp.

Plant Manager . . . . .M.D. Douglas

1952

GMC Truck & Coach Div. of General Motors Corp.

General Manager . . . . .R.M. Kyes
Truck General Sale Manager . . . . .J.E. Johnson
Coach General Sales Manager . . . . . .H.E. Listman
Manufacturing Manager . . . . .P.J. Monaghan
Chief Engineer . . . . .C.J. Bock
Purchasing Agent . . . . .J.P. McManus
Service Manager . . . . .A.A. Shantz
Personnel Director . . . . .E.A. Maxwell
Comptroller . . . . .V.P. Blair

1953

GMC Truck & Coach Div. of General Motors Corp.

General Manager . . . . .P.J. Monaghan
Truck General Sale Manager . . . . .R.C. Woodhouse
Coach General Sales Manager . . . . . .E.P. Crenshaw
Manufacturing Manager . . . . .T.E. Wilson
Chief Engineer . . . . .C.J. Bock
Purchasing Agent . . . . .J.P. McManus
Assistant General Truck Sale Manager . .A.A. Shantz
Personnel Director . . . . .E.A. Maxwell
Comptroller . . . . .V.P. Blair
Advertising Agency . . . . .Kudner Agency, Inc.

1954

GMC Truck & Coach Div. of General Motors Corp.

General Manager . . . . .P.J. Monaghan
Truck General Sale Manager . . . . .R.C. Woodhouse
Coach General Sales Manager . . . . . .E.P. Crenshaw
Manufacturing Manager . . . . .T.E. Wilson
Chief Engineer . . . . .C.J. Bock
Purchasing Agent . . . . .J.P. McManus
Assistant General Truck Sale Manager . .A.A. Shantz
Personnel Director . . . . .E.A. Maxwell
Comptroller . . . . .V.P. Blair
Advertising Agency . . . . .Kudner Agency, Inc.

1955

GMC Truck & Coach Div. of General Motors Corp.

General Manager . . . . .P.J. Monaghan
Truck General Sale Manager . . . . .R.C. Woodhouse
Truck Fleet Division Manager . . . . .A.S. McEvoy
Coach General Sales Manager . . . . . .E.P. Crenshaw
General Manufacturing Manager . . . . . .T.E. Wilson
Chief Engineer . . . . .C.V. Crockett
Purchasing Agent . . . . .J.P. McManus

Assistant General Truck Sale Manager . .A.A. Shantz
Personnel Director . . . . .E.A. Maxwell
Comptroller . . . . .V.P. Blair
Advertising Agency . . . . .Kudner Agency, Inc.

1956

GMC Truck & Coach Div. of General Motors Corp.

General Manager . . . . .P.J. Monaghan
Truck General Sale Manager . . . . .R.C. Woodhouse
Truck Fleet Division Manager . . . . .A.S. McEvoy
Coach General Sales Manager . . . . . .E.P. Crenshaw
General Manufacturing Manager . . . . . .T.E. Wilson
Chief Engineer . . . . .C.V. Crockett
Purchasing Agent . . . . .J.P. McManus
Personnel Director . . . . .E. A. Maxwell
Comptroller . . . . .V. P. Blair
Public Relations Director . . . . .B. W. Crandell
Advertising Agency . . . . .Kudner Agency, Inc.

1957

GMC Truck & Coach Div. of General Motors Corp.

General Manager . . . . .P.J. Monaghan
Truck General Sales Manager . . . . .R.C. Woodhouse
Executive Assistant to
General Manager Dealer Relations . . . .W.L. VandeWater
Coach General Sales Manager . . . . . .E.P. Crenshaw
General Manufacturing Manager . . . . . .T.E. Wilson
Chief Engineer . . . . .C.V. Crockett
Purchasing Agent . . . . .J.P. McManus
Personnel Director . . . . .E.A. Maxwell
Comptroller . . . . .V.P. Blair
Public Relations Director . . . . .B.W. Crandell
Advertising Agency . . . . .Kudner Agency, Inc.

1958

GMC Truck & Coach Div. of General Motors Corp.

General Manager . . . . .P.J. Monaghan
Truck General Sales Manager . . . . .R.C. Woodhouse
Executive Assistant to
General Manager Dealer Relations . . . .W.L. VandeWater
Coach General Sales Manager . . . . . .E.P. Crenshaw
General Manufacturing Manager . . . . . .T.E. Wilson
Chief Engineer . . . . .C.V. Crockett
Purchasing Agent . . . . .J.P. McManus
Personnel Director . . . . .E.A. Maxwell
Comptroller . . . . .R.L. Ganter
Public Relations Director . . . . .B.W. Crandell
Advertising Agency . . . . .Kudner Agency, Inc.

1959

GMC Truck & Coach Div. of General Motors Corp.

General Manager . . . . .P.J. Monaghan
Truck General Sales Manager . . . . .R.C. Woodhouse
Executive Assistant to
General Manager Dealer Relations . . . .W.L. VandeWater
Coach General Sales Manager . . . . . .C.F. Dick
General Manufacturing Manager . . . . . .T.E. Wilson
Chief Engineer . . . . .C.V. Crockett
Director of Purchasing . . . . .J.P. McManus
Personnel Director . . . . .E.A. Maxwell
Comptroller . . . . .R.L. Ganter
Public Relations Director . . . . .B.W. Crandell
Advertising Agency . . . . .McCann-Erickson, Inc.

1960

GMC Truck & Coach Div. of General Motors Corp.

General Manager . . . . .C.J. Werner

GMC executives outside what is probably the old Rapid St. office sometime between 1910 and the early 1920s. Note the original GMC logo stenciled on the door. (© General Motors Corp.)

Truck General Sales Manager . . . . .R.C. Woodhouse
Coach General Sales Manager . . . . . .C.F. Dick
General Manufacturing Manager . . . . .T.E. Wilson
Chief Engineer . . . . .C.V. Crockett
Director of Purchasing . . . . .J.P. McManus
Personnel Director . . . . .E.A. Maxwell
Comptroller . . . . .R.L. Ganter
Public Relations Director . . . . .B.W. Crandell
Advertising Agency . . . . .McCann-Erickson, Inc.

1961
GMC Truck & Coach Div. of General Motors Corp.
General Manager . . . . .C.J. Werner
Truck General Sales Manager . . . . .R.C. Woodhouse
Coach General Sales Manager . . . . . . .C.F. Dick
General Manufacturing Manager . . . . . .T.E. Wilson
Chief Engineer . . . . .C.V. Crockett
Director of Purchasing . . . . .J.P. McManus
Personnel Director . . . . .E.A. Maxwell
Comptroller . . . . .R.L. Ganter
Public Relations Director . . . . .B.W. Crandell
Advertising Agency . . . . .McCann-Erickson, Inc.

1962
GMC Truck & Coach Div. of General Motors Corp.
General Manager . . . . .C.J. Werner
Truck General Sales Manager . . . . .R.C. Woodhouse
Coach General Sales Manager . . . . . . .C.F. Dick
General Manufacturing Manager . . . . . .T.E. Wilson
Chief Engineer . . . . .H.O. Flynn
Director of Purchasing . . . . .J.P. McManus
Personnel Director . . . . .E.A. Maxwell
Comptroller . . . . .R.L. Ganter
Public Relations Director . . . . .J.A. Castle
Advertising Agency . . . . .McCann-Erickson, Inc.

1963
GMC Truck & Coach Div. of General Motors Corp.
General Manager . . . . .C.J. Werner
Truck General Sales Manager . . . . .R.C. Woodhouse
Coach General Sales Manager . . . . . . .C.F. Dick
General Manufacturing Manager . . . . . .T.E. Wilson
Chief Engineer . . . . .H.O. Flynn
Director of Purchasing . . . . .J.P. McManus
Personnel Director . . . . .E.A. Maxwell
Comptroller . . . . .J.D. Mintline
Public Relations Director . . . . .J.A. Castle
Advertising Agency . . . . .McCann-Erickson, Inc.

GMC service training expert Jim Olsen demonstrates the workings of the Fuller R96 10-speed Load Ranger transmission to four service personnel around 1958. (© General Motors Corp.)

1964
GMC Truck & Coach Div. of General Motors Corp.
General Manager . . . . .C.J. Werner
Truck General Sales Manager . . . . .R.C. Woodhouse
Coach General Sales Manager . . . . . . .C.F. Dick
General Manufacturing Manager . . . . . .T.E. Wilson
Chief Engineer . . . . .H.O. Flynn
Director of Purchasing . . . . .J.P. McManus
Personnel Director . . . . .E.A. Maxwell
Comptroller . . . . .J.D. Mintline
Public Relations Director . . . . .J.A. Castle
Advertising Agency . . . . .McCann-Erickson, Inc.

1965
GMC Truck & Coach Div. of General Motors Corp.
General Manager . . . . .C.J. Werner
General Sales Manager . . . . .R.C. Woodhouse
Coach Sales Manager . . . . .C.F. Dick
Director of Defense Products . . . . .S.G. Little
General Manufacturing Manager . . . . . .T.E. Wilson
Chief Engineer . . . . .H.O. Flynn
Director of Purchasing . . . . .J.P. McManus
Director of Reliability . . . . .W.W. Edwards
Personnel Director . . . . .E.A. Maxwell
Comptroller . . . . .J.D. Mintline
Public Relations Director . . . . .J.A. Castle
Advertising Agency . . . . .McCann-Erickson, Inc.

1966
GMC Truck & Coach Div. of General Motors Corp.
General Manager . . . . .C.J. Werner
General Sales Manager . . . . .R.C. Woodhouse
Truck Sales Manager . . . . .R.C. Stelter
Coach Sales Manager . . . . .E.F. Lewis
Director of Defense Products . . . . .S.G. Little
General Manufacturing Manager . . . . . .T.E. Wilson
Chief Engineer . . . . .H.O. Flynn
Director of Purchasing &
Production Control . . . . .W.W. Edwards
Director of Purchasing . . . . .R.K. Russell
Director of Reliability . . . . .N.F. Trost
Personnel Director . . . . .E.A. Maxwell
Comptroller . . . . .J.D. Mintline
Public Relations Director . . . . .J.A. Castle
Advertising Agency . . . . .McCann-Erickson, Inc.

1967
GMC Truck & Coach Div. of General Motors Corp.
General Manager . . . . .M.J. Caserio
General Sales Manager . . . . .R.C. Stelter
Sales Manager Coaches & Trucks-Retail .E.F. Lewis
Director of Defense Products . . . . .S.G. Little
General Manufacturing Manager . . . . . .T.E. Wilson
Chief Engineer . . . . .H.O. Flynn
Director of Purchasing &
Production Control . . . . .W.W. Edwards
Director of Purchasing . . . . .R.K. Russell
Director of Reliability . . . . .G.A. Brundrett
Personnel Director . . . . .E.A. Maxwell
Comptroller . . . . .J.D. Mintline
Public Relations Director . . . . .J.A. Castle
Advertising Agency . . . . .McCann-Erickson, Inc.

1968
GMC Truck & Coach Div. of General Motors Corp.
General Manager . . . . .M.J. Caserio
General Sales Manager . . . . .R.C. Stelter
Sales Manager Coaches & Trucks-Retail .E.F. Lewis
Vehicle Safety Audit . . . . .S.G. Little
General Manufacturing Manager . . . . . .B.T. Olson
Chief Engineer . . . . .H.O. Flynn
Director of Purchasing &
Production Control . . . . .W.W. Edwards
Director of Purchasing . . . . .M.D. Walker
Director of Reliability . . . . .G.A. Brundrett
Personnel Director . . . . .E.A. Maxwell
Comptroller . . . . .J.D. Mintline
Public Relations Director . . . . .J.A. Castle
Advertising Agency . . . . .McCann-Erickson, Inc.

1969
GMC Truck & Coach Div. of General Motors Corp.
General Manager . . . . .M.J. Caserio
General Sales Manager . . . . .R.C. Stelter
Sales Manager Coaches . . . . .E.R. Stokel
Sales Manager Trucks . . . . .T.L. Harris
Vehicle Safety Audit . . . . .S.G. Little
General Manufacturing Manager . . . . . .B.T. Olson
Chief Engineer . . . . .H.O. Flynn
Director of Purchasing &
Production Control . . . . .W.W. Edwards
Director of Purchasing . . . . .M.D. Walker
Director of Reliability . . . . .G.A. Brundrett
Personnel Director . . . . .E.A. Maxwell
Comptroller . . . . .R.G. Courter
Public Relations Director . . . . .F.E. Cronin
Advertising Agency . . . . .McCann-Erickson, Inc.

1970
GMC Truck & Coach Div. of General Motors Corp.
General Manager . . . . .M.J. Caserio
General Sales Manager . . . . .R.C. Stelter
Sales Manager Coaches . . . . .E. R. Stokel
Sales Manager Trucks . . . . .T.L. Harris
Director of Systems Data Processing . . .R.J. Sullivan
General Manufacturing Manager . . . . . .R.W. Podlesak
Chief Engineer . . . . .W.W. Edwards
Director of Production,
Materials Control & Materials Handling . .W.D. Noon
Director of Purchasing . . . . .M.D. Walker
Director of Reliability . . . . .G.A. Brundrett
Personnel Director . . . . .E.A. Maxwell
Comptroller . . . . .R.G. Courter
Public Relations Director . . . . .F.E. Cronin
Advertising Agency . . . . .McCann-Erickson, Inc.

1971
GMC Truck & Coach Div. of General Motors Corp.
General Manager . . . . .M.J. Caserio
General Sales Manager . . . . .R.C. Stelter
Director of Systems Data Processing . . .R.J. Sullivan
General Manufacturing Manager . . . . . .R.W. Podlesak
Chief Engineer . . . . .W.W. Edwards
Director of Engineering . . . . .H.O. Flynn
Director of Production,
Materials Control & Materials Handling . .W.D. Noon
Director of Purchasing . . . . .G.R. Fitzgerald

Director of Reliability . . . . .G.A. Brundrett
Personnel Director . . . . .E.A. Maxwell
Comptroller . . . . .R.G. Courter
Public Relations Director . . . . .F.E. Cronin
Advertising Agency . . . . .McCann-Erickson, Inc.

1972
GMC Truck & Coach Div. of General Motors Corp.
General Manager . . . . .M.J. Caserio
Director of Reliability . . . . .G.A. Brundrett
Divisional Comptroller . . . . .R.G. Courter
Public Relations Director . . . . .F.E. Cronin
Chief Engineer . . . . .W.W. Edwards
Director of Purchasing . . . . .G.R. Fitzgerald
Personnel Director . . . . .E.A. Maxwell
Director of Production,
Materials Control & Materials Handling . .W.D. Noon
General Manufacturing Manager . . . . . .R.W. Podlesak
General Sales Manager . . . . .R.C. Stelter
Director of Systems Data Processing . . .R.J. Sullivan
Product Planning Manager . . . . .B.M. Wilton
Advertising Agency . . . . .McCann-Erickson, Inc.

1973
GMC Truck & Coach Div. of General Motors Corp.
General Manager . . . . .A.C. Mair
Director of Reliability . . . . .G.A. Brundrett
Divisional Comptroller . . . . .R.G. Courter
Public Relations Director . . . . .F.E. Cronin
Chief Engineer . . . . .W.W. Edwards
Director of Purchasing . . . . .G.R. Fitzgerald
Director of Personnel . . . . .E.A. Maxwell
Director of Production,
Materials Control & Materials Handling . .W.D. Noon
General Manufacturing Manager . . . . . .R.W. Podlesak
General Sales Manager . . . . .R.C. Stelter
Product Planning Manager . . . . .B.M. Wilton
Director of Advertising . . . . .R.T. Jennings
Advertising Agency . . . . .McCann-Erickson, Inc.

1974
General Motors Truck & Coach Div. of General Motors Corp.
General Manager . . . . .A.C. Mair
General Manufacturing Manager . . . . . .J.D. Wisner
Director of Supplier Relations . . . . .G.A. Brundrett
Director of Public Relations . . . . .F.E. Cronin
Director of Product Planning . . . . .B.M. Wilton
Director of Reliability . . . . .T.A. Maxwell
Director of Public Transportation . . . . . .E.R. Stokel
Director of Purchasing . . . . .G.R. Fitzgerald
Divisional Comptroller . . . . .R.G. Courter
Chief Engineer . . . . .W.W. Edwards
Director of Production,
Materials Control & Materials Handling . .W.D. Noon
General Sales Manager . . . . .R.C. Stelter
Director of Advertising . . . . .R.T. Jennings
Advertising Agency . . . . .McCann-Erickson, Inc.

1975
GMC Truck & Coach Div. of General Motors Corp.
General Manager And
General Motors Vice President . . . . .A.C. Mair
General Manufacturing Manager . . . . . .J.D. Wisner
Director of Supplier Relations . . . . .G.A. Brundrett

Director of Public Relations . . . . .F.E. Cronin
Director of Production & Materials Control   E.C. Mosner
Director of Personnel . . . . .E.A. Maxwell
Director of Systems & Data Processing .J.V. Stingley
Manager of Product Planning . . . . .E.B. Blair
Director of Reliability . . . . .T.A. Maxwell
Director of Public Transportation . . . . . .E.R. Stokel
Director of Purchasing . . . . .G.R. Fitzgerald
Divisional Comptroller . . . . .R.G. Courter
Chief Engineer . . . . .W.W. Edwards
Director of Production &
Materials Control . . . . .W.D. Noon
General Sales Manager . . . . .R.C. Stelter
Director of Advertising . . . . .R.T. Jennings
Advertising Agency . . . . .McCann-Erickson, Inc.

1976
GMC Truck & Coach Div. of General Motors Corp.
General Manager . . . . .R.W. Truxell
General Manufacturing Manager . . . . . .J.D. Wisner
Director of Supplier Relations . . . . .G.A. Brundrett
Director of Public Relations . . . . .F.E. Cronin
Director of Purchasing,
Materials Control & Traffic . . . . .E.C. Mosner
Director of Reliability . . . . .T.A. Maxwell
Director of Personnel . . . . .E.A. Maxwell
Director of Systems &
Data Processing . . . . .J.V. Stingley
Manager of Product Planning . . . . .E.B. Blair
Director of Public Transportation . . . . . .E.R. Stokel
Director of Purchasing . . . . .G.R. Fitzgerald
Divisional Comptroller . . . . .R.G. Courter
Director of Engineering . . . . .W.W. Edwards
Director of Production &
Material Control Systems . . . . .W.D. Noon
General Sales Manager . . . . .J.E. Conlan
Director of Advertising . . . . .R.T. Jennings
Advertising Agency . . . . .McCann-Erickson, Inc.

1977
GMC Truck & Coach Div. of General Motors Corp.
General Manager and
General Motors Vice President . . . . .R.W. Truxell
General Manufacturing Manager . . . . . .J.D. Wisner
Director of Supplier Relations . . . . .G.A. Brundrett
Director of Public Relations . . . . .F.E. Cronin
Director of Purchasing,
Materials Control & Traffic . . . . .E.C. Mosner
Director of Reliability . . . . .T.A. Maxwell
Director of Personnel . . . . .J.R. Miller
Director of Systems &
Data Processing . . . . .J.V. Stingley
Manager of Product Planning . . . . .E.B. Blair
Director of Public Transportation . . . . . .E.R. Stokel
Director of Purchasing . . . . .C.E. Code, Jr.
Divisional Comptroller . . . . .R.G. Courter
Director of Engineering . . . . .W.W. Edwards
Director of Production &
Material Control Systems . . . . .W.D. Noon
General Sales Manager . . . . .J.E. Conlan
Director of Advertising . . . . .R.T. Jennings
Advertising Agency . . . . .McCann-Erickson, Inc.

1978
GMC Truck & Coach Div. of General Motors Corp.
General Manager and

General Motors Vice President . . . . .R.W. Truxell
General Manufacturing Manager . . . . . .J.D. Wisner
Director of Public Relations . . . . .F.E. Cronin
Director of Purchasing,
Materials Control and Traffic . . . . .E.C. Mosner
Director of Reliability . . . . .T.A. Maxwell
Manager of Product Planning . . . . .E.B. Blair
Director of Public Transportation . . . . . .E.R. Stokel
Director of Purchasing . . . . .C.E. Code, Jr.
Divisional Comptroller . . . . .R.G. Courter
Director of Engineering . . . . .W.W. Edwards
General Sales Manager . . . . .J.E. Conlan
Manager of Advertising . . . . .R.T. Jennings
Advertising Agency . . . . .McCann-Erickson, Inc.

1979
GMC Truck & Coach Div. of General Motors Corp.
General Manager and
General Motors Vice President . . . . .Robert W. Truxell
General Manufacturing Manager . . . . . .Jay D. Wisner
General Sales Manager . . . . .James E. Conlan
Director of Reliability . . . . .Thomas A. Maxwell
Director of Planning . . . . .Richard A. Pennell
Director of Public Transportation . . . . . .Edward R. Stokel
Director of Purchasing . . . . .Donald J. Cassady
Divisional Comptroller . . . . .Robert C. Shannon
Director of Engineering . . . . .Dean D. Forester
Director of Public Relations . . . . .Frank E. Cronin
Manager of Advertising . . . . .Richard T. Jennings
Advertising Agency . . . . .McCann-Erickson, Inc.

1980
GMC Truck & Coach Div. of General Motors Corp.
General Manager and
General Motors Vice President . . . . .Robert W. Truxell
General Manufacturing Manager . . . . . .Jay D. Wisner
General Sales Manager . . . . .James E. Conlan
Director of Reliability . . . . .Thomas A. Maxwell
Director of Planning . . . . .Richard A. Pennell
Director of Public Transportation . . . . . .Edward R. Stokel
Director of Purchasing . . . . .Donald J. Cassady
Divisional Comptroller . . . . .Robert C. Shannon
Director of Engineering . . . . .Dean D. Forester
Director of Public Relations . . . . .Frank E. Cronin
Advertising Manager . . . . .James E. Wenzel
Advertising Agency . . . . .McCann-Erickson, Inc.

1981
GMC Truck & Coach Div. of General Motors Corp.
General Manager and
General Motors Vice President . . . . .Robert W. Truxell
General Manufacturing Manager . . . . . .Jay D. Wisner
General Sales Manager . . . . .James T. Riley
Director of Reliability . . . . .Thomas A. Maxwell
Director of Planning . . . . .Richard A. Pennell
Director of Public Transportation . . . . . .Edward R. Stokel
Director of Purchasing . . . . .Frank E. Cooney
Divisional Comptroller . . . . .Robert C. Shannon
Director of Engineering . . . . .D. Dean Forester
Director of Public Relations . . . . .Frank E. Cronin
Advertising Manager . . . . .James E. Wenzel
Advertising Agency . . . . .McCann-Erickson, Inc.

1982

GMC Truck & Coach Div. of General Motors Corp.

General Manager and
General Motors Vice President and
Group Vice President Worldwide
Medium and Heavy Truck &
Bus Operations . . . . .Robert W. Truxell
General Manufacturing Manager . . . . . .Jay D. Wisner
General Sales Manager . . . . .James T. Riley
Director of Reliability . . . . .Thomas A. Maxwell
Director of Planning . . . . .Richard A. Pennell
Director of Public Transportation . . . . . .Edward R. Stokel
Director of Purchasing . . . . .Frank E. Cooney
Divisional Comptroller . . . . .Robert C. Shannon
Chief Engineer, Truck . . . . .Paul O. Larson
Director of Public Relations . . . . .Frank E. Cronin
Advertising Manager . . . . .James E. Wenzel
Advertising Agency . . . . .McCann-Erickson, Inc.

1983

General Motors Truck & Coach Operations

Vice President General Motors Corp. and
Group Executive, Truck & Bus Group . . .Donald J. Atwood
General Manager Truck and
Bus Manufacturing Div. . . . . .Robert L. McKee
General Manufacturing Manager . . . . . .Ross M. Haun
Manager, GMC Truck &
Coach Operations . . . . .John D. Rock
General Sales Manager . . . . .James T. Riley
Advertising Manager . . . . .James E. Wenzel
Director of Public Relations . . . . .Donald C. Huss
Director of Public Transportation . . . . . .Edward R. Stokel
Advertising Agency . . . . .McCann-Erickson, Inc.

1984

General Motors Truck & Coach Operation

Vice President General Motors Corp.
and Group Executive,
Truck & Bus Group . . . . .Donald J. Atwood
General Manager Truck and
Bus Manufacturing Div. . . . . .Robert L. McKee
General Manufacturing Manager . . . . . .Ross M. Haun
Manager,
GMC Truck & Coach Operations . . . . . .John D. Rock
Advertising Manager . . . . .Candace M. Robbins
General Director, Truck Sales . . . . .Duncan A. Brodie
Director of Public Relations . . . . .Donald C. Huss
Director of Public Transportation . . . . . .Edward R. Stokel
Advertising Agency . . . . .McCann-Erickson, Inc.

1985

General Motors Truck & Coach Operation

Executive Vice President
General Motors Corp.. . . . . .Donald J. Atwood
General Motors Vice President &
Group Director of Operations . . . . .Charles Katko
General Manager Truck and
Bus Manufacturing Div. . . . . .Patrick J. Coletta
Manager, GMC Truck &
Coach Operation . . . . .John D. Rock
Advertising Manager . . . . .Candace M. Robbins
General Director, Truck Sales . . . . .Duncan A. Brodie
Director of Public Relations . . . . .Donald C. Huss
Director of Public Transportation . . . . . .Edward R. Stokel
Advertising Agency . . . . .McCann-Erickson, Inc.

1986

General Motors Truck & Coach Operation

Executive Vice President
General Motors Corp.. . . . . .Robert C. Stempel
General Motors Vice President &
Group Executive . . . . .Charles Katko
General Motors Vice President &
Group Director of Operations . . . . .Patrick J. Coletta
Manager, GMC Truck &
Coach Operation . . . . .John D. Rock
Advertising Manager . . . . .Candace M. Robbins
General Director, Truck Sales . . . . .Duncan A. Brodie
Director of Public Relations . . . . .Donald C. Huss
Director of Public Transportation . . . . . .Edward R. Stokel
Advertising Agency . . . . .McCann-Erickson, Inc.

1987

General Motors Truck & Coach Operation

General Motors Vice President &
Group Executive . . . . .Charles Katko
General Motors Vice President &
Group Director of Operations . . . . .Patrick J. Coletta
General Manager GMC
Truck & Coach . . . . .John D. Rock
Advertising Manager . . . . .Candace M. Robbins
General Director, Truck Sales . . . . .Duncan A. Brodie
Director of Public Relations . . . . .Donald C. Huss
Director of Public Transportation . . . . . .John Jarrell
Advertising Agency . . . . .McCann-Erickson, Inc.

1987

GMC Truck Div. of General Motors Truck Group

General Motors Vice President &
Group Executive . . . . .Charles Katko
General Motors Vice President &
Group Director of Operations . . . . .Patrick J. Coletta
General Manager GMC
Truck & Coach . . . . .John D. Rock
Advertising Manager . . . . .Candace M. Robbins
General Director, Truck Sales . . . . .Duncan A. Brodie
Director of Public Relations . . . . .Donald C. Huss
Director of Public Transportation . . . . . .John Jarrell
Advertising Agency . . . . .McCann-Erickson, Inc.

> *GMC Class-8 truck operations merged with Volvo-White
> Truck Co. to form Volvo GM Heavy Truck Corp. of
> Greensboro, N.C. Official start of new company Jan. 1,
> 1988.
> **GMC Coach Operations sold to Greyhound Corp. effec-
> tive Jan. 1, 1987. Becomes Transportation Mfg. Corp., of
> Roswell, N.M., under former GM executive John Nasi.

1988

GMC Truck Div. of General Motors Truck Group

GM Truck and Bus Group

General Motors Vice President &
Group Executive . . . . .Charles Katko
General Motors Vice President &
Group Director of Operations . . . . .Patrick J. Coletta
General Sales Manager . . . . .Duncan A. Brodie
Director of Public Relations . . . . .Donald C. Huss
Group Director of Engineering . . . . .William B. Larson

GMC Truck Division

General Manager . . . . .John D. Rock
Director of Marketing . . . . .Richard M. Lee
National Advertising Manager . . . . .Candace M. Robbins
Advertising Agency . . . . .McCann-Erickson, Inc.

1989

GMC Truck Div. of General Motors Truck Group

GM Truck and Bus Group

General Motors Vice President &
Group Executive . . . . .Clifford J. Vaughan
General Motors Vice President &
Group Director of Operations . . . . .Patrick J. Coletta
Director of Public Relations . . . . .Donald C. Huss
Group Director of Engineering . . . . .William B. Larson

GMC Truck Division

General Manager . . . . .John D. Rock
General Sales Manager . . . . .Ray E. Rota
Director of Marketing . . . . .Richard M. Lee
National Advertising and
Publications Manager . . . . .William P. Middlekauff
Director of Medium-
Duty Truck Operations . . . . .Frank L. Schweibold
Medium-Duty Sales Manager . . . . .Michael J. Wattai
Advertising Agency . . . . .McCann-Erickson, Inc.

1990

GMC Truck Div. of General Motors Truck Group

GM Truck and Bus Group

General Motors Vice President &
Group Executive . . . . .Clifford J. Vaughan
General Motors Vice President &
Group Director of Operations . . . . .Patrick J. Coletta
Director of Public Relations . . . . .Donald C. Huss
Group Director of Engineering . . . . .William B. Larson

GMC Truck Division

General Manager . . . . .John D. Rock
Director of Marketing . . . . .Richard M. Lee
General Sales Manager . . . . .Ray E. Rota
National Advertising and
Publications Manager . . . . .Sandra L. Dellinger
Director of Medium-
Duty Truck Operations . . . . .Frank L. Schweibold
Medium-Duty Truck Sales Manager . . . .Michael J. Wattai
Advertising Agency . . . . .McCann-Erickson, Inc.

1991

GMC Truck Div. of General Motors Truck Group

General Manager . . . . .Lewis B. Campbell
Director of Marketing . . . . .Richard M. Lee
General Sales Manager . . . . .Ray E. Rota
National Advertising and
Publications Manager . . . . .Sandra L. Dellinger
Director of Medium-
Duty Truck Operations . . . . .Frank L. Schweibold
Medium-Duty Truck Sales Manager . . . .Michael J. Wattai
Advertising Agency . . . . .McCann-Erickson, Inc.

1992

GM Truck & BusGroup

GM Vice President and Group Executive .Clifford J. Vaughan
GM Vice President and
Group Director of Operations . . . . .Guy D. Briggs

GMC Truck Div. of General Motors Truck Group

General Manager . . . . .Lewis B. Campbell
Director of Marketing . . . . .Frederick E. Cook
General Sales Manager . . . . .Ray E. Rota
National Advertising and
Publications Manager . . . . .Sandra L. Dellinger

Martin J. Caserio (center) and Robert C. Stelter (right) get a demonstration of the Toroflow V-6 diesel engine from a lab technician in 1969. (© General Motors Corp.)

Director of Medium-
Duty Truck Operations . . . . .Frank L. Schweibold
Medium-Duty Truck Sales Manager . . . .Michael J. Wattai
Advertising Agency . . . . .McCann-Erickson, Inc.

1993

GM North American Truck Platforms (NATP)

GM Vice President and Group Executive Clifford J. Vaughan
GM Vice President and
Group Director of Operations . . . . .Guy D. Briggs

GMC Truck Div. of General Motors Truck Group

General Manager . . . . .Roy S. Roberts
General Sales Manager . . . . .Ray E. Rota
Director of Marketing . . . . .Frederick E. Cook
Director of Consumer Influence and
Business Operations . . . . .Warren E. Christell
Director Dealer Network Operations . . . .Michael J. Wattai
Director of Public Relations . . . . .Tom R. Klipstine
Advertising Agency . . . . .McCann-Erickson

1994

GMC Truck Division and GM North American Truck Platforms (NATP)

General Manager . . . . .Roy S. Roberts
General Director of Marketing . . . . .Frederick E. Cook
General Sales Manager . . . . .Ray E. Rota
Director of Consumer Influence and
Business Operations . . . . .Warren E. Christell
Director Dealer Network Operations . . . .Michael J. Wattai
Director of Public Relations . . . . .Tom R. Klipstine
Advertising Agency . . . . .McCann-Erickson

1995

GMC Truck Division and GM North American Truck Platforms (NATP)

Vice President and General Manager . . .Roy S. Roberts
General Sales Manager . . . . .Frederick E. Cook
General Marketing Manager . . . . .Ray E. Rota

Director Dealer Network Operations and
Sales Administration . . . . .William P. Middlekauf
Director of Engineering and Planning . . .Warren E. Christell
Director of Public Relations . . . . .Carl E. Sheffer
Advertising Agency . . . . .McCann-Erickson

1996

Pontiac GMC Div. of General Motors

General Manager . . . . .Roy S. Roberts
Communications Director . . . . .Darwin E. Allen
GMC Category Director . . . . .Frederick E. Cook
Finance Director . . . . .Michael L. Heisel
Pontiac Category Director . . . . .Lynn C. Myers
Marketing Services Manager . . . . .Michael O'Malley
General Sales and Service Manager . . .Elwood M. Schlesinger
Personnel Director . . . . .Gay G. Tosch
Advertising Agency (GMC only) . . . . . . .McCann-Erickson, Inc.

GM Truck Group

GM Vice President and
Group Executive . . . . .Thomas J. Davis
GM Vice President and
General Manager . . . . .Guy D. Briggs
GM Vice President and
Group Director of Engineering . . . . .Thomas G. Stephens
Group Director of Communications . . . . .Kathleen A. Tanner

1997

Pontiac GMC Div. of General Motors

General Manager . . . . .Roy S. Roberts
Communications Director . . . . .Darwin E. Allen
GMC Category Director . . . . .Frederick E. Cook
Finance Director . . . . .Michael L. Heisel
Pontiac Category Director . . . . .Lynn C. Myers
Marketing Services Manager . . . . .Michael O'Malley
General Sales and Service Manager . . .Elwood M. Schlesinger
Personnel Director . . . . .Kirk Hobolth
Advertising Agency (GMC only) . . . . . . .McCann-Erickson, Inc.

GM Truck Group

GM Vice President and
Group Executive . . . . .Thomas J. Davis
GM Vice President and
General Manager . . . . .Guy D. Briggs
GM Vice President and
Group Director of Engineering . . . . .Thomas G. Stephens
Group Director of Communications . . . . .Kathleen A. Tanner

1998

Pontiac GMC Div. of General Motors

General Manager . . . . .Roy S. Roberts
Communications Director . . . . .Darwin E. Allen
Pontiac-GMC Category Director . . . . . . .Lynn C. Myers
Finance Director . . . . .Michael L. Heisel
Marketing Services Manager . . . . .Michael O'Malley
General Sales and Service Manager . . .Elwood M. Schlesinger
Advertising Agency (GMC only) . . . . . . .Ammirati, Puris: Lintas

GM Truck Group

GM Vice President and
Group Executive . . . . .Thomas J. Davis
GM Vice President and
General Manager . . . . .Guy D. Briggs
GM Vice President and
Group Director of Engineering . . . . .Thomas G. Stephens
Group Director of Communications . . . . .Kathleen A. Tanner

1999

Pontiac GMC Div. of General Motors

General Manager . . . . .Lynn C. Myers
Communications Director . . . . .Darwin E. Allen
General Manager Sales and Service . . .Elwood M. Schlesinger
Advertising Agency (GMC only) . . . . . . .Ammirati, Puris: Lintas

GM Truck Group

GM Vice President and
Group Executive . . . . .Thomas J. Davis
GM Vice President and
General Manager . . . . .Guy D. Briggs
GM Vice President and
Group Director of Engineering . . . . .Thomas G. Stephens
Group Director of Communications . . . . .Kathleen A. Tanner

2000

Pontiac GMC Div. of General Motors

General Manager . . . . .Lynn C. Myers
Communications Director . . . . .Johannes M. Reifenrath
Director of Advertising and
Sales Promotion . . . . .Mark-Hans Richer
Advertising Agency (GMC only) . . . . . . .Ammirati, Puris: Lintas

2001

Pontiac GMC Div. of General Motors

General Manager . . . . .Lynn C. Myers
Communications Director . . . . .Mary T. Henige
Director of Advertising and
Sales Promotion . . . . .Mark-Hans Richer
Advertising Agency (GMC only) . . . . . . .Lowe Lintas & Partners

Note: 1942 and 1949-2001 personnel list compiled by John A. Gunnell and Donald E. Meyer.

Chapter 15

GMC Sales and Production Numbers

GMC Truck Unit Sales
1909-1925

(General Motors figures as published in *My Years With General Motors*.)

1909 (a)	372
1909 (b)	102
1910	656
1911	293
1912	372
1913	601
1914	708
1915	1,408
1916	2,999
1917	5,885
1918	8,999
1919	7,730
1920	5,137
1921	2,760
1922	5,277
1923	6,968
1924	5,508
1925	2,865

(a) Fiscal year ending September 30, 1909

(b) Three months ending December 31,1909

© GMC Truck was not included with corporation figures from July 1, 1925, through September 30, 1943, when it was part of Yellow Truck & Coach Manufacturing Co.

GMC New Truck Registration Figures 1929-1939

(As compiled by R.L. Polk & Co.)

1929	17,568
1930	9,004
1931	6,919
1932	6,359
1933	6,602
1934	10,449
1935	11,442
1936	26,980
1937	43,522
1938	20,152
1939	34,908

•During these years, the operations of the Yellow Truck & Coach Manufacturing holding company were not consolidated into the accounts of General Motors Corp. so, unfortunately, there are no records of GMC truck production.

GMC Trucks Model-Year Production 1936-1939

1936	30,930
1937	56,996
1938	31,346
1939	34,265

GMC Trucks Calendar-Year Production 1936-1939

1936	35,355
1937	57,350
1938	20,640
1939	44,000

GMC Trucks Model-Year Production 1940-1941

1940	49,125
1941	101,168

GMC Truck and Coach Calendar-Year Production
1940-1949

Year	Trucks	Coaches	Combined
1940	59,313	2,347	61,660
1941	111,382	2,421	113,803
1942	148,111	2,395	150,506
1943	136,461	0	136,461
1944	151,02	1,965	152,992
1945	110,110	3,016	113,126
1946	33,850	2,439	36,289
1947	61,918	5,506	67,424
1948	92,677	5,362	98,059
1949	83,840	2,176	86,016

GMC Truck and Coach Calendar-Year Production
1950-1959

Year	Trucks	Coaches	Combined
1950	110,528	2,251	112,779
1951	127,447	4,367	131,814
1952	119,469	2,415	121,884
1953	114,123	2,531	116,654
1954	76,243	2,809	79,052 (*)
1955	104,759	2,888	107,647
1956	91,485	2,912	94,397
1957	69,675	3,108	72,783
1958	61,768	2,405	64,173
1959	75,411	2,119	77,530 (*)

(*) Industry trade journals of this period indicated that GMC figures were "estimated" and there may be very slight variations in calendar-year production totals from one reference to another because of this.

GMC Truck and Coach Calendar-Year Production
1960-1969

Year	Trucks	Coaches	Combined
1960	100,521	3,806	104,327
1961	72,085	2,911	74,996
1962	89,789		
1963	101.234		
1964	110,521		
1965	136,705		
1966	127,294		
1967	130,659		
1968	148,479		
1969	150,180		

(*) Calendar-year production of trucks and coaches given as a combined total after 1961. After 1968, all GMC light-duty trucks built by Chevrolet and all GM medium- and heavy-duty trucks built by GMC.

GMC Truck and Coach Calendar-Year Production
1970-1979

Year	Trucks	Coaches	Combined
1970	121,833		
1971	170,085	1,870	171,955
1972	193,537	1,795	195,332
1973	242,930	1,850	244,780
1974	215,811	2,425	218,236
1975	192,915	2,038	194,953
1976	288,644	1,856	290,500
1977	318,462	507	318,969
1978	372,444	1,339	373,783
1979	335,662	1,719	337,381

(*) Total calendar-year production with motor homes included was 247,825 in 1973; 219,316 in 1974; 197,008 in 1975; 293,997 in 1976; 321,009 in 1977; and 375,000 in 1978. There were no motor homes built in 1979, when production of all trucks and coaches combined came to 337,881 units.

GMC Truck and Coach Calendar-Year Production
1980-1982

Year	Trucks	Coaches	Combined
1980	171,207	2,495	173,702
1981	173,251	1,957	175,208
1982	223,171	1,135	224,306

GMC Truck and Coach Operation Calendar-Year Production 1983-1986

1983	262,538	1,264	263,802
1984	321,553	527	322,080
1985	355,540	945	356,485
1986	358,915	662	359,577

GMC Truck Div. of GM Truck Group Calendar-Year Production 1987-1989

1987	373,424	435	373,859
1988	386,528	NA	386,528
1989	372,168	NA	372,168

(*) Calendar-year production of trucks and coaches given as a combined total.

• GMC Class-8 truck operations merged with Volvo-White Truck Co. to form Volvo GM Heavy Truck Corp. of Greensboro, North Carolina. Official start of new company was January 1, 1988. GM continued producing Brigadiers in Pontiac until mid-1988, but ceased other Class-8 output there in 1987.

• GMC Coach Operations sold to Greyhound Corp. effective Jan. 1, 1987. Becomes Transportation Manufacturing Corp. of Roswell, New Mexico, under former GM executive John Nasi. Some partly finished coaches built late in 1987 were shipped to Roswell, but included in GMC production totals.

GMC Truck and Truck & Bus Calendar-Year Production 1990-1992

Year	
1990	326,885
1991	288,569
1992	341,856

GMC Truck and GM NATP— Calendar-Year Production 1993-1995

1993	403,385
1994	445,105
1995	456,034

Pontiac-GMC Division (Truck) and GM Truck Group

Calendar-Year Production 1996-1999

1996	454,797
1997	477,560
1998	450,915
1999	559,772

(*) Calendar-year production of trucks and buses given as a combined total.

GMC Light-Duty Truck Model-Year Production
1974-2001

Series	Production

1974
C1500	72,196
C2500	39,996
C3500	7,073
Value Van	5,416
Jimmy	11,883
Suburban	8,204
Sprint	4,502
Vandura	18,898
Rally	4,571
Total	**172,739**

1975
C1500	56,704
C2500	30,934
C3500	11,385
Value Van	1,596
Jimmy	10,861
Suburban	8,263
Sprint	3,988
Vandura	12,320
Rally	2,677
Total	**138,728**

1976
C1500	95,032
C2500	48,321
C3500	15,319
Value Van	3,880
Jimmy	18,551
Suburban	13,960
Sprint	5,884
Vandura	15,898
Rally	3,848
Total	**220,693**

1977
C1500	114,418
C2500	52,933
C3500	25,727
Value Van	7,556
Jimmy	21,013
Suburban	18,821
Sprint	7,118
Vandura	20,560
Rally	6,458
Total	**276,152**

1978
C1500	102,154
C2500	42,452
C3500	25,349
Value Van	6,321
Jimmy	21,013
Suburban	18,395
Caballero	7,661
Vandura	32,391
Rally	3,969
Total	**259,705**

1979
C1500	120,430
C2500	41,491